THE
TASTER'S
GUIDE
TO BEER

The Taster's Guide to Beer

Brews and Breweries of the World

BY Michael A. Weiner

COLLIER BOOKS

A DIVISION OF MACMILLAN PUBLISHING CO., INC.

NEW YORK

COLLIER MACMILLAN PUBLISHERS

LONDON

Macmillan Publishing Co., Inc.
866 Third Avenue, New York, N.Y. 10022
Collier Macmillan Canada, Ltd.

Library of Congress Cataloging in Publication Data:

Weiner, Michael A.
  The taster's guide to beer.

  Bibliography: p.
  1. Beer.   2. Brewing.   I. Title.
TP577.W4   641.2′3   76-30364
ISBN 0-02-625600-2
ISBN 0-02-082470-X pbk.

Designed by Philip Grushkin

First Collier Books Edition 1977

THE TASTER'S GUIDE TO BEER *is also published in a hardcover edition by Macmillan Publishing Co., Inc.*

Printed in the United States of America

CONTENTS

INTRODUCTION

Is "the worst the best?" I understand that in Italy a visitor inquiring about the best cheese in a locality is usually directed to the most modern cheese factory. The taster is told to avoid the "worst" makers—those small, untidy rooms in the poorer sections of town where ancient methods of production are followed. In many cases the "worst" cheese *is* the best, because it is made of pure dairy products and allowed to age naturally, without any artificial coloring or flavors. Similarly, some of the world's "worst" brewers (in terms of physical appearance of the brewery—usually antiquated factories without impressive "quality-control" panels, stainless steel dials, and gleaming tile floors) produce the best beers.

This is not to say that brewing by ancient methods with dilapidated equipment will guarantee a quality beer. Some "traditional" brewers have been producing the same insipid beer for generations and selling it to indiscriminate drinkers on the strength of massive advertising campaigns which capitalize on nostalgia-invoking images

It is only too easy to pass judgment on brewers who use certain shortcuts to economize in a highly competitive business, and to lose sight of the enormous problems involved in brewing on a grand scale. The best way to gain some insight into these difficulties of brewing a tasteful, unadulterated beer is to brew your own. I suggest the skeptics try it just to see what's involved, even in a two-bucket brewhouse.

Then, wandering through the vast network of huge pipes and mammoth tanks at a local brewery, observing the refrigerated storage bins which hold thousands of gallons in secondary fermentation, the doubters may begin to appreciate the need for some of the shortcuts taken in brewing for a massive marketplace. A tour of a brewery, and an attempt to make a palatable beer at home will do much to make the beer drinker who likes to pay a low price understand the need both to minimize the risks and keep down the price.

Some very high-quality beers are available, both domestic and imported, which are worth their high price. The common beers, which are usually less expensive (high price alone is, of course, no indication of quality), should be reserved for everyday drinking or avoided completely by those willing to pay the price for a pure, wholesome beer.

Of course, the exacting beer drinker may first get acquainted with the truly masterful commercial brewers who brew only with barley, malt, pure hops, water and yeast, and who use no additives or preservatives. To be able to brew beautiful beer, following very strict codes based on hundreds of years of tradition, utilizing relatively modern equipment, and still turn a profit is a feat indeed in a world of ersatz boosted by educated Babbits.

Having examined the making of beer in Chapter 4, a detailed inspection of some of the beers of the world may be interesting for the regional drinker. Therefore, in Chapter 5 beers, both domestic and imported, arranged according to nation, will be examined.

Obviously, some limit had to be imposed on the number of beers which are profiled. Fortunately, the brewers themselves imposed some such limits. In order to present as many beer profiles as possible, we mailed questionnaires to all American breweries, the larger Canadian companies, and representative breweries around the world. In addition, requests for information were circulated among various national brewers' societies who, it was assumed, would encourage their members to respond.

The best-known European breweries responded immediately. In the United States the largest (Anheuser-Busch) and the smallest (Anchor Steam Beer) breweries responded in detail; not all of the American breweries, however, felt that it was in their best interests to respond to the questionnaire. In the end, I think you will find more than enough brews and breweries of the world to whet your appetite for knowledge about the universal drink, beer.

THE
TASTER'S
GUIDE
TO BEER

1

Beginnings of a Shikker*

Shikker: Hebrew term for one who overindulges in intoxicants; drunk.

And Malt does more than Milton can
To justify God's ways to man.

—A. E. HOUSMAN

BEER seems to make people want to talk and we may as well begin with a true beer story. A Danish medical friend tells me of a peculiar case of chronic alcoholism. It seems that a male patient was turning up drunk at the hospital, showing a high level of alcohol in his blood, and all the time insisting that he did not drink. This problem confused both patient and physician for months. One day the "dry" alcoholic had to be operated on for a routine appendectomy, whereupon it was discovered he possessed an extra little segment of intestine. In this circular sac (which jutted off the intestine) portions of the victim's food would get trapped long enough for fermentation to take place. Thus the alcohol in his blood. A true story from the annals of medical history.

Aside from a few ceremonial glasses of sweet wine, beer was the first alcoholic beverage I took in quantity. While I've since enjoyed more than a few beers around the world I do not consider myself a taste expert. I've not sat at Brussels to consider candidates for the Gold Medal, nor have I served under a famous Cologne brewmaster. I've never even taken a basic course in brewing.

I am an avid beer drinker and consider this my chief qualification. As an anthropologist I was interested in the peculiarities of various malted beverages and why different regions have given rise to their own special formulas. In Bamberg, Germany, for example, why is smoked beer, such as *Rauchbier* or *Doppelbock*, preferred while *Altbier* is the favored brew in the Rhineland, or *Budvar Budweiser* the choice in Budweis, South Bohemia?

Each type (and there are many other types in Germany) is made very differently and consumed by faithful followers who would as soon switch to a beer brewed outside their communities as marry outside their village.

As an economic–botanist I wanted to understand how various strains of yeast, varieties of cereals, clones of hops, and sources of water lent their particular qualities to the finished beer.

Finally, an almost paranoid interest in food purity has compelled me to attempt to determine the deleterious effects of the numerous additives that find their way into most mediocre beers.

WHY READ ABOUT BEER?

"But," someone recently asked, "why bother reading about beer when I can spend the same money drinking the stuff and learn for myself?"

This man is precisely the type of person who would most benefit by reading about the beer he is drinking. He, and people like him who have gone back to beer after doing the required wine-tasting tour, would now like to speak authoritatively and articulate their likes and dislikes with a vocabulary suitable to this different genre.

The pleasure of any food or beverage is naturally augmented when we know why we like a certain taste, when we are able to identify our preferences. True, the tastes of man the social animal are easily influenced by advertisements and the opinions of others, but when alone, people usually do what pleases only themselves. This applies to food and drink. We may pretend to enjoy something in the company of friends to avoid hurting their sensibilities. We may actually believe we like the taste of a new beer, for example, in the company of a friend who recommended it after he returned from the little town in Germany where it is made. But when alone, we may find the beer too bitter, too dark, too strong. The ability to articulate your likes and dislikes, based on a grasp of the craft of brewing, should be one dividend you acquire from *The Taster's Guide to Beer*.

Good beer, like good bread, requires choice ingredients and the hand of a master craftsman. All bread is not alike, as we are now rediscovering, and as many knew all along. There is plain white, enriched white, white mixed with whole wheat and other flours, pure stone-ground whole wheat and a host of other grains. Each may be baked with a whole line of additives or none at all. Various oils or shortenings may be used, and so on. Similarly, beer can be made with pure barley malt, or with cheaper substitutes such as corn, rice or even corn grits. The conversion of starchy grains into fermentable sugars can be speeded up by adding sugar or even various enzymes. Particularly fine varieties of hops may be added, or cheap hop oils substituted.

A brewer may have water available which is just right for his needs—hard water for British pale ales and bitters, soft water for lagers and stouts—or he may add chemical salts to condition his water to his needs.

In the brewing process itself various shortcuts are available (just as t.v. dinners are faster than the real thing). Storage and ageing are important, as are the storage vessels. Experienced drinkers can taste the difference between beer stored in wooden barrels and that stored in aluminum.

The drinking container also makes a difference. The same beer imbibed from a can, a stein or a conical glass, may taste differently.

This book, it is hoped, will give the reader awareness of these differences. Perhaps as a result the cost-conscious brewmasters will be able to look their accountants in the eye and say, "Either we do it the old way or they'll stop drinking it altogether." Only a consumer who can distinguish his preferences and be articulate about them will be able to produce arguments for change to an otherwise indifferent manufacturer.

WHAT IS TASTE?

Taste is a highly complex phenomenon and beer tasting is no exception to this. Taste experts often differ as to what constitutes a great beer, a good one, a mediocre one and one that might mercifully be called inadequate.

One taster might favor bitter ales, and rate even the finest Pilsener below a mediocre ale. Another might prefer sweet stouts, and so on. Moreover, an individual's taste may change from time to time if not within the same day. Taste, like the human organism, is as variable as the wind, especially when it comes to beer.

Nevertheless, while taste is highly subjective, there are certain differences which most drinkers can learn to detect, if they have not already done so intuitively. But first we must define taste.

Taste, as registered in the taste buds of the mouth and throat, divides itself into sweet, sour, salty and bitter. The flavor of a substance is a *combination* of the impressions received when that substance is taken into the mouth: taste, aroma (burnt, fragrant, pungent, sharp, and acidic), feeling sensations, and sometimes aftereffects.* In fact, when we say taste we are actually referring to the flavor of a substance.

The entire mouth, and especially the tongue, is very responsive to sensations induced by the temperature at which a beer is served and the amount of carbonation (whether it is flat or lively). Chemicals used in brewing can also be detected. Excessively sour substances will cause salivation, while tannin-related compounds will cause a "puckery or drawing sensation."

Beer drinkers are quick to detect and very sensitive to negative flavor characteristics, such as metallic, bitter or rancid ones. Beers are often rejected on such grounds and just as frequently if they are "flat" or "watery."

The typical drinker is quick to detect such crude taste impressions on the first beer, but by his own admission "after the first you can't tell the difference." Sometimes a freshly poured bottle of beer or a refilled mug will give a strong flavor impression, even though it may be caused by a sourness or bitterness in the newly poured beer. This is because the flavor impression arises from the overall drinking experience: the flavor of the refill may, in fact, reflect the taste of the first good drink.

Anne J. Neilson has pointed out "that every step in the complex technology of brewing—from selection of raw materials to packaging and even

---

*S. E. Cairncross and L. B. S. Jöström, *"Flavor Profiles—A New Approach to Flavor Problems,"* Food Technology* (1950), Vol. 4 (8): 308–311.

retail handling—can have an effect on the flavor of the product the consumer drinks."*

This flavor scientist evaluated the effects of the brewing process, raw materials, packaging and storage on flavor, and drew the following conclusions:

1. The flavor of daily production beer will vary no matter how carefully controlled it is. . . . For every beer there is . . . [an] identity [that] sets it apart from every other beer. This identity . . . is almost never one specific characteristic [but a] blended complex.

2. [Flavor is changed by age and abuse.] For most beers, storage at 100°F. (37°C.) for more than a week is too much abuse. . . . For other beers, flavor stability is such, or (and this is important) their market is such, that temperatures higher than 100°F. must be used [to evaluate their flavor].

3. The effects of heat on stored beer are often summarized by the word "oxidized." The flavor changes of such oxidized beer can better be described as "less fragrant," "more bitter" and, as having "plus tongue bite." [The descriptive words used to articulate flavor changes in the following table may be of value to the interested drinker.]

Flavor Changes Incurred During Aging of Beer as Depicted by the Flavor Profile

Basic Profile Amplitude 2½		Aging Profile Amplitude 1	
Carbonation	2	Carbonation	1
Fruity-estery fragrance	2	Estery fragrance	1½
Sourness	2	Amyl alcohols	1
Grain fragrance	1	Sourness	2
Bitterness	1	Bitterness-lingering	2
Yeast fragrance	1	Autolyzed yeast	1
Hop fragrance	½	Old grain fragrance	1
		Weedy hop fragrance	1
		Tongue bite	1

*Anne J. Neilson, "Significance of the Flavor Profile to the Master Brewer," *Technical Quarterly of the Master Brewers Assn. of America* (1966), Vol. 3 (1): 69–75.

4. Changes in the finished beer resulting from changes in the raw materials are of [extreme importance]. The flavor fullness of a beer is quite influenced by the type of malt used . . . for example, the shift from Kindred to Traill to Trophy and Larker malt can pretty much be portrayed in the changes in description of feeling factors—sometimes astringent, sometimes viscous and sticky.

5. A change to dry hopping or, more drastically, to hop extracts, influences the type of hop fragrance and the fruity-estery fraction as well as influencing the basic taste bitterness.

6. The importance of a change in yeast culture is . . . considerably underestimated. [There are] obvious differences in beer aroma resulting from fresh versus used yeast versus autolyzed yeast. . . .

7. [Different packaging materials have their effects on flavor, the extremes being represented by fresh draught beer and canned beer. Even an amateur drinker recognizes the difference between these extremes. However, what confounds even the master brewer is assessing the effects of shifting from one variety of packaging to another.] The shift away from the export bottle; the shift to the tab-top cans; new can liners; plastic crowns. . . .

8. The flavor of the beer packaged in a new package is not the same as that packaged in the old tried and true. These flavor differences are often insidious, because usually nothing tastes obviously wrong; the beer just tastes a little different.

PSYCHOLOGICAL FACTORS AFFECTING BEER TASTE

The Institute for Design Analysis in San Francisco reported in 1962 that the label is capable of changing the taste of beer, at least in the mouths and minds of the consumer "with average taste sensitivity."

In a by now classic test involving ninety-six beer drinkers and eight brands of lager beer it was shown that the average beer drinker:

a) cannot distinguish between brands,

b) changes his evaluation once a brand is identified,

c) reacts differently when the brand name only is exposed than when the actual label is exposed.

As an example, one brand, B, "was considered a light-tasting beer until its brand name became known. Then it was classed as overwhelmingly heavy-tasting. Its flavor then . . . became what the consumers *thought* it should be. In addition, brand E, classified first as strong in alcohol content, became weak; and brand B, rated as weak, became strong."

In another test "brand B was consistently rated first when the brand name only was given, and also when the actual label was shown. But brand H, in eighth place when the consumers knew it only by the printed overlap, moved into fourth place when its label was shown."

Apparently then a small midwestern brewer was right when he recently said "the average consumer drinks advertising . . . he doesn't care what he puts down his throat." No doubt the brewers have heeded the study by the Institute for Design Analysis and other blind taste tests which tend to confirm the conclusions. As a result more money is spent on market-

CULVER PICTURES

Ox-horn tankard with cover, London, 1561.

ing and packaging than on the physical product.* Nondiscriminatory palates now accept some of the least distinguished beer in the world.

Liking for beer tends to be an acquired taste. In the United States 63 percent of all beer drinkers are men and 37 percent women. Younger women show a preference for cocktails, but immediately after marriage their drinking habits change. Men begin to drink more at home, and women have a tendency to start drinking beer at this time, possibly to share in a pleasure enjoyed by their husbands.

Many women whom I interviewed (age twenty-five and over) find beer refreshing and satisfying after many years of wine drinking. The feeling expressed was that the sweetness of wine makes them drink more without quenching thirst. To these women, beer has a tartness that limits the amount consumed, while completely satisfying thirst.

It is surprising that beer has for so long been considered a man's drink. In early times a great part of the brewing trade was in the hands of ale-wives and brewesses. Down to the close of the fifteenth century the London brewing trade was run mostly by women. As late as the seventeenth century the brewing of ale and beer for household consumption was still considered the special province of the housewife and her female servants.

When then did beer acquire this strictly masculine association? My pet theory is that following Prohibition the brewers, anxious to disassociate their product from "the hard stuff" yet unwilling to risk losing male drinkers who would not want a weak beverage, created in the public mind the idea that beer is "a drink of moderation . . . for the strong man."

This was done to head off future prohibitionist onslaughts. By establishing beer in a separate category (note that the license to sell beer and wine is more easily obtainable in most locales than the license for hard liquor sales) the brewers hoped to avoid a repetition of the 1920's, when hundreds were forced to close their plants permanently, while others shifted their production to soft drinks until the storm had passed.

THE ART OF STORING, SERVING AND DRINKING BEER**

If beer is kept too long in bottles, casks or cans it gradually loses its subtle flavor; so if you are a true connoisseur of beer you will prefer it straight from a fresh barrel. Carefully stored in an even temperature in total darkness there is a great chance that it will retain a full brewery cellar freshness.

Be certain your beer is stored upright. Laying it flat like wine exposes more of the liquid to the air in the bottle and hastens its demise. Buy from a

---

*Of an average price of $1.07 for a sixpack, packaging costs neary 30¢, while the beer itself costs a little over one half cent. *The Chemical Additives in Booze,* p. 35.

**Adapted from *The Art of Enjoying Continental Beer,* Brewery Hürlimann AG Zurich.

distributor who can assure you that his stock is fresh. Beer is lifeless after three to six months on the shelf.

The Serving

The serving of beer is also an art, and it is worthwhile learning to do it correctly. When pouring beer it is best to let it run along the side of the glass. Hold the glass at a slight angle, pour a little, then stop to allow the first froth to settle; then fill the glass full so that a fine, frothy head stands just a little above the rim of the glass.

The Eyes

The beer drinker drinks both with his eye and his palate, and the look of the beer is all-important. First look at the froth—one and one-half to two inches is the ideal height. If you are drinking from a tankard you can carefully blow away some froth to assure this. The amount of froth depends on the temperature of the beer. If the beer is too cold the froth will be weak; if too warm there will be too much froth.

Even such things as too warm a glass, rough places on the inside of the glass, dust specks, etc., can encourage bubbles to form. If the froth consists of bubbles of different size, and the big bubbles form on the outside against the glass then the glass has not been washed properly or bears traces of grease. Glasses, in fact, must be perfectly clean. The slightest film of grease, fat, oil or soap will cause the head to collapse and the beer to lose sparkle and flavor. Use soapless or greaseless detergent. Rinse in running water. Air-dry only, since even a trace of oil or soap from a towel will destroy the foam.

As the beer is drunk the froth sinks naturally with the beer level, becoming thinner and thinner as the glass is emptied, but staying compact, white to yellowish in color, and sticking firmly to the glass. After each mouthful, as the level of beer sinks, loose rings of foam should stay adhering to the inner surface of the glass.

The froth bubbles contain carbonic acid gas. They are surrounded by a network of protein molecules. As the froth rises the small bubbles unite to form bigger ones and they finally all burst when they reach the air at the top of the glass. The layer of froth will only rebuild itself if sufficient carbonic acid gas is released continuously from the beer.

There must be enough bubble builders, albuminoids and peptones, that is, proteins, in the beer to start with. Thin beers contain less of these bubble builders. A high alcohol content results in less froth, but a high hop content will give the beer a good head. So take a good look at the beer in your glass—even before you taste it, you can tell whether it has a strong, satisfying flavor.

Under certain circumstances the protein molecules in beer cling together until they become so large that they make the beer cloudy and form sediment at the bottom of the bottle. To prevent this the matured beer is passed into cold-storage tanks where it is stored at a temperature near freezing point. This stabilizes the haze-producing protein molecules in a form which ensures their removal during the subsequent filtration. Old beers froth better than young beers because of these tightly clinging protein chains. So it's impossible to have a perfect head of froth and perfect freshness. The brewer must aim for a happy medium, not too much protein, and not too little. Each batch of beer is different. The brewer must be flexible and use all his skill and judgment at each brewing, for it is impossible to calculate the correct quantity of protein in advance.

Now you should look closely at the color of the beer. Light beer varies from a pure, clear yellow to a rich, deep yellow, a light gold yellow, or a greenish yellow. Dark beer should be a deep, thick brown or gold-brown. Vienna Type beers are the color of "married" beers, that is, light and dark mixed.

Pilsner is a light, pale lager-type beer with a high percentage of hops, and Munich a sweeter, dark one (similar in character to a British mild ale). The darker color results from drying the malt at a higher temperature, and the pigment itself is a compound of proteins and sugar that have resisted fermentation. By looking closely at the color you can tell at once whether the beer is cloudy. The cloudiness may be caused by the yeast (as in most Czechoslovakian beers) which should give it an excellent flavor. More frequently it is caused by protein substances or occasionally by lactic acid bacteria. This kind of cloudiness is not harmful but it is detrimental to the flavor.

This muddy type of beer is known as blind, veiled or opalescent beer. Fortunately most of the beers served to us are clear and brilliant to the last drop.

In intense cold, however, some beers become cloudy despite all the care that has been taken in their manufacture, because the protein molecules cling together. They lose this bitter-tasting haziness if warmed up. Such beers are particularly full-flavored with a beautiful frothy head.

The Hand

Now, at last, comes the big moment when you actually grip the glass. The interesting thing is, you not only drink with your eyes, and your palate, but with your hand too. If the glass is covered with condensation (a mug or tankard insulates its contents better) then merely holding the glass gives you the sensation that your thirst is being quenched. The coolness to the touch of the glass is itself satisfying and foreshadows the coolness of the beer. The ideal temperature for light beers is between 8° and 10°C.

(45 to 50°F.), and for dark ones between 10° and 12°C. (50 to 54°F.).

Some beer drinkers like their beer warmer, but they should realize they are sacrificing both froth and flavor.

The Nose

Before drinking a good-looking beer it should be smelled.

Light beers of the Pilsner type should have a fine, subtle hop aroma, dark beers a good malt aroma. They should all smell pure, clean, beery, perhaps of hops but never of yeast, in short—agreeable and a little titillating. Smell the beer and you will find its faults more easily than by tasting. Your sensitive nose will register any smell of pasteurization, any stale, sour smell, or any lactic-acid smell at once. So bottled beers should be sniffed at the bottle mouth as soon as they are opened. In that small amount of gas the aroma of the whole bottle is concentrated.

The Lips

There are many delights in a glass of beer. Just as very few hold the ear above the glass of fresh beer and listen dreamily to the popping bubbles of froth, even fewer pay attention to the sensation of their lips while drinking, although these are of paramount importance. The lips confirm the temperature sensations of the hand, and appreciate the texture of the beer container, whether thick or fine glass, stone, china, silver, tin or wood. Each material has a different flavor and this harmonizes subtly with the exciting aroma of the beer and almost at the same moment the first taste impression.

The Flavor

Now we have come to the heart of the matter, the taste of the beer, its most essential, vital characteristic. Persons of discernment can distinguish clearly between the taste of the actual mouthful, that is, the sensation which the beer first creates in the mouth, the sensation in the nose and throat during swallowing, and then the final sensation in the mouth, nose and throat once the beer is swallowed. The various taste sensations are felt by different parts of the tongue. Sweetness, for instance, is felt only on the tip of the tongue, spicy and salty at the sides of the tongue, bitter and acrid at the back. Everything depends on that first, decisive impression. If the taste pleases us we smack our lips, make an exclamation of delight, and are satisfied. If we call a beer full-flavored we mean that it's got body and is strong and tasty. This, as we know, is caused by the protein and the unfermented sugar, called together rest extract, and by the alcohol (3 to 3.5 percent by weight in lager beer). A beer can therefore be pure, and yet not

full-flavored. It is empty, light, thin, lifeless, even watery, because it is lacking in alcohol and rest extract.

Both are necessary to give the beer body and a heart. If the alcohol is obtrusive in flavor, the beer is called winey or spirited. Of course, if you're suffering the torments of thirst you're likely to overlook little faults of flavor, but they will come to light sooner or later. The most full-flavored beer of all is unfiltered beer served straight from the storage barrel, but, as we said before, it is unfortunately cloudy. Malt gives the beer its distinctive, characteristic flavor but hops also play an important part. As you approach the beer you should be faintly conscious of the smell of the hops but not too conscious. The first sip brings the flavor of the hops, and this can be delicate or quite strong. But the hop flavor should vanish when the first sip is swallowed, and not linger in the after-drink sensation.

If it does linger, then the beer is rough, scratchy or even unpleasantly bitter. The tannin resulting from excessive malt extraction, and the use of hard water in the brewing process can also cause roughness. In a hot, thirsty summer, distinctly hopped beer is very refreshing, but in winter a stronger, malt-flavored, lightly hopped beer is more enjoyable. The food you are eating or have just eaten, while you drink, also affects the flavor of the beer; but there are other things that influence it, too. The carbonic acid gas (a result of the action of yeast on the sugars) gives the beer its piquancy, and causes that pleasant prickling sensation in the tongue and throat. The carbonic acid gas makes the beer taste good; it warms the stomach and has the same beneficient action on digestion as the carbonic acid in mineral waters. If the open bottle is left standing about, the carbonic acid disappears and the beer becomes flat and weak.

CULVER PICTURES

Porcelain drinking cups from Munich and Dresden.

There are two further taste faults which have not been mentioned. One is the tang of yeast caused by yeast cells disintegrating in the beer. Although it means extra vitamins in the beer, it is at the expense of flavor, which is no longer pure. Bottled beer that has stood in the sun, or glasses of beer that have been exposed to sunlight in your backyard, on the patio, or at the beach, also lose their flavor and get a sun taste.

There are also additional flavors, peculiar to individual breweries, which are proudly called "house flavors," because the brewers maintain that customers like them. And it's a sad fact that one can indeed lose one's discrimination and become accustomed to a flavor that is less than perfect.

The Container

A very important question, for flavor does not solely depend on the beer itself—its container also influences it. The drinking horn, once handed down from generation to generation, may no longer be in fashion, but our choice of drinking vessels—mugs, tankards, beakers, and glasses—is still very wide.

Glasses are most commonly used; either schooners—tall glasses containing about fourteen fluid ounces—or mugs. The beer looks much better in schooners, the shape giving it a good head, but it tastes cooler when served in a mug. Mugs have another advantage—you can lean your face over the cool beer in a mug and enjoy the aroma, but over a schooner there is hardly enough room for your nose.

If the glass narrows toward the top, a beautiful head will form. The shape of the glass forces the froth into a little tower as the beer is poured. The froth should re-form itself constantly, and many glasses have thick, heavy glass bottoms to ensure this. Because these bottoms are always a little warm they cause the carbonic acid gas to rise in the beer.

They also give the glass a firm base. If the glasses narrow toward their base, the area of froth lessens with every mouthful, but it becomes thicker. Nowadays beer is sometimes served in tulip glasses which are probably the most beautiful glasses in appearance. But they are difficult to wash and therefore have a higher breakage rate than others. The feel, the taste, the smell of the beer container should all, if possible, be in harmony with the character of the drink. There are, for instance, wooden beer mugs, lined with brewer's pitch, which are a joy to drink from. The resiny smell is a delightful complement to light beers and blends perfectly with strong ones. Dark beer tastes particularly good in a silver tankard; it stays fresh for a long time and the cool touch of silver at each mouthful of cool beer is an extremely pleasant sensation. But wooden and silver tankards are impractical in restaurants and bars. Some English public houses use pewter tankards, heavy and beautiful, with a dull sheen. Pewter has a taste and smell all its own and some people prefer it with a dark beer. English porter and English ale taste particularly good in pewter tankards.

Lager beer, pretzel, and pipe.

Sixteenth-century Rhenish stoneware mugs.

The traditional Swiss or German big stoneware mug, with or without a lid, has a neutral taste and smell. For the majority of drinkers it is probably a little too large, but for those with somewhat excessive thirsts it is, undoubtedly, ideal.

It has the great advantage of keeping the beer cool for a very long time, but as it narrows a little toward the top, washing it is difficult and one can never be quite certain that it is clean. Its narrow neck also gives the drinker the false impression that the mug contains a lot of froth and not much beer.

It is strange that dark beer tends to be drunk from thick, opaque containers, so that you are not aware of any cloudiness present (fortunately it is harmless) while light beer, which is clear and brilliant, is usually drunk from transparent glasses. But there's no doubt that clear, light yellow beer looks better served in a glass than in any other container.

A SAMPLE BEER TASTE TEST

Informal beer-tasting parties are an excellent way to enjoy and learn about beers from around the world. Below is a standard form I have devised for recording flavor impressions. For best results simply hand out a sheet like this to each taster.

To be sure the label is not affecting the impressions you are recording, pour the sample beers into identical glasses in another room. Bring them to your taste panel already filled but unidentified, keeping a record of the brand name for yourself. Although you could conduct the blind test by presenting the beer containers in paper sacks, it is better to serve the beer in identical glasses since shape or type of container influences the test. Some people are biased against cans, others prefer tall bottles, and so on.

It is important to taste only one type of beer at any given sampling. Lagers should be tasted separately from ales, or stouts, or other types of beer. Dark beers should all be tasted at one time. Never mix dark beers with lagers or stouts. The results will be meaningless. It would be like trying to draw meaningful taste impressions about tea and coffee by tasting samples of both beverages at the same sitting.

After your guests have filled in Part II of the form, you can show them the bottles (or cans) and complete Part I together, discussing the possible causes of negative impressions. We have already seen how various factors in the brewing and serving of beer can affect taste. Two more points might also be considered. *Temperature*—Remember, many beers, especially the better ones, are brewed to be served at' temperatures much below the "ice-cold" level preferred in the United States. *Perishability*—How long have the beers been in storage? Bad tastes, such as "rustiness" or "skunkiness" may be due to the perishable nature of beer.

If snacks must be served, stick to neutral foods such as soda crackers, graham crackers, dry toast or a fine, mild cheese. Remember, salty foods

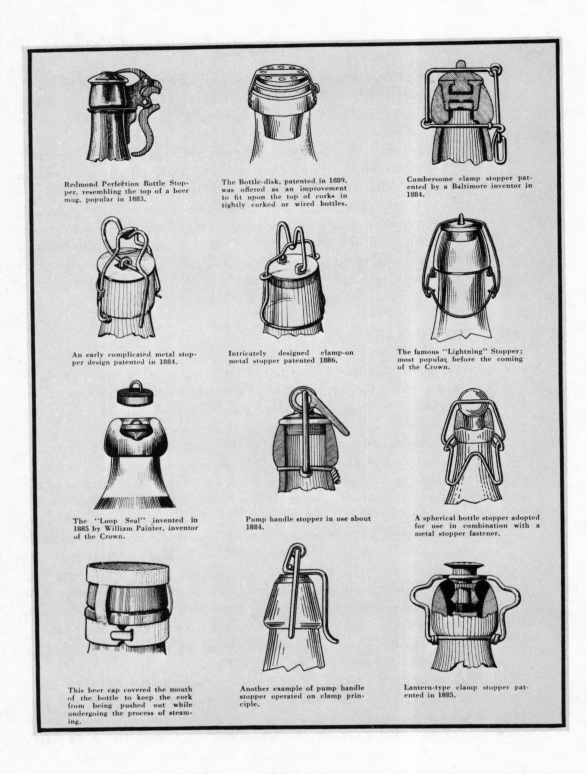

Redmond Perfection Bottle Stopper, resembling the top of a beer mug, popular in 1883.

The Bottle-disk, patented in 1889, was offered as an improvement to fit upon the top of corks in tightly corked or wired bottles.

Cumbersome clamp stopper patented by a Baltimore inventor in 1884.

An early complicated metal stopper design patented in 1884.

Intricately designed clamp-on metal stopper patented 1886.

The famous "Lightning" Stopper; most popular before the coming of the Crown.

The "Loop Seal" invented in 1885 by William Painter, inventor of the Crown.

Pump handle stopper in use about 1884.

A spherical bottle stopper adopted for use in combination with a metal stopper fastener.

This beer cap covered the mouth of the bottle to keep the cork from being pushed out while undergoing the process of steaming.

Another example of pump handle stopper operated on clamp principle.

Lantern-type clamp stopper patented in 1885.

will affect flavor impressions, as will hot and spicy foods. If, however, you generally drink beer with a favorite snack then taste your beers while enjoying your indulgence. But don't expect a tightly controlled set of results. As for complex gourmet specialties, I suggest you save these to follow the formal tasting ceremony. Afterwards, drink and eat as you please!

BEER PROFILE FORM

PART I. *Physical*

Brand _____   Type

Brewer _____   (lager, ale, etc.) _____

Country _____   Place of Purchase _____

Container   Storage

(can, keg, bottle) _____   (warm or refrigerated?) _____

PART II.

A. *Visual* (*Look* at your beer.)

clear _____   Color

cloudy _____   (pale, amber, brown,

                         black, etc.) _____

Head   a. no head _____

          b. small head _____

          c. full, rich head _____

          d. too much foam _____

Sediment visible   yes _____

                      no   _____

B. *Aromatic Qualities* (*Smell* your beer.)

pleasant aroma _____

unpleasant aroma _____

no aroma _____

Aroma description (check as many as are appropriate)

    nutty _____   fruity _____

    rancid _____   yeasty _____

    hoppy _____   malty _____

    cheesy _____   other (describe) ___

                                   _____

C. *Flavor* (*Taste* your beer.)

lively, sparkling _____   good body _____

flat _____   "thin," watery _____

                       heavy body _____

Flavor description (check as many as are appropriate)

    metallic _____   malty _____

    astringent _____   yeasty _____

    acidy _____   salty _____

    sour _____   sweet _____

    bitter _____   dry _____

Aftertaste

    none _____   mild _____   pronounced _____

D. *Rating* (From 0 to 7 steins)

2

Beer–the Universal Drink

No civilization has found life tolerable without . . .
the things that provide at least some brief escape from reality.

—WILL DURANT, *Life of Greece*

IN PREHISTORIC TIMES

Drinking fermented beverages is as widespread as civilization itself, and from all indications the practice is as old as civilization. The empire of Bacchus is not worldwide, but it does include practically all lands where men have learned to raise grain in fields or trees in orchards, or to herd cattle and horses, camels and goats.*

Anthropologists have devoted an entire symposium to the question "Did Man Once Live by Beer Alone?" Scholars have debated whether our prehistoric ancestors discovered bread or beer first.

Despite ancient books, clay tablets and the like, our knowledge of brewing in ancient (and even medieval) times is not exact, but, rather, shrouded in myth and legend.

The most that can be stated with certainty is that the beers of prehistoric and ancient nations were produced from grains, by fermentation or decomposition. The motive for preparing these beverages was no doubt the desire to escape the sheer routine of living, a desire that has tormented at some time in their lives all men who have achieved comparative security and an adequate supply of food. Of course, the early fermented beverages were also nutritious, not having been subjected to the great changes in temperature that modern pasteurization and refrigeration produce, which often kill most life-giving properties.

The nature of fermentation and the intoxication arising from it were probably revealed to our ancestors by pure accident. Someone left a batch of half-chewed barley in a closed dish, still moist, ate the altered leftovers a few days later and found himself delightfully changed. The accident was repeated; other villagers tried the stuff, and the art of brewing was gradually developed. As civilizations advanced, the preparation of such beverages also advanced and the use of them increased. Excessive use eventually forced individuals and whole societies to limit their intake as a

*Science Newsletter, September 9, 1933, p. 166.

result of a wider experience of the consequences. So might go the evolutionary theory.

In any case the development of beer certainly did not proceed from a beginning in which the four principal ingredients—a malted grain, water, yeast and hops—were used by the primitive brewer. No doubt the principles of brewing and knowledge of the values of each ingredient (the microscopic yeast was unknown to prehistoric man) came slowly, through a long series of trials.

Some primitive peoples still produce fermented beverages by methods which have probably not changed in thousands of years.

In parts of South America, Africa, southern Asia and the western Pacific Islands, palm toddy (more like a wine) is frequently drunk. The sugary sap of palm trees is allowed to ferment in the depression left when the central bud is cut off. Toddy is not intoxicating while fresh but becomes so if imbibed after it has stood for only a few hours.

In early times in countries where there were many bees men learned to dilute and then ferment their honey into mead.

Fermented beerlike beverages are various and many. In the following list the important varieties are arranged alphabetically by country of origin:

AFRICA:
Millet beer called *booza*(!) or *pombe*.
Maize beer called *wheedah*.
Cassava beer called *peewore*.

AMERICA:
Persimmon beer in North America.
Corn and quinca beer known as *chicha* in South America.
Sweet potato beer known as *vinho de batatas* in Brazil.

ASIA:
Steamed rice is hydrolyzed and fermented into *sake* in Japan.
Wheat or barley beer known as *tar-asun* in China.
Sorghum beer known as *sorgho*.

MEXICO:
Agave sap is fermented into *pulque*.

RUSSIA:
Barley and rye malt with added fruits and cold water are baked into *kvass* (quass).

Of course, these less-known varieties are in addition to ale, wheat beer, cider, ginger beer, porter and stout.

The desire for an intoxicant has even led nomadic tribes in central Asia to ferment an animal product—the milk of mares and camels—to make *kumiss,* a popular drink.

BEVERAGES OF THE ANCIENTS*

Records of former civilized or semicivilized nations of Asia, existing thousands of years before the Christian era, have been found—records which disclose at least partial information, and enable us to draw fairly accurate conclusions and get a vivid picture of the conditions at the time. We owe this to the linguists and antiquarians of past centuries who mastered the old writings of India, China and Persia, the hieroglyphics on the monuments and the inscriptions of Egypt, Babylon, and so forth, translated and deciphered them, and thereby filled, year after year, the gaps in the history of former ages, and made us able to reconstruct them.

China

Long before Confucius (died 478 B.C.) and Mencius (died 288 B.C.), who occasionally cautioned against the excessive use of wine and spirits, intoxicating drinks must have existed, and made it necessary for the imperial government to take measures against the practice of inebriety. "The Announcement about Drunkenness," issued about the year 1116 B.C. by the government, furnishes us with information about the excessive use of spirituous drinks among all classes of people in those days. The "Shoo-King," or "History," and the "She-King," or "Book of Ancient Poetry," also contain many references to the drinking of wine and spirits. Here's a sentence from the "Shoo-King": "Spirits are what men will not do without. To prohibit them and secure a total abstinence from them is beyond the power even of sages." It appears that the peace of the country was threatened by the general intemperance which had taken hold, and that the most stringent measures had to be resorted to.

It is not always clear what was meant by "spirits" in this connection. They are mentioned together with wine frequently in the "She-King" and other writings of those and previous times, which also contain many descriptions of the bibulous behavior and amusements of the people. Here, for instance, is an ode about the agricultural employment of the people:

And with the grain make spirits 'gainst the spring
Which to the bushy eyebrows comfort bring—

and—

Good spirits, in two vessels kept, they take—

---

*Abridged from *One Hundred Years of Brewing* (Chicago: H. S. Rich and Co., 1903; reprinted by Sonja and Will Anderson, Newtown, Conn. 1973), Chapter 2.

or—

> Full of spirits soft and good;
> It excites no conduct rude,

and further—

> I've strained and made my spirits clear.

It appears that the grain used was rice, and that the beverage, which of course had to be subjected to fermentation in order to obtain its exhilarating qualities, was strained and clarified before use.

The art of distilling alcoholic beverages or "spirits" in the modern sense was not known in China until the eleventh century, and very probably not until much later. It appears quite certain that during the preceding period the wine and beerlike beverages were made from cereals, chiefly rice. It may be added that there is a Chinese beer today called *tarasun*, which is made of barley and wheat, the hops which are used being prepared in the form of bricklike masses.

It is also of interest to learn that the ancient customs associated with drinking, which we meet in China in the most approved and perfect form more than a thousand years before Christ, as, for instance, the merry-go-round drinking from the filled horn, the "here's-to-you" drinking, the toasting, and so on, are found in later periods among people of Germanic countries.

India and Persia

The knowledge we possess of ancient India we owe, as we do our information about China, to the sacred books, the *Rig-Veda*, which covered a period of about 1000 B.C. Members of the Aryan race, the ancient Hindus and Persians are related to the Germanic nations, being the Asiatic branch of the Indo-European people. These facts are noteworthy for the reason that even the history of beer and of the materials used in its production, as well as the history of drinking and of religious acts, in which offerings of intoxicating beverages were made to the gods, may be construed as proof of their ancient origin.

The religion of the Hindus, the eastern Aryans, was originally monotheistic in character. In later periods, it developed into a polytheistic system, as expressed in the "Books" or "Vedas" still existing (written 800 to 900 B.C.), and finally degenerated into avowed polytheism and schism.

The worship of the gods was a service of intoxication, for the priests and for the people. The gods appeared to their worshipers as beings requiring alcoholic stimulants, who performed their godly functions and blessed mankind with their gifts only when in a state of drunkenness. A number of quotations from the Sanskrit literature, translated by eminent authorities, will suffice to show that the "Aryan conception of the gods was but a reflection of the character of the people themselves." A prayer to Indra, the chief of the gods, to whom an offering is made of the intoxicating beverage *soma* (to be referred to hereafter), contains the passage: "Come hither, O Indra, to our sacrifices! Drink of the *soma*, O *soma* drinker! thine intoxication is that which gives us abundance of cows. Come hither, O Indra, and intoxicate thyself!"

Without being in a state of drunkenness, Indra was not apparently considered competent to satisfy the wishes of the people and to act upon his own will. In a hymn to the same god, each verse finishes with the lines:

> In the intoxication which *soma* has caused him,
> See what Indra has accomplished.

At their drunken ceremonies they not only called on Indra for his blessing, but invited him to attend in person: "Called by us, O Indra, sit down and intoxicate thyself with us, thy friends!"

Soma was drunk to excess by both priests and people, and the conviviality in tippling between mankind and the gods is splendidly illustrated by the following appeal to one of the latter: "Very old in your favor and your auspicious friendship, reviewing again that auspicious friendship, may we now in your society intoxicate ourselves with *soma*?"

As to the nature of the beverage *soma*, Samuelson, from whose translation of the *Rig-Veda* we have quoted above, says: "The drink (*soma*) is believed to have been prepared from the juice of a creeper (*asclepias*). After being cleaned and macerated in water, the plant was pressed between two stones, and the juice which flowed from it was diluted with water, and strained through ram's wool. This juice was then mixed with malt and warm milk or clarified butter and was allowed to ferment."

Another intoxicating beverage was the *sura*, the drink of the common people, much more intoxicating than *soma*, and made from an Indian grass (*panicum*), water, honey, curds, melted butter and barley. In later years "spirits of rice" is also called *sura*, but its use was prohibited by the mandates of Mamis, a reformer of the Brahmin religion (about the sixth century B.C.), a fate which also befell a beverage extracted from sugar dregs, and another made from the flowers of *madhura* (*bossia latifolio*).

The *Mahabharata*, an ancient Indian epic concerned the quarrels of two rival royal families, describes the coronation of an emperor and various offerings and ceremonies which relate to our subject. A combination of barley and *soma* juice, which may be dignified with the name of beer, was first offered to the element of fire and then to the emperor, who, as he drank it, repeated an invocation. He then offered gifts to the priests, in-

THEY HAD "CEILING PRICES"
ON A CUP OF BEER IN BABYLON
4000 YEARS AGO!

Beer was so popular 4000 years ago that King Hammurabi found it necessary to impose wise regulations on the price that Bit-Sikari (ancient taprooms) might charge for it.

C. SCHMIDT & SONS, INC. • IN PHILADELPHIA SINCE 1860

Schmidt's
Beer & Ale
SINCE 1860 • SINCE 1774*

*Predecessor: Rob't Smith Ale Brewery

CARRYING ON THE FINEST TRADITIONS OF BREWING IN ONE OF AMERICA'S MOST MODERN BREWERIES

© 1945, C. S. & SONS, INC.

cluding a cartload of barley. The epic thus describes the effect of the so-called beer upon the imperial drinker: "The effect of this beer, like the enjoyment of some exquisite food, thrills the body of the Kshatriya, who is inaugurated by means of Indra's great inauguration ceremony, just as pleasantly and agreeably as when the son feels such an excess of joy when embracing his father, or the wife when embracing her husband, as to lose all self-command."

The old Persians (or Parsees), according to their sacred book, the *Zend-Avesta,* were also at times addicted to drink, and we find among them the same beverages and religious libations as in India. The *soma* of the Hindus was their *homa,* or *haoma,* and the *sura* was the *hura* of the Zend language. *Bonga,* another beverage, strongly intoxicating, is named, which was probably prepared from flaxseed, the material still used in Arabia, India and by some tribes of Africans. Though drunkenness was a violation of the religious tenents of Zoroaster, intoxicating beverages were included by him among the offerings at religious rites. His followers did not become as intoxicated as the Brahmins, even though, as Herodotus tells us, and as the Germanic people did in later times, they discussed public affairs while under the influence of wine. Both palm and grape wine were known to the Persians, and their effects frequently played a part in war and politics.

Palestine

The beverages of the Jews, or the Semitic race, were, according to the Bible, products of the grape, tomato, palm, apple, date and other fruits, drunk in both fermented and unfermented state, and therefore called by different names. It is generally accepted that the name *tirosh* was applied to the unfermented, the name *yayin* to the fermented grape juice, while *schechar* was the designation of the other beverages collectively. The disputes as to the sinfulness of the use of wine, owing to its intoxicating influence, and the righteousness of the use of *must* as a nonintoxicating wine, which have been and are still carried on by the temperance people, we may here disregard entirely. It is a fact, however, that wine had a part in the ritual of the Jewish religion—even as other intoxicating beverages had among the above-mentioned peoples—and was among the offerings to Jehovah.

The Jewish people were, as a rule, less addicted to strong drink than the above-mentioned nations, the Persians and Hindoos, and for that reason did not experience any periods when the people or the state stood in danger of ruin from drunkenness, although there was frequent occasion for admonition and advice concerning the benefits of sobriety.

We have no historical record of beverages prepared from any kind of grain by the Jews,* and in a country like Palestine, rich and prosperous up to the time of its conquest by the Romans and the wars of devastation that followed, with a soil abounding with grape and palm and fruits of all kinds, there seems to have been no necessity for such. However, rabbinic tradition indicates that the use of hops to prevent leprosy was discovered by the ancient Hebrews during the Babylonian captivity, in the seventh and eighth centuries B.C.

Egypt

In this country we meet the first and at the same time oldest reliable information concerning a beverage which may be designated as beer,** the history of which, be it mythical or authentic, bears more directly upon the subject in hand. The myth that Osiris and Isis were the inventors of beer is based upon the religious view of nature at that time, personifying the physical forces useful or harmful to mankind and representing them as gods. Osiris represents life—he is the "King of Life." Isis, the "queenly spouse," is the Earth. Nature is aroused from its slumber and seminated by Osiris. For the legend of beer, this religious and poetic background represents the worship of both as the inventors of the amber juice of barley; for history it at least demonstrates that the art of beer brewing was of very ancient origin, even in Egypt. A similar conclusion, as will be shown, was reached much later, in defining the Latin word *cerevisia* (beer) to be a compound of *Ceres*, the goddess of agriculture, and *vis*, the Latin for strength.

Even in the old Egyptian fable of the creation mention is made of beer. When the sun god, Rê, looked down upon his human creatures he beheld the heartless war goddess Hathôr, who had descended upon earth to bathe in the blood of sinful men. So fierce was she in her vengeance that in one city every street swam in blood. Then Rê concluded he would put an end to the murders. He caused great quantities of Delala fruits to be brought from the Elephantine Island, and "gave these to the god Seklet, who is in Heliopolis, that he should grind same." When their barley was being crushed for beer, these Delala fruits were mixed with it, together with the blood of men, and thus seven thousand cases of beer were prepared. This beer, made from human blood, barley and Delala fruits, the compassionate Rê caused to be poured out before the bloodthirsty goddess, until the whole vicinity overflowed with it. This had a wonderful effect: "When the

---

*William Emboden, *Narcotic Plants* (New York: Macmillan Publishing Co., Inc., 1972), p. 103.

**An Assyrian tablet of 2000 B.C. lists beer among the foods Noah used in provisioning the Ark. There were numerous types of beer in ancient Babylon. An ancient tablet in New York's Metropolitan Museum of Art lists dark beer, pale beer, red beer, threefold beer, beer with a head, without a head and so on. The beer was sipped through a straw—in the case of royalty a golden one—long enough to reach from the throne to a large container kept alongside. *See Brewing In Canada* (Ottawa: Brewers Association of Canada, 1963), p. 2.

goddess Hathôr came next morning she found these fields overflowed so she saw her likeness in the shining surface. She drank greedily of the liquor and was pleased with it; drank until she became drunk and forgot all about the men." So it happened that enough men were left alive to repeople the land of Egypt.

Beer, or at least some sort of decoction of barley, is mentioned in the *Book of the Dead,* a record of the ancient Egyptian kings, which scholars claim is about five thousand years old.

It is related that Osiris, in about the year 2017 B.C., found barley wine in the Egyptian city of Pelusium. It is also told how, about 3000 B.C. in the land of the Nile four kinds of beer were known. The historian Herodotus (494 B.C.) speaks only of a barley wine known to the Egyptians, and even asserts that the grape is not found on the soil of Egypt. A native of Greece, where the grape had been cultivated since the earliest days of history and where the pleasures of wine-drinking were freely enjoyed, Herodotus obviously was an entire stranger to the Egyptian juice of barley. He relates: "Their beverage is a wine prepared by them from barley, there being no grapes in their country." Of "barley wine," or "barley drink," as it is always called by the Greek writers, we also hear in many other parts of

Asia Minor and Eastern Europe, for example, from Strabo and Xenophon. Pliny (A.D. 23), speaking of Egyptian beer, says that it is made from grain soaked in water; and as a wine-drinking Roman he deplores the fact that so much skill is wasted in the production of a beverage of that kind, adding that by this a means had been discovered for becoming drunk even with water.

It appears, however, that the Egyptian beer was not as innocuous a beverage as has thus been pictured. Students of that period especially seem to have had a strong predilection for beer-drinking. A passage from the letter of a teacher to his scholar furnishes us with a picture of the dangers of the habit of beer-drinking and saloon-frequenting for the Egyptian student, and proves that youth has been the same at all times, or at least was no better in former ages than today. Our quotation is taken from the *Papyrus Sallier I* and *Papyrus Anastasi IV*, and says:

I am told that you neglect your studies, have a desire for enjoyments, and go from tavern to tavern. Whoever smells of beer (*hagu*) is repulsive to all; the smell of beer holds people at a distance, it hardens your soul. . . . You think it proper to run down a wall and to break through the board gate; the people run away from you. You beat them until sore. . . . Do not give the mugs a place in your heart; forget the goblets; . . . you sit in the hall, you are surrounded by the nymphs; you arise and act foolishly. You sit in front of the girl, you are rubbed with oil, a wreath of burrs is around your neck; you beat your stomach like a drum, you stumble, you fall upon your stomach, you are smeared with filth.

This shows that the beer of Egypt was hardly a temperance drink, but by fermentation had acquired the requisite amount of alcohol. That it was made from malted grain is not only shown by the various designations of the barley, but also by the discovery of barley malt in the ruins of ancient Egypt. No mention is made of hops anywhere, but this does not preclude the possibility that certain spices were used as a substitute for them.

There is another designation for beer besides the above-mentioned *hagu*: the name *zend*, which the Greek writers call *zythos*, has been preserved to the present day in the *zyto* of the Poles and Bohemians. *Zythos* is mentioned in the *History of Plants*, whose Greek author, Theophrastus, lived about 300 B.C. Diodorus assures us that the ancient Egyptians had a strong beer that they named *zythos*, and a weaker named *eurmi*. The first seems to have been a mixture, for according to other writers it possessed the odor of wine and seems to have been some sort of root beer. At Pelusium in the earlier times a much-relished beer was exported even to Greece and Rome. The characteristic of this beer arose from the special ingredients, roots, etc., which gave it its agreeable taste.

It is known that Egypt was a country so richly endowed by nature that its agricultural transactions were very important. The cultivation of grain not only supplied the country with its own necessary breadstuffs but also supplied the surrounding nations. This is demonstrated by the incident in the Bible when Joseph in Egypt "opened all the store houses," and his brothers traveled there to buy grain. The construction of such granaries is illustrated in the sketches found on the tombs of the kings of Thebes, and as described in Wilkinson's *Ancient Egyptians*. The granaries were apart from the dwelling and were enclosed by a separate wall; some of the rooms in which the grain was housed appear to have had vaulted roofs. These were filled through an aperture near the top, to which the men ascended by steps, and the grain, when wanted, was taken out from a door at the base.

Greece and Rome

Greeks and Romans, being richly blessed with grapes, did not require beverages other than wine and had no desire to use the beverages of surrounding nations, whom they considered barbarians. We have seen how Pliny could not understand why the Egyptians wasted so much skill and labor upon an inferior waterlike beverage. During the first centuries of the Christian era the barbarians still addicted to the use of barley wine were a target for the mockery and satire of historians and poets of civilized nations.

It is a mistake to assume that Greeks or Romans had anything to do with the extension of the use of beer, either from Greece to the north, or from Rome to Spain and Gaul; it can be shown that beer, or similar beverages prepared from cereals, were native to the latter countries or had been brought thither by the migrations from Asia to Europe, together with a knowledge of brewing. The Greeks and Romans sought hilarity, pleasure, recreation and inspiration in wine; their poets sing hymns to the godlike grape; their songs of revelry are songs of praise to Dionysus-Bacchus; the pleasures of life are sipped from the wine goblet. However, a beerlike beverage played a part in certain religious ceremonies. Closely connected with Dionysus is the goddess Demeter, whose worship was transferred from Greece to Rome, where it became connected with the worship of Ceres. Sacred feasts, the Cerealia, were celebrated with great pomp and with plays; they were the origin of the designation *cerevisia* for beer, and from them the fruits of the field also received the name cereals.

We now leave the age and the peoples of the old civilized world, who with the exception of Egypt contributed little to the history of beer. We will turn to the nations of Europe, who at that time were slightly or not at all affected by civilization of any kind and who, devoted to agriculture, prepared from grain the beverages used at drinking carousals and the festivals of the gods.

FROM MEDIEVAL TIMES TO THE PRESENT*

In the Christian age beer really came into it own, perhaps largely through the influence of the monasteries which brewed and improved the beer. Monasteries were the centers of learning of all kinds, both scholarly and technical, and religion touched every aspect of life. In many areas the monks built the first breweries, as they pioneered the hotel business by

---

*Insofar as the art of brewing was significantly improved in premedieval times in several nations, the individual historical developments are treated in Chapter 5, especially under "British beers," and "German beers." *See Brewing in Canada*, pp. 2–5.

providing hospitality to pilgrims and other travelers during the Middle Ages. With the usual close association of ale and bread, the brewery in the monastery was built next to the bakehouse.

Three saints are listed as patrons of brewing, and they are very distinguished members of the Christian hagiology indeed: St. Augustine of Hippo, author of the *Confessions* and the most influential of the early Christian philosophers; St. Nicholas of Myra, better known to us as Santa Claus; and the Evangelist, St. Luke, "The Beloved Physician." But there are a myriad of other saints involved with brewing: St. Thomas à Becket, the later martyred Archbishop of Canterbury, when he went to France in 1158 to seek the hand of a French princess for Prince Henry of England, brought with him as gifts several barrels of English ale. He was

An alewife.

elected by the Brewers' Company, one of the London Guilds, as their patron saint.

The Irish saints were also apparently partial to beer. St. Patrick is said to have had among his household a brewer, a priest named Mescan. St. Columban when doing missionary work in Germany came across a crowd of people around a huge cask of beer to be consumed during a ceremony of sacrifice to the pagan god Woden. This was too much for St. Columban, who in his wrath blew upon the cask, which instantly fell apart. The

CULVER PICTURES

Collecting taxes from a fifteenth-century French brewer.

1115.—The Tabard.

" In Southwark at the Tabard as I lay,
Ready to wenden on my pilgrimage
To Canterbury with devout courage,
At night was come into that hostelry
Well nine and twenty in a company
Of sundry folk, by adventure yfall
In fellowship, and pilgrims were they all,
That toward Canterbury woulden ride."

Canterbury Tales.

*Chaucer's pilgrims on their way to Canterbury
spent their first night at the Tabard Inn.*

heathen congregation expressed their penitence after this stern rebuke, and the saint, who had really nothing against beer, increased by a miracle the small amount of beer which had not run away. St. Bridget, who lived a few generations before St. Columban, is credited with changing water into beer for ill-fed lepers.

The involvement of beer with religion is found in many parts of Europe.° St. Arnould is regarded as the patron saint of brewers in Belgium. Munich, one of the great beer cities, bears on its municipal coat of arms the "Munchner Kindl," the figure of a child in a monk's robe, holding a stein of beer.

As in ancient times, the brewers in the medieval period were women. This strikes a strange note today, when a female brewmaster (or perhaps brewmistress) is almost unheard of. Yet beer has always been regarded as that unusual commodity, a "food-drink," and women have always been the cooks. Once the monasteries had established the techniques, the alewives took over the business of brewing.

These women had to contend with the multifarious medieval laws governing quality, quantity and price—legislation clearly indicating the importance of beer in everyday life. The role of bread and beer in the English diet is evident from the price regulations which had been imposed on these commodities by the thirteenth century. There was an Assize of Bread and Ale, a special court, probably as early as the Norman Conquest, to set fair prices for these two basic commodities.

The great events in the lives of the people in medieval England carried the name "ale." It was the tradition for the bride to sell ale on her wedding day, to defray the expenses of the wedding; hence the words "bride ale," which has become "bridal." Funeral feasts of medieval Danes were called "grave ales," with the ale served to keep the departed's ghost away. The familiar church bazaar may well have originated with the "give ale" of the Middle Ages. Then there were "cuckoo ales" on the day the first cuckoo is heard. (This was celebrated as late as 1821 in Shropshire.) There were "college ales," "lamb ales," "clerks' ales."

Ale was the drink of both nobleman and noble lady—as well as peasant. When Queen Elizabeth set out to tour her realm she would send special couriers ahead to test the ale in the town she was to visit. If it wasn't to the Queen's taste, she would have a supply of her own favorite brew

---

°According to the traditions of the Anglo-Saxons, ale was utilized for casting out devils by the following recipe and ritual:

> For one possessed of a devil or fiend-sick: A number of herbs having been worked up in clean ale, the patient was to sing seven masses over the worts, then to add garlic and holy water, and was to drink the mixture out of a church bell. [Garlic has always been a recognized means of exorcising devils, as most students of the occult or witchcraft are aware.] The person possessed was then to give alms and to pray for God's mercies.

> —From Frank A. King, *Beer Has a History*
> (London: Hutchinson's Scientific and Technical Publications), p. 15.

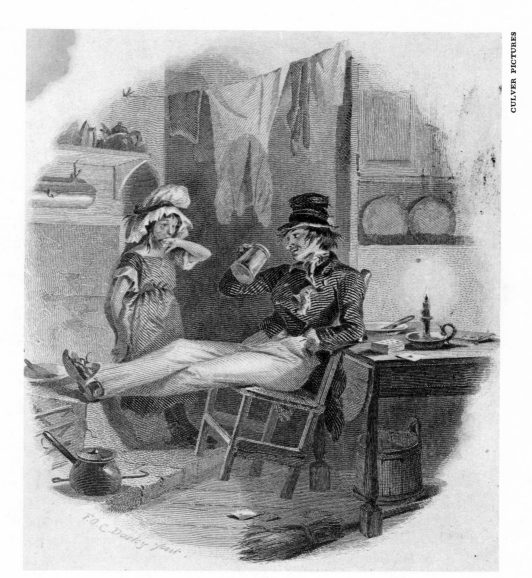

Dick Swiveller to the Marchioness in Dickens'
Old Curiosity Shop: "Your health. You will excuse
my wearing my hat, but the palace is damp
and the marble floor is—if I may be allowed
the expression—sloppy."

expressed from London in time for her arrival. And when her great rival, Mary Queen of Scots, was imprisoned in Tutbury Castle, her special ale from Burton-on-Trent was sent to Mary.

Individual consumption was substantial, in part, no doubt because of the shortage of drinkable water. Ladies-in-waiting at the court of Henry VIII were allowed a gallon of beer (160 ounces) for breakfast alone. (Pretty considerable when one realizes that Canadian adults average only 10.4 ounces for a whole day.)

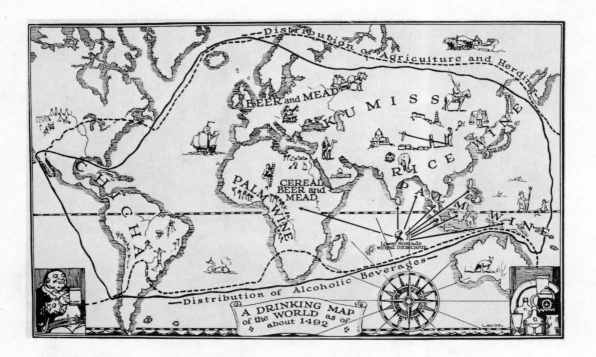

Because ale was so important to the people's daily diet, the government was constantly concerned with its quality. Much has been written about the quaint custom of the British ale conners, who tested the quality of the brew by pouring some on a bench and sitting with their leather breeches in the puddle for a half hour or so. If there was sugar in the ale, or it was impure, the breeches would stick to the bench.

However, the ale conner was a serious official with a responsible job, who had to decide the price at which the ale could be sold, or whether it should be sold at all. (Shakespeare's father was an ale conner.) Ale had to be produced to suit all pocketbooks, and some had to be available to sell very cheaply to the poor.

As the discovery of America began to open up new continents, beer moved with the explorers. In fact Christopher Columbus on his final voyage to America, in 1502, found the natives of Central America making a first-rate brew ". . . of maize, resembling English beer." The French explorers in the north brought with them a tradition of brewing, and the first commercial brewery in Canada was founded by the intendant, Jean Talon, to control the intemperate use of strong drink. The Pilgrim Fathers, who landed at Plymouth Rock instead of farther south as they had planned, did so at least partly because of lack of beer. The journal of one of the Mayflower's passengers, in an entry dated December 19, 1620, said: "We could not now take time for further search or consideration; our victuals being much spent, especially our beer. . . ."

The later centuries witnessed improvement in the quality of beer, and in the method of distribution. Dr. Alexander Nowell, Dean of St. Paul's from 1560 to 1602, is credited with the discovery that beer can be kept for long periods in stoppered bottles. Dr. Nowell, described by Isaak Walton as "a dear lover and constant practiser of angling," left a bottle of ale on the river bank while fishing. Returning a few days later he discovered the bottle and removing the stopper he found "no bottle, but a gun, so great was the sound at the opening thereof." Further, he found the flavor of the ale improved, contrary to our usual experience with sun-warmed beer!

During the seventeenth century, beer fought off the competition of a flood of exotic new drinks, ranging from French brandy to chocolate, tea and the latest novelty, coffee. In eighteenth-century England—and later, in Ireland—the brewing of porter became a substantial business.

The growth of cities saw the development of the great breweries. Improved transport made famed beers from one city or country available to discerning customers in another. Two eighteenth-century Russian rulers, Peter the Great and Catherine the Great, became devotees of the English beer from Burton-on-Trent, and shipments for the royal household arrived regularly in St. Petersburg.

The history of beer is still developing. New production techniques are being discovered—but the beer is still produced through natural fermentation, in the old, old way. New types of drinking vessels—bottles, cans, glasses, mugs—have replaced the ancient jars and containers of earthenware, wood, pewter or leather, but bastioned by tradition, the beverage remains unchanged.

The adjacent "drinking map" was prepared by Dr. John M. Cooper, anthropologist of the Catholic University of America in Washington, D.C.* He learned that the arts of brewing beer and fermenting wine did not originate in one place and then spread to the rest of the world. Individual cultures developed their own fermented beverages.

---

*Science News Letter, Dr. Frank Thone, September 9, 1933, p. 167.

3

**Beer
and
Health**

I T may be unwise in a book written primarily for people who have more than a fondness for beer to present negative arguments about its values. However, a counterpoint is necessary in this chapter, both to balance the book (which leans heavily on information provided by the brewing industry), and to justify the author who, at this point in his "research" (drinking steadily and reading about, as well as talking to people about beer for well over three years), is by no means certain that daily consumption of even the purest of brews is necessarily beneficial to the human organism.

Heinrich E. Jacob* argues that an alteration in bodily type from leanness to corpulence in Northern Europe was "the outcome of beer swilling," and that the supersaturation of the body with carbonic acid counteracts the chief function of respiration, which is to eliminate excess water and CO_2, while providing O_2 to the cells via the bloodstream. These points are worth considering, especially by those of us who consume beer regularly.

BEER AND BODILY SHAPE

At the opening of the humanist epoch, there was a fairly sudden change in bodily type in northwestern and northeastern Europe. The Scots, the English, the Dutch, the Danes, the Norwegians, the Swedes, the Finns, and, above all, the Low Germans, began to put on flesh. Especially the leaders —princes, artists, men of learning, generals, priests, persons of taste or of musical genius—were fat folk. An amazing transformation! Never since the world had been turning on its axis, or at least since human beings had dwelt on its surface, had the belief been prevalent that obesity was in any way synonymous with health, power, genius and dignity. Yet from 1400 to 1700 this belief inconspicuously gained predominance throughout northern Europe.

A large number of notables during that period were in fact exceedingly

*Heinrich E. Jacob, *Coffee: The Epic of a Commodity* (New York: The Viking Press, 1935).

Beer is mother's milk to him.

stout: kings Gustavus Adolphus and Henry VIII, the German general Frundsberg, Martin Luther, Humanist and writer Willibald Pirckheimer, sculptor Peter Vischer, author Hans Sachs, composers George Frederick Handel and Johann Sebastian Bach, Christian IV of Denmark, and countless others.

To us these worthies look unpleasantly fat. They themselves regarded their potbellies as so natural that they would have been puzzled to learn that we should think it necessary, for aesthetic reasons, to moderate their outlines. No sculptor today, working on a memorial statue of Gustavus Adolphus, the Protestant hero who fell at Lützen, would dream of presenting him with the huge belly which the king really possessed. In those days leanness was looked upon as morbid. It is true that Erasmus of Rotterdam, Prince Eugene and Frederick the Great, who were of the asthenic type, were also by no means healthy persons. But if we were to meet them today in dinner jacket or lounge suit, we should regard them, precisely because of their leanness, as much healthier than, say Bach or Handel, if met under similar circumstances.

It was only in northern Europe that this "monstrous regiment" of the fat prevailed. Southern Europe retained its lean and sinewy type. Men of the wine-drinking countries, the Spanish, the inhabitants of central and southern France, the Italians and the Greeks, the Hungarians and Danubian vintners, did not share, or shared very little in, the inflation of bodily type. For the inflation was the outcome of a new mode of nutrition, the outcome of beer swilling.*

Carbonic Acid

The citizen's day began and ended with beer. A good draught to wet your whistle at the start; at the noonday meal a beer soup; and at supper, of course, there must be egg-flip made with beer. Raisin-beer and sugar-beer, fish and sausages boiled in beer, beer in all conceivable forms, to say nothing of abundant draughts of plain beer when paying visits, talking business, attending baptisms and funerals. The body was deluged with carbohydrates, which were transmogrified into fat. When we remember that the main purpose of the process of respiration is to rid our blood of carbonic acid, we can see that the unceasing supersaturation of the human organism with H_2CO_3 cannot fail to have effect on the individual and on the community.

Beer is a food. In addition to alcohol and water, it contains albumin, dextrin, nutritive salts and sugar. A liter of good beer contains five grams of albumin, and fifty grams of carbohydrates. The fact that these nutritive

---

*Beer actually has a *lower* caloric value than wine. Beer contains 42 cals/100 gm; table wine 85 cals/100 gm. The relative amounts consumed may explain why beer drinkers got fat while wine drinkers stayed thin.

You are what you drink is illustrated by this engraving from Mew and Ashton's Drinks of the World *(1892).*

substances are introduced into the organism in a fluid and readily as-similable form, accompanied by effervescent carbonic acid, alone accounts for the revolution in the appearance of the human figure.

Heinrich E. Jacob believes that the temperance movement was a de-sirable one if for no other reason than that a slimming of the population was more readily begun. Certainly no one can argue that beer is not to some degree fattening like all alcoholic beverages. (*See* Charts: Caloric Content of Beer and Nutritive Values of Beer.)

In twentieth-century Scandinavia there has been a very effective tem-perance movement, and the Nordic slimness and persistent youthfulness bear witness to the fact. Goethe longed for a similar movement among the Germans. Of all the enemies of excessive beer drinking no one had keener insight than he. Writing to Knebel, tutor to the princes at the court of Weimar, he said that beer dulled the nerves and thickened the blood. "If our people go on swilling beer and smoking as they now do, for another three generations, woe to Germany! The effect will first become noticeable in the stupidity and poverty of our literature, and our descendants will declare themselves greatly astonished thereat!"

I cannot help but wonder if the excesses of the Third Reich were a fulfillment of Goethe's prophecy.

HOPS AND HEALTH

The healthful properties of beer owe much to the hops which are added during brewing. The brewer adds hops to aid in the preservation of beer and to give it a tart flavor. Perhaps few people realize that *Humulus lupulus* was once an official part of the United States Pharmacopoeia, and its medicinal properties highly valued. It was prescribed in the form of infusions, tinctures and extracts for its tonic, soporific and stomachic properties.

It is only reasonable that a plant which exerts preservative properties on a beverage which would otherwise be a perfect medium for the growth of bacteria must be antibacterial, at least to some degree. As mentioned earlier, rabbinical tradition has it that ancient Hebrews discovered that the use of hopped ale offered protection against leprosy, an infection of bacterial origin.

Medical writers continued to extol the virtues of these delicate blossoms of the hop, until the age of synthetic medicines, the present century. As an ethnobotanist and antiquarian I cannot omit a summary page of these writings.*

Until they were recently trumpeted forth in the advertisements of a certain patent medicine, the medicinal properties of hops were not generally known outside the medical profession. Old medical writers, however, must have been profoundly aware of them. William Coles, herbalist, in his *History of Plants,* published in 1657, states that certain preparations of hops are cures for about half "the ills that flesh is heir to." Another old writer declares the young shoots of the hop, eaten like asparagus, are very wholesome and effectual to loosen the body (the poorer classes in some parts of Europe still eat the young hops as a vegetable), the head and tendrils good to purify the blood in scurvy and most other cutaneous diseases (which scurvy is not) and the decoctions of the flower and syrup thereof useful against pestilential fevers. Juleps and apozems were also prepared from hops for hypochondriacal and hysterical affections; and a pillow stuffed with hops was used to induce sleep. This last method, by the way, was taken advantage of by the medical advisers of George III. That unfortunate king, when in a demented state, always slept on such a pillow. Another writer tells us that the Spaniards were in the habit of boiling a pound of hop roots in a gallon of water, reducing it to six pints, and drinking half a pint when in bed of a morning, in the belief that it possessed the same properties as sarsaparilla. Dr. Brooks, in his *Dispensatory,* published in 1753, concurs with the older writers on the subject.

Observations and Experiments on the Humulus Lupulus of Linnaeus,

---

*John Bickerdyke, *The Curiosities of Ale and Beer* (London: Spring Books, 1889; reprinted 1965), pp. 85–86.

with an account of its use in Gout and other Diseases, is the title of a pamphlet by a Mr. Freake, of Tottenham Court Road, published in 1806. The author states that a patient of his, who was in need of a bitter tincture, found all the usual remedies disagreed with him, and after numerous unsatisfactory experiments, fell back upon a preparation of hops, which appeared to answer his purpose. This led Mr. Freake to try further experiments with the hop, and he came to the conclusion that it was an excellent remedy for the pains of gout, acting sometimes when opium failed.

Hops have also been employed with good effect in poultices. Dr. Trotter, in one of his medical works, quotes a letter from an assistant of Dr. Geach, once senior surgeon of the Royal Hospital at Plymouth, in which the writer says that he had experimented with hops during six months, and found that a poultice made of a strong decoction of hops, oatmeal and water was an excellent remedy for ulcers, which should first be fermented with the decoction.

In the introduction to Murray's *Handbook of Kent* it is stated that invalids are occasionally recommended to pass whole days in hop grounds. In hop gardens the air is no doubt impregnated with lupulin, so there may be something in this.

At the present day lupulin is often used in medicine. Lupulin was the name given by Ives to the yellow dust covering the female flower of hops. Later, Ives, Chevallier and Pellatus gave that name, not to the dust, but to the bitter principle it contains. The recognized preparations of hops are an infusion, a tincture and an extract. Dr. John Gardner, in one of his works on medicine, says that "bitter ale, or the lupulin in pills which it forms by simply rubbing between the fingers and warming, are the best forms for using hops in dyspepsia and feeble appetite, which they will often relieve." The lupulin powder is easily separated from the hops by sieving. A hop bath is also recommended by Dr. Gardner to relieve pain in certain internal diseases. It is made thus: two pounds of hops are boiled in two gallons of water for half an hour, then strained and pressed, and the fluid added to about thirty gallons of water. This bath has been much praised. Hop beer (without alcohol) is another preparation of the plant which has been recommended.

In the same book, the author of an old pamphlet (London, 1641) declares that warm beer is healthful, and cold beer injurious. "Cold beer is very pleasant when extreme thirst is in the stomach; but what more dangerous to the health? Many by drinking a cup of cold beer in extreme thirst, have taken a surfeit and killed themselves. Therefore we must not drink cold beer because it is pleasant, but hot beer because it is profitable."

To make beer "more heady," some nineteenth-century brewers added the fruits of *absinthium* or wormwood (*Artemisia absinthium*) to their hops. Absinthe, the drink shrouded in mystery, was compounded of this herb with a host of other aromatics. Until about fifty years ago wormwood had been used in medicine, going back to ancient times. Linnaeus, Boerhaave and many other great naturalists extolled "its good effects in many disorders," including hypochondriasis.

This last named virtue of wormwood may explain why the following drink was said to "restore self-respect and interest in one's surroundings when even Tahiti rum failed." The following drink (let's call it a "Dr. Weiner") was prepared for Paul Gauguin before he left Tahiti to die in the Marquesas. "It was made of a portion of absinthe, a dash of grenadine—a syrup of the pomegranate fruit—the juice of two limes, and half a pint

Beer improperly prepared or negligently stored
was once a common source of disease, as
illustrated in this engraving from Mew and Ashton's
Drinks of the World *(1892).*

of siphon water." The "receipt" for this potent South Seas concoction was left in Tahiti many years ago by the physician to Robert Louis Stevenson.

Allergies and Beer

A highly complex product like beer may contain small traces of certain ingredients which may occasionally cause allergic reactions. (Allergic reactions have even been seen with human milk.)

A recent publication* lists many components not usually associated with a glass of beer. People subject to allergic reactions might scan the following list for an offensive fraction: carbon dioxide, fluoride, hydrogen sulfide, phosphate, sulfur dioxide, calcium, copper, iron, magnesium, potassium, sodium, methyl alcohol, ethyl alcohol, higher alcohols, diacetyl, acetaldehyde, lactic acid, hexoses, tannins, isohumulones, proteins, ammonia, thiamine, riboflavin, pantothenic acid, pyridoxine, nicotinic acid and biotin.

---

*C. D. Leake and M. Silverman, *Alcoholic Beverages in Clinical Medicine* (Chicago: Year Book Medical Publishers, 1966).

CULVER PICTURES

Kentish hop gardens, 1880.

An Alsatian hop yard, 1880.

Additives in Beer

By far the most threatening fractions in beer are those contributed by additives and preservatives. These have been given wide coverage by the press recently. Representative Benjamin Rosenthal (Democrat, New York) has read a list of food and chemical additives used in beer-making into the Congressional Record.

Seventy members of the House of Representatives have co-sponsored a bill which would require brewers and manufacturers of other alcholic beverages to list all ingredients on their labels. It is surprising that alcoholic beverages are at present exempt from the labeling laws which apply to most other foods and beverages.

Congressman Rosenthal, basing his comments on a recent publication of the Center for Science in The Public Interest* said "most of the chemicals are probably safe. However, some of the additives have not been adequately tested, and many individuals are allergic to certain others.

Much of the present concern with additives in beer grew out of a seri

---

The Chemical Additives in Booze.

The beginning
of your pint

is the brewers' most important raw material
lped to make it a better crop for the farmers

of fatal heart attacks among heavy beer drinkers between 1964 and 1966. Mere alcohol was not to blame. It was discovered that cobalt sulfate, used at that time by several brewers to make thick, lasting heads, upset the metabolism of heart cells. Researchers believe that cobalt locks up alpha lipoic acid, which is needed by the vitamin thiamine to complete an essential reaction in a metabolic pathway of the Krebs Cycle. The heart cells of the beer drinkers were thus destroyed by energy starvation.

While cobalt has since been banned in beer, consumer advocates insist that all additives must be listed on labels, to enable patients with known allergies to avoid those that affect them. To elucidate: even a little peanut butter may be fatal to individuals who are hypersensitive to peanuts. In the booklet *The Chemical Additives in Booze* Dr. Jean Mayer, Harvard nutritionist, reported that one such individual died after eating ice cream that contained peanut butter. Had the manufacturer been required to list this ingredient the boy might have been spared this "accidental" death.

A list of some of the chemical additives which may be used in beer-making follows. While all brewers do not use all of these ingredients (or any of them for that matter—some brewers use *no* additives) many brewers continue to do so. Brewers in Germany, Switzerland and Luxembourg are the only brewers in the world who are prohibited by law from using anything but barley malt, hops, water and yeast in their beers. However, export beers of these countries are only required to meet the standards of the country which imports them. This means that, for example, a fine German beer, which is additive free in Germany, could enter other countries containing some chemicals. The only exception is Bavarian beers. Brewed to the strictest code in the world, beers from this region (a state of West Germany whose largest cities are Munich, Nürnburg and Augsburg) are the same whether produced for the local market or for abroad.

Chemicals Sometimes Used in Beer-Making*

Name of Chemical	Purpose
gum arabic propylene glycol alginate (PGA) peptones	To stabilize foamy heads
ethylenediaminetetraacetic acid (EDTA)	To prevent gushing when container is opened

*For further information *see* Thomas E. Furia, *Handbook of Food Additives,* 2nd ed. (Cleveland: Chemical Rubber Co., 1972).

Name of Chemical	Purpose
various proteases (papain, bromelain, etc.)	Chill-proofing (to dissolve particles which may cloud beer under refrigeration)
ascorbic acid (vitamin C), isoascorbates, sodium bisulfite, sodium hydrosulfite, sodium metabisulfite, potassium metabisulfite	Antioxidants (prevent oxidation and subsequent loss of flavor and color)
various enzymes	To speed up conversion of starch to sugar during malting
heptyl paraben hydroxybenzoate	Preservative
caramel, F.D. & C. Blue No. 1, Red No. 40 and Yellow No. 5	Artificial colors
acetic acid, adipic acid, anethole, benzaldehyde, citric acid, decanal, ethanal, ethyl acetate, ethyl isobutyrate, ethyl maltol, gentian extract, grapefruit oil, isoamyl-acetate, isoamyl butyrate, isobutyl acetate, juniper berries, lemon oil, licorice root, lime oil, malic acid, methyl anthranilate, nootkatone, octanol, orange oil, quassia extract, sodium citrate, sucrose, octaacetate, tartaric acid, terpineol	Flavoring and coloring

The addition of chemical agents to beer is an ancient practice. Adulteration has probably occurred from the time man began depending upon others for his foods and beverages. Public food inspectors were early assigned to check on manufacturers, and in 1309 English wine inspectors were required to take an oath to protect the public from unscrupulous wine makers.

Ale conners were later created to insure the strength and quality of the brew. As described by Frank A. King,[*]

---

[*]*Beer Has a History*, p. 21.

He would enter an inn unexpectedly, draw a glass of ale, pour it on a wooden bench, and then sit down in the little puddle he had made. There he would sit for thirty minutes by the clock. He would smoke, he would drink with all who asked him, but he would be very careful not to change his position in any way. At the end of the half hour he would make as if to rise, and this was the test of the ale, for if the ale was impure, if it had sugar in it, the tester's leather breeches would stick fast to the bench, but if there was no sugar in the liquor no impression would be present; in other words, the tester would not 'stick to the seat.'

Present-day food inspectors use more technologically accurate methods to assay purity but the entire subject of adulteration is conspicuously absent from the curriculums of universities and even of medical courses. Basic

PLZEŇSKÝ PRAZDROJ V OBRAZECH

To test the honesty of beer and brewer, an alderman would pour beer onto a bench and bid the brewer sit on it and in it. When the beer dried, the alderman would bid the brewer rise. If the bench stuck to his leather trousers, then the beer was adjudged honest; if it didn't, then the brewer was punished. Or so the story is told in Plzeňský Prazdroj V Obrazech. *In Frank A. King's* Beer Has a History *the story is the same but the conclusion is just the opposite. The medieval woodcuts shown here seem to support the Czechoslovakian version of the story.*

education on the potential dangers of the substances we imbibe daily should be offered even at the lower grade levels. The consumer must not assume that "the government is keeping an eye on them." The cobalt incident, the high probability that the common meat and fish preservatives, the nitrates and nitrites, are carcinogenic (they are used in pressed meats, frankfurters, etc., even while they are highly suspect), would indicate a lax governmental agency, more interested in protecting manufacturers from the demands of consumers than protecting consumers from unconscientious manufacturers.

The beer drinker must be made aware of the possibilities of contamination in his favorite brew (as well as in all foods and beverages). Accidents do occur. In London, at the turn of the century, six thousand people were affected by and seventy died from arsenic poisoning that was transmitted by contaminated beer. The contamination had originated not with the brewers but with the producers of brewing sugars—glucose and invert sugar. Nor was the brewing sugar producer himself at fault. He was using sulfuric acid that had been accidentally manufactured from highly arsenical iron pyrites.

Caloric Content of Beer*

	Number of Calories
Beer—pint (12 ounces)	144.0
Rum (1¼ ounces with 4 ounces of cola)	134.9
Dry gin (1¼ ounces with 4 ounces of ginger ale)	120.9
Scotch whiskey (1¼ ounces with 4 ounces of soda)	79.4
Rye whiskey (1¼ ounces with 4 ounces of ginger ale)	121.1
Martini (2 ounces of gin and ½ ounce French vermouth)	142.3
Manhattan (2 ounces of rye and ¾ ounce Italian vermouth)	159.6
Milk (12 ounces)	229.5
Ginger ale (12 ounces)	126
Cola (12 ounces)	168
1 Doughnut	210
2 Eggs	162
2 medium frankfurters	206
Peanuts (½ cup)	392
Plain milk chocolate bar (1½ ounces)	226
Cream cheese (1 ounce)	106
Apple pie (3¼-inch sector)	246

*In *Brewing Art and Science,* Brewers Association of Canada.

Nutritive Values of Beer*

An Analysis of Beer (12-ounce bottle)

Protein	1.6–1.7 gm
Fat	0.0 gm
Carbohydrates	15.9 gm
Water	92%
Ethyl Alcohol	3.8%
Solids and Extracts	4.2%

Vitamins and Minerals

Calcium	15 mg.
Phosphorus	93 mg.
B_1 Thiamine	18.7 mcgm
B_2 Riboflavin	40–100 mcgm
B_6 Pyridoxin	185 mcgm
Niacin	2250–3750 mcgm
Pantothenate	185–375 mcgm

---

*In *Brewing Art and Science,* Brewers Association of Canada.

4

Brewing: The Act and the Art

BEFORE looking into the commercial brewhouses and some of their products I think it would be interesting to investigate the making of beer at home (i.e., the production of relatively small quantities of beer for non-commercial purposes). In earlier times many a household and tavern brewed its own beer, according to its own taste.* The art of brewing, at least in limited quantities, does not demand great chemical and scientific knowledge nor a few years of apprenticeship to a Bavarian master. However, some knowledge of the basic materials is desirable—barley, wheat, rice, corn, oats and sugar, as well as water, hops, yeast, finings and primings. This will help explain the commercial *brewing processes*—cultivation, harvesting, malting, mashing, hopping, fermenting, filtering, fining, priming, refrigerating, pasteurizing, racking and packaging.

The basic materials are common to both home brews and commercial beers, while the brewing processes obviously must be much more simple for the limited production demands of a kitchen or basement workshop than for a massive commercial brewhouse.

By learning about beer from the ground up the reader should gain a working knowledge of the beer they regularly drink, as well as an understanding of some of the problems facing those who make beer on a massive scale. To be able to recognize the various tastes, flavors, aromas and colors of beer, a basic knowledge of the raw materials used in brewing is essential. To appreciate the finer points of the art of brewing, it is first necessary to understand the procedures in the *act* of brewing.

In the days when homemade beer was as common as homemade bread** only malt, hops, water and yeast was utilized. Today, even home brews contain ingredients other than these. The list of ingredients multiplies in

---

*Before attempting to make beer at home, one should check and comply with all federal, state, and local laws.

**As an example of consumption: in seventeenth-century England an average household drank 36 gallons of beer. Beer was taken at every meal, and water was imbibed only when no other beverage was available.

commercial beers, where the brewer must provide and maintain many qualities over relatively long periods (a "good" color, a beer that does not foam out of the bottle or can when opened but maintains a foamy head when poured, a nonrancid taste, no sediment, to name a few). In addition, many means exist to recover foul or stale batches of beer which add yet further to the list of components of a basic, simple drink.

The making of beer, or any fermented malt beverage, depends basically upon the transformation of sugar into alcohol by the action of yeast. Since cereals which contain starch, such as barley, rye, maize, rice, oats, sorghum, tapioca or soy, are utilized in making beers, special methods are required to change the starch into sugar. One such method is malting. Starch is not fermentable in its original state; it must first be converted to sugar, which is fermentable by yeasts.

Whereas all sugars necessary for conversion into alcohol are derived solely from malted grains in "true beers," home brews generally rely upon the addition of sugar to increase the speed of fermentation, reduce the cost of utilizing expensive malted grains, and increase the alcoholic content of the final brew. It must be pointed out that most commercial brewers now add various sugars during brewing for the same reasons. In Germany, Switzerland and Luxembourg it is illegal to employ sugar; these regions recognize beer as a drink made only from barley malt, hops and water. (While it is not illegal to add sugar or substitute cheaper grains in the production of beer in other countries, some conscientious brewers adhere to the same standards as the brewers in the above-mentioned nations. This will be discussed further when we investigate some commercial beers of the world. The brewing laws in Pilsen, Czechoslovakia, are even stricter.)

Imitation Beers. Some writers categorize those brews which utilize only grains for the required sugar as true beers. Imitation beers are those made by use of malt extract and sugars. For the purposes of this brief outline home brews will be referred to as imitation beers, since most people choose to add sugar, employ malt extract and cut corners in other ways as well. The reader will soon realize that many, if not most, of our commercially produced beers also fall into this category.

This is not to say that so-called imitation beers are not excellent in taste and very satisfying. They are not however as superlative in quality as those brewed according to the strict Bavarian code. In this light it will become easy to understand how a home brew can be made that is as good, if not better, than most commercial brews. Both brews can be made of the very same ingredients and by similar methods. The home brewer however has one great advantage: he does not have to add those questionable substances often utilized by the commercial brewer to retain desirable qualities over a period of time and under adverse conditions.

Good beer, like good food, requires good ingredients as well as a care and skill. Since most home brewers buy their ingredients prepackaged, the following guidelines will be useful only to those individuals who have access to a variety of each component.

BASIC MATERIALS

Malts

> *Should be chosen by its round body, sweet smell, and thin skin; if it bites easy, you may rely upon its being good; if, on the contrary, you should find it hard, it has not had due attention paid to it in the malting. . . .*
>
> —B. Parkes, *The Domestic Brewer* (1821)

From the date of the above recommendation it appears that even in the good old days ready-malted barley was employed by the home brewer. The malting process is time-consuming and relatively complex. For these reasons it is generally avoided by home brewers who use malt extract in conjunction with ready-malted barley. The malting of barley will be outlined when we examine the production of commercial beers, but for the moment we may as well look at the basis for all malt, the grains.

High quality barley is the most desirable grain for brewing. It produces the best-tasting beer, with characteristics unmatched by brews made from the less expensive grains—corn, rice, oats or rye. According to a Munich brewhouse an ancient saying "malt is the soul of beer" is taken to mean only barley malt by the world's best brewers. Those who claim to use the best corn, rice, oats or rye are simply evading the fact that barley is the preferred grain. The others are simply less expensive substitutes.

Hardy barley will grow from the Arctic to the semitropics; in the Andes at 11,000 foot elevations, to as low as the basin of the great Sahara. It is probably this ecological diversity and its status as the oldest of all cultivated grains that makes barley the standard grain for beer. However, all barleys are not useful to the brewer. The most particular brewers grow their own barley from carefully cultivated seed strains.

High protein content is not desirable in brewing. High protein means high nitrogen and this means in turn a lessened amount of carbohydrates. Since ample starch is necessary for conversion to malt, a high protein barley makes for difficult malting and retards the conversion of starch into sugar. On the other hand, nitrogen does speed up fermentation, once the yeast has been added, and produces an active, foamy brew. This can be troublesome to the brewer, who must create a sparkling beverage that looks clear in the glass. (In the old days when steins were used, nitrogenous particles or "sediment" went unobserved; today people prefer glasses and demand a clear if less nutritious drink.)

Two main types of barley are used in brewing: two-row barley and six-row barley. Both refer to the number of rows of fertile flowers, hence the number of rows of barleycorns that are produced prior to harvest. Six-row barley is generated from the type where all the flowers are fertile, and produce three barleycorns which result in six rows. Two-row barley is generated from the type where only one of each of the three flowers is fertile. The six-row variety gathers more sunlight and is subsequently richer, indicating a high nitrogen content. Thus, two-rowed types, with a *low* protein content, are preferred for brewing.

In looking over barley, with an eye toward making a few gallons of beer, select a soft, mealy endosperm (internals) and thin hull. This indicates a low nitrogen content and less trouble during malting. Grains should also be even in size, have finely wrinkled hulls, and be dry and sweet.

While home brewers usually buy their barley already malted, the conscientious commercial brewer must undertake the difficult process of malting. For this reason a barley with good germinating properties is essential. There is general agreement that two-row barley, in addition to having more desirable rounder grains than six-row types, generally malts better. The largest producers of brewer's barley in Europe are France, Great Britain and Denmark. Considerable quantities are also cultivated in Germany, Czechoslovakia, Poland, Holland, Austria and Spain.

While most brewers buy malt already made, a few make their own. Fewer still are those who grow their own crop.

Malt Extracts

These are laboratory products derived from barley and other cereal grains. While not chemicals per se, they are adjuncts, and much cheaper than pure barley. Most home brews are made largely with such extracts (and exhibit the characteristic "nutty" flavor) but superior beers are never "enriched" with them, although most average beers rely on them. A combination of malt extract and malted barley is the most common compromise, both for the home brewer who hasn't the desire to malt his grains or pay the price for pure malted barley, and for the brewer out to make a palatable beer as quickly as possible and at the lowest price.

Other Grains

Not only do the other grains cost less to purchase initially but smaller quantities of them are required to make beer. They have relatively high starch contents and therefore convert easily to the malt sugar required during fermentation. Beer made with corn, rice, wheat, potatoes, oats, rye or tapioca may be stronger (in alcohol content) and less expensive than barley beer, but such beers are often of poorer quality, lacking the flavor and aroma of the pure barley brews.

Corn and rice are frequently used in domestic U.S. beers which are extremely light, pale, and brilliant. Both grains contain a lot of oil which must be removed by cracking, cooking and then rolling them into flakes. Flaked maize is a common ingredient in most domestic home-brewing kits.

Oat malt is used in oatmeal stouts which have unique flavor and better nutritive qualities than other types of grain beer.

Wheat malt is often used to stimulate yeast growth, improve the stability of the finished product, and promote flavor and body. It is difficult to malt this grain which makes wheat an expensive raw material. Especially strong English ales were made in Elizabethan times from wheat malt, as was also the famous Berliner Weissbier. Today, several excellent local beers in Belgium are brewed from wheat.

Rye malt is favored by Ken Shales, a British home brewer and author, who states that his stouts are "smoother and have a slightly greater head retention" when rye is used in place of barley.

While other grains are frequently employed in commercial brews they are not too desirable for home brews, since the overall saving in substituting them for barley malt is not significant and "the risks of making poor beers, which do not ferment or clear well, are much increased."

Hops

> *Must be chosen by their bright green colour, sweet smell, and clamminess when rubbed in the hand.*
> —B. PARKES, *The Domestic Brewer* (1821)

Although since ancient times hops have been valued for their medicinal properties, appreciation of the flavor they impart to beer is of more recent origin. In England until the time of Henry VII, beer was brewed without the use of hops. Today many so-called ales and light lagers (especially in the United States) are made with just a small quantity of these attractive blossoms. Introduced into English beers in the fifteenth century, hops were first looked upon as a dangerous adulterant and then prohibited as a "wicked weed." In those days they were used primarily to preserve beer, and for their soporific and other medicinal properties. Many other herbs were preferred for flavoring beer—balsam, broom, centaury, dandelion, hay, mint, tansy and wormwood, to name but a few. Today the bitter flavor and characteristic beer aroma come from hops. The very significant tranquilizing properties of beer are not derived solely from its alcoholic content. The glandular hairs of the familiar hop cones contain lupulin, a sedative and hypnotic drug that was recognized in *The Pharmacopoeia of the United States* between 1831 and 1916. The famous hop-pillows of King George III (1787) were used instead of opiates to calm his nerves and to promote sleep, as we have seen.

The flavor, head retention and over-all character of a beer will be strongly influenced by the type of hop used. It is important to use the best variety available. Determining which variety is best can only be undertaken by the serious home brewer willing to experiment with various types. Some prefer to blend their hops, producing a custom crafted brew.

The following types are frequently used in brewing:

Bullion. This American grown hop is noted for its marked bitterness. It is particularly favored by brewers of stouts and for beers aged exceptionally long. Rarely used by itself, due to its strength, it is often blended with milder varieties.

Hallertau. This Bavarian hop is very popular in light beers, particularly those made of both barley malt and grain adjuncts. It is the hop of choice in those regions of Germany where lagers are preferred.

Saaz. From Czechoslovakia, this variety is ideal for lagers, being mild, slightly aromatic, delicate and slightly dry.

Fuggle. This is probably the favorite of the British brewers. Used for over 100 years, this Kentish hop is noted for its strong flavor. It is particularly useful for stronger beers such as brown ales.

Golding. Developed over 160 years ago, in Kent, England, this variety is frequently used in light ales due to its milder flavor.

Hops for commercial purposes are grown chiefly in the United States, Germany (Spalt hops, Tettnang hops, Hallertau hops), Czechoslovakia

LONDON ILLUSTRATED NEWS

A visit to a brewery in 1847: the ale rounds.

(Saaz hops), France, England, Japan, Spain and China. While each brewer has his preferences and tries to use the same variety consistently, he is sometimes forced to accept whatever species he can get, with a resultant inconsistency in the final product. That is one reason why from time to time the same brand may taste different. For instance Hürlimann Breweries of Switzerland uses mainly German Hallertau hops, but occasionally resorts to Saaz hops, as well as to small quantities of hops from the Swiss hop gardens in the region of Stammheim.

Hop Extracts

To reduce shipping and storage costs, lower the required boiling time and lessen the overall amount of hops required many brewers now use hop extract. While one manufacturer assures me that hop extracts actually enhance the taste of beer (because undesirable hop oils are evaporated) some of the world's oldest breweries still employ only whole, unrefined hops.

Both hop powder and hop extract are commercially available. Whereas the former is made from fresh hops without using organic solvents (leaf and stem portions are mechanically removed) in the extract form hop resins are removed with methylene chloride, a relatively safe organic solvent. This chemical, being very volatile like ether, is distilled from the hops by heat. There is no danger that methylene chloride is ingested from beers brewed with hop extract. The only thing missing may be the full flavor characteristics which come from using whole hops. At least this is the consensus of masters who brew beers such as Pilsner Urquell, Tuborg, Lowenbrau Zurich and others. The only possible danger associated with methylene chloride is that the worker in the hop-extract plant who inhales the fumes for long periods is exposing himself to possible poisoning from too much carboxylhemoglobin in his blood—one of the same compounds formed when cigarettes are smoked. But the home brewer needn't consider using hop concentrates. Dried whole hops are available at a cost low enough to warrant their use.

Water

The nature of a particular water is determined by the salts dissolved in it, and this in turn influences the character of the beer. Water with a high calcium content is described as hard, and with a low content as soft. The salt content of the water depends on the soil through which the rain seeps before collecting at the source. While today the majority of the world's breweries modify natural water to conform to a brewer's ideal, some are fortunate enough to be able to utilize what is drawn from their own wells. For instance, England's high quality pale ales and bitter beers are brewed at Burton-on-Trent, where the water contains a relatively high quantity of

A visit to a brewery in 1847: the stables.

calcium sulphate (gypsum). This aids in the separation of unwanted husks from the malt, which in turn helps to produce a clear finished beer. Similarly, the characteristics of water in other regions of Britain have made local beers what they are. Thus, Hampshire is known for its bitter, and Ireland is famous for her stouts.

Many American brewers attempt to capitalize on their waters, too. Genesee draws its brewing water from the spring-fed Hemlock Lake reservoir. This water is then run through sand and gravel filters and later through charcoal filters. Coors beer is brewed from Rocky Mountain spring water, exactly as it comes from the ground—without the need of any corrective salts. Olympia beer is made with water from Tumwater Falls, Washington, which the brewers claim is "recognized throughout the world as one of the finest natural brewing waters for the production of a pale Pilsen-type beer."

Yeast*

According to Andrew Cambell,

> The real nature of yeast was little comprehended until Pasteur published the results of his researches in 1876. The old-time brewers knew that to add yeast or barm or "Godes good" caused the wort to ferment, and although violent fermentation ceased after a time, the ale stored in cask or bottle continued to work slowly. If kept too long it would become thick and ropy.

---

*Strictly speaking yeast is *not* an ingredient of beer. It is an essential agent but is not present in the finished brew.

Yeast is not so much a material as a living cellular organism that feeds on nitrogenous and other substances and reproduces itself, at the same time altering the nature of the substances in which it is working. The enzymes in yeast attack the sugars in the wort and break them into carbon dioxide and alcohol.

In reproduction yeast multiplies itself many times, creating a surplus that can be used for more brewing and for sale to distillers and to food and chemical manufacturers. Brewing yeast is not sold directly to bakers. They draw their supplies from the distillers. Brewers' yeast can be treated so that the bitterness from the hops is removed, and then mixed with distillers' yeast.

The brewery scientist carefully selects and develops a pure strain of yeast. There is an important difference here between Britain, whose brewers have long held that a rather less pure strain produces a better-flavoured beer, and Scandinavia, where a really pure strain is sought. The scientist strives to keep wild yeasts out of the brew, for if stray cells permeate the beer after racking and filtration they will ferment any remaining carbohydrates. In some beers this is desired and allowed for, in others it will cause cloudiness or *haze*. The modern brewery is constructed so that the air can be conditioned and purified, and stray yeast cells virtually eliminated.

—*The Book of Beer*, p. 34

Other Ingredients

Home brewers who imitate their less conscientious commercial cousins, sometimes color their beer to alter the appearance of the finished brew. To create various shades of beer, from light to dark, by regulating the amounts of roasted malts present in the wort is a perfectly acceptable practice among quality beer craftsmen. In addition, tannins that come from hops and barley during brewing add naturally to the color of the finished beer. However, the home brewer who attempts to influence the final color of his brew by adding *burnt sugar, caramels* or *syrups* (some even use *gravy browning*!) is definitely stepping out of this fraternity of craftsmen. Only cheap bootleggers, imitation commercial beer makers and superficial home brewers alter the final color to influence the eye of the drinker. However as pointed out by Andrew Campbell, the color of a beer can affect our opinion of its taste. Before we smell the aroma, let alone taste the flavor, we form some opinion about a beer simply by looking at its color.

The "head" on a beer should arise from fermentation in the bottle. Yeast splits starches into carbon dioxide and sugar. The CO_2 is what gives the beer its head. If carbon dioxide is forced into the beer artificially, either by gas cylinders or by cooling, the beer may no longer be considered naturally effervescent. Such processes yield a carbonated or artificially conditioned product.

Beers which rapidly form a vigorous head of foam on pouring generally fall flat just as quickly. Other beers, which may be slower to foam, or which develop an insignificant head, often keep their effervescence throughout the tenure of the drink and are in a sense more desirable than the showy foamers, especially where the foamy head has been artificially induced.

As a final note for the home brewer who sometimes adds head-improving materials such as quillaia bark, root licorice solutions and gum acacia, it is best to remember that while these materials tend to thicken the head they very definitely ruin the flavor. Such substances are best left to the manufacturers of fire-fighting foams who can put such raw materials to a more productive use.

COMMERCIAL BREWING

Home brewing began to decline toward the end of the eighteenth century. As the industrial boom expanded, people moved to towns, and beer shops became popular. Factory workers no longer had the land necessary to grow the raw materials for brewing at home, and the low price of the beer produced by the numerous brewing establishments finally discouraged the working family from continuing the craft. Brewing was left to the leisured classes, and to people living in the country.

In considering the commercial beers we have inherited today, a few basic questions must be kept in mind. Is there a significant difference between the beers commonly available in your neighborhood bar? That there is a difference in taste is obvious. Certainly dark beers have a flavor and aroma distinct from light beers; tart ales reveal a more pronounced hop aroma than soft, mellow lagers; sweet bock beers are different from robust, bitter porters and stouts. But is there a real difference in quality? Are some domestic beers genuinely brewed of better raw materials, by superior methods, and aged for greater lengths of time than others? Or are all domestic brews mere variations of the chemist's schemes—adequate for the occasional thirst-quenching cold beer but in no way equal to the higher-priced imports? On the other hand, are the imports truly superior in quality and taste or merely the lucky inheritors of that foreign "mystique"?

First, there are very definite differences in quality among domestic beers. All are not brewed by approximately the same methods, from the same formulas or aged for similar lengths of time. As an example, Utica Club, a product of the West End Brewing Co. in Utica, New York, is aged for six to eight weeks. This compares very favorably even with such a superior import as Tuborg, a Danish beer, which may be aged for six weeks (regular lagers), nine weeks (Gold Label Export) or twelve weeks (their strongest beers). We should add that by contrast the majority of domestic beers are aged for less than thirty days. Many experienced home brewers age their beer for up to twelve months—a length of time

A visit to a brewery in 1847: store vats.

obviously not feasible for a commercial brewhouse, yet one that was commonly employed until the first half of the nineteenth century.

As for the ingredients used, again not all domestic beers are alike. It is common practice for most brewers to purchase malt from specialized suppliers, but Genesee is one of the few breweries in America which continues to make its own malt—a delicate art in itself. The firm utilizes corn as the only adjunct in brewing Genesee Lager Beer, with thrice-filtered water from spring-fed Hemlock Lake Reservoir, and avoids using any preservatives, chemicals or minerals in the brewing process.

Coors is another pure, superior domestic brew. Made principally from barley, which is malted at the brewery, with a short-grained variety of rice from the San Joaquin and Sacramento Valley of California as the only adjunct, *Coors* uses absolutely no additives in their processing, nor any corrective salts in the Rocky Mountain spring water. The Coors brothers take even greater pains in their packaging and transportation techniques. It is a well-known fact that keg or draught beers generally taste better than bottled or canned beers. This is because draught beer is unpasteurized and consequently more flavorful, although it must be consumed within a week of leaving the brewery. Coors is one of the very few domestic beers that is not pasteurized after being canned or bottled. It is packaged cold, under aseptic conditions, and shipped to the marketplace (which averages about 1,000 miles from the brewery in Golden, Colorado), in either insulated or refrigerated transportation equipment. Coors distributors are then required to refrigerate the beer they warehouse, and to deliver it to the

LONDON ILLUSTRATED NEWS

A visit to a brewery in 1847: portion of the great brewhouse.

LONDON ILLUSTRATED NEWS

A visit to a brewery in 1847: bobbing the beer.

retailers in refrigerated trucks. Approximately 80 percent of the retail outlets cooperate with this refrigerated marketing concept and take delivery of this beer directly into their cold boxes. Consequently, Coors may be one of the very few true beers in the United States. It is not only well brewed, but by not being pasteurized, this beer maintains all the taste and aroma associated with fresh draught beer.

This domestic beer, as well as others which will be treated in the next chapter, compares favorably with the best the Old World has to offer. In fact many U.S. beers are even superior to European brews, especially when one considers that even the finest European brews are altered for export. As we have seen, export beers are usually made with additives and preservatives to protect the delicate liquid food from deteriorating with the rocking motion of transport ships.

At the risk of disappointing the reader who is anxious for an immediate list, by rank, of the world's best beers, I invite the serious drinker to ponder first the various types of beer and how they are made.

WHAT IS BEER?

Beer as we know, is generally defined as a fermented grain beverage, where starch is first broken down into fermentable sugars and then transformed into alcohol and carbon dioxide. The essential ingredient is *grain,* as in wine it is the *fruits* of the plants that are fermented. However, these definitions do overlap. For example, in the beverage *chicha* in South America several different parts of plants are fermented together, including grains of corn and fruits of various herbs.

As described earlier beer is flavored with a bitter herb such as hops, but formally by the addition of any of a number of aromatic plants.

At present beer belongs to many different types. At one time the words ale and beer were used to describe two different beverages. Ales did not contain hops while beer did. Today, the word beer is sometimes used specifically as a synonym for lager—America's favorite malt beverage—which introduces a note of confusion. All of the types that follow are beers. Each is brewed by the use of malt from some grain, though the type of grain may vary; each contains some quantity of hops, a top or bottom-fermenting yeast to start fermentation, and, of course, each depends upon water for its liquid base.

The simplest division—that between light and dark beer—is more confusing than helpful. Lager beers come in both light and dark varieties, while some writers prefer to categorize stouts, Scotch ales and Burtons as dark beers, relegating ales to the light category.

For simplicity then, definitions will be limited to lagers, ales, porters, stouts and bock beer, each being a variety of beer.

TYPES OF BEER

Lager

This is the most popular type of beer in the United States. Ninety percent of the amber, light beer served in this country is lager, which simply means a beer which has been "stored" or "stocked," the name coming from the German verb *lagern* 'to store.' It refers to earlier times, when German monks stored beer in cool mountain caves during the hot months of summer.

While the better lagers are today stored or aged for up to three months, some domestic lagers are aged for as little as one week. Lager beer is brewed in this country with adjuncts such as corn or rice, while most European lager is brewed from barley malt. A smaller quantity of hops is used than in ale which gives these beers only a mild hop aroma and flavor.

In North America lager is fermented at temperatures between 50° to 60°F. Fermentations take longer periods of time than ale fermentations and are less vigorous. Continental brewers conduct lager fermentations at between 41° and 54°F. and for longer time periods and they are even less vigorous than American lager fermentations. Alcoholic content of lagers ranges between 3.2 percent and 4 percent. (Any malt beverage sold in the United States which is more than 5 percent alcohol cannot be sold as beer. If it contains a higher percentage of alcohol it must be termed malt liquor, stout, porter or ale. This explains why many European lagers are imported into the United States with the words "malt liquor" hastily stamped on their labels.)

Lager beer is usually produced with bottom-fermenting yeast. This means that the yeast settles to the bottom of the fermenting vat when the fermentation is completed. The lager itself is drawn off, leaving the yeast in the tank. With beers that are brewed with top-fermenting yeast, such as ales and stouts, the yeast rises to the top in a froth during fermentation and is skimmed off.

Light lager

This beer is pale golden in color, light-bodied and generally strongly carbonated and has a soft, mellow, dry taste. Lagers are all filtered during brewing, which allows them to be refrigerated without any risk of hazing or clouding. However, some nutritional value is lost, especially as compared with unfiltered stouts and porters. Most light U.S. beers are light lagers. Examples are Coors, Olympia and Rainier from the western states; Budweiser, Michelob, Schlitz and Miller from the central states; and Rheingold, Piels, Schaefer, Genesee and Utica Club from the eastern states.

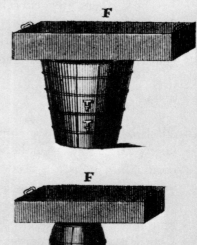

FRONTISPIECE.

A. *Moveable Fire place.*
B. *Cylindrical Boiler to be placed on* A. C. *Cover for* B.
D. *Extracting perforated Cylinder to be placed within* B.
E. *Centre.* D^o
F F. *Coolers, one to pack within the other.*
G. *Machine ready for use, the Cover raised to shew the internal*

London. Published by Wetton & Jarvis, & T. Boys.

Imported light lagers are quite numerous. The most well known being Germany's Löwenbräu, the Philippines' San Miguel, Holland's Heineken, Norway's Ringnes, Ireland's Harp Lager, Canada's Labatt Pilsner and Molson, Mexico's Carta Blanca and Dos Equis, Japan's Kirin, Denmark's Carlsberg, and Germany's Wurzburger, Dortmunder Union and Beck's.

The archetype of light lagers is *Pilsner Urquell*. This beer is the only one brewed in Pilsen, Czechoslovakia, and thus the only true *pilsner* in the world. It is a lager and not a separate type of beer. Pilsner type beers are brewed to try to capture the unique flavor of the Czech import, which is a dry, light-bodied, pale beer.

Dark lagers

These are brewed by the same techniques as light lagers but are made dark in color in various ways. The color of true dark lagers is derived from the addition of roasted barley. Imitation dark lagers are made with caramel or with an extract of roasted barley malt, both methods being less time-consuming and less costly than roasting and adding barley in precise amounts.

Dark lagers are generally more aromatic, creamy-headed and sweeter than light lagers. Examples are Löwenbräu Dark Special, San Miguel Dark and Carlsberg Special Dark Lager, a particularly excellent brew, with a gentle bouquet of hops, and true dark amber coloration with a ruby tinge.

Ale

Ale is brewed from the same basic ingredients as lager: barley malt, hops, yeast, water and a smaller amount of adjuncts, such as flakes of rice and corn. More hops are used and fermentation is done with top-fermenting yeast.

Ales are more aromatic than lagers, with a more pronounced hop flavor and aroma, more full-bodied and higher in alcoholic content, ranging from 4 percent to 5 percent.

Ballantine Ale is perhaps the best known domestic example with its strong aroma and light amber color. Other domestic ales include Pabst Old Tankard and Neuweiler Cream Ale from the Ortlieb Brewery. However, most U.S. ales are simply lagers flavored artificially with "ale flavor." One need only compare Britain's golden Bass Pale Ale, which has a more pronounced malt flavor, is deeper bodied and mellower than our domestic ales.

Ale is the most popular type of beer in Britain and is there further subdivided into light and strong.

The staple drink of the British saloon bar, known as draught bitter, is brewed from pale-ale malts, with a small amount of corn and rice flakes added to make the beer clear and sparkling. It is more heavily hopped than the "milds" (staple of the pubs), but not necessarily more bitter, simply more aromatic and drier.

Strong ales are very special beers and have an extremely limited public. Brewed privately, as celebration drinks (such as *King's Ale* by Bass to commemorate a visit of King Edward VIII), or in limited commercial production as with Young's *Celebration Ale*, the strong ales are the alcoholic equivalents of wine. Strong ales are on the dark side, and have a rich ruby hue with a brown to reddish tinge. Some are highly carbonated, others mildly so or not at all. Some brewers filter their ale, others let them mature in the bottle.

Two celebrated strong ales available commercially are Benskin's Colne Spring Ale and Bass No. 1 Barley Wine. Examples of other strong British ales include Barclay's Winter Brew, and Younger's No. 1 Strong Scotch Ale on draught, and their bottled King of Ales.

We learn from Andrew Campbell in his *Book of Beer* that:

> Strong ales are the present-day descendants of the barley wines of the Egyptians, of the *Beer of the Notables, Nubian Beer,* and the later *Huff-Cup, Nipitatum* and *Dragon's Milk*. Today they still have fine names: *Stingo, Dragon's Blood, Royal Toby, Rouser, Old Tom, Double Courage, Colne Spring, Final Selection,* but many brewers adhere to the simple description of *Barley Wine*. A custom when farmers and landowners brewed was the preparation of a particularly powerful brew for consumption by the tenants and landworkers on the occasion of the annual reckoning, when payment of rent and dues was accompanied by feasting and drinking; a pleasant custom that is commemorated in Friary, Holroyd and Healy's, Dale's and other brewer's *Audit Ale*. Audit ales were also brewed by other property-owning institutions including the colleges of Oxford and Cambridge.

Among the strongest of all fermented barley beverages in the world is Russian Imperial Stout, brewed by the London firm of Courage. This beer is aged for *two years* and is about twice as strong as Guinness Stout. Brewed originally for the Russian trade, especially for Catherine the Great who ordered it for her own drinking and that of her court, the beer has a smooth, full flavor with the rich sweetness of barley malt, while at the same time transmitting the bitter taste of hops.

Porter and Stout

These distinctly British brews are varieties of ale. They are fermented as ales are, using top-fermenting yeast. In addition to the ale ingredients, roasted barley or malt are included, or barley and various sugars. Some brewers use malted or flaked oats as well. Although color varies from light to dark within each type, porter is generally lighter in color and of a lower alcoholic content than stout, while also less bitter.

While many native British stouts have sweetish flavors, Guinness Stout, from Ireland, has a bitter taste. Guinness is well hopped, and brewed without sugar, reaching perfect drinkability within three or four days of bottling, when it pours as a heavy, rich, nearly black, creamy-headed brew.

Bickerdyke's *Curiosities of Ale and Beer* (1889) explains some theories

LÖWENBRÄU MUNICH

Three scenes at a medieval brewery: preparing the brew;
cleaning and filling the kegs; delivering the finished product.

about the origins of porter and stout in eighteenth-century England. (Incidentally, "porterhouse" steaks were sold in the taverns where porter was sold.)

It appears that in the early years of last century the lovers of malt liquors in London were accustomed to regale themselves upon three classes of these beverages; they had ale, beer, and twopenny. Many who preferred a more subtle combination of flavours than either of these liquors alone could impart, would ask for *half-and-half*, that is, half of ale and half of beer, half of ale and half of twopenny, or half of beer and half of twopenny. Others again—and these were the real connoisseurs of malt liquors—would call for a pot of three threads, or three thirds, *i.e.*, one-third of ale, one-third of beer, and one-third of twopenny. The drawer would therefore have to go to three different casks, and through three distinct operations, before he could draw a pint of liquor. But the hour had come—and the man. One Ralph Harwood, whose name is too little known to an ungrateful posterity of beer-drinking Britons, some time about the year 1730, kept a brewhouse on the east side of High Street, Shoreditch. In that year, or perhaps a little earlier, as this great man brooded over the inconvenience and waste occasioned by the calls for the "three threads," which became more and more frequent, he conceived the idea of making a liquor which would combine in itself the several virtues of ale, beer, and twopenny. He carried the idea into action, and brewed a drink which he called "Entire," or "Entire Butts." It was tasted; it was approved; it became the fruitful parent of a mighty offspring; and from that day to this has gone on increasing in name and fame.

Visitors to the great brewery in Brick Lane are shown a hole from which steam issues to the accompaniment of awful rumbling noises. "In there once fell a man," they are told—"a Negro. Nothing but his bones were found when the copper was emptied, and it is said that the beer drawn off was of an extraordinary dark colour. Some say this was the first brew of porter. "Oh yes" (this in answer to a question), "we soon learnt how to make it without the Negro." We must confess that we have some doubts as to this account of the origin of porter. We do not believe that brew could have been much darker on account of the accident, though no doubt, under the circumstances, it contained plenty of "body." A similar tale is told of nearly every London porter brewery, and later on it will be found in verse.

It seems to be to some extent a moot point among the learned how porter obtained its present name, for no record seems to have been kept of its christening. Harwood, no doubt, stood godfather to his interesting infant, but, as we have seen above, he called it "Entire"; and how or when it came to be known as porter is not quite clear. There are several theories on the subject, each more or less plausible. One is that being a hearty, appetizing, and nourishing liquor, it was specially recommended to the notice of the porters, who then, as now, formed a considerable proportion of the Shoreditch population. Pennant, in his *London,* seems to have held this view; he calls it "a wholesome liquor, which enables the London porter-drinkers to undergo tasks that ten gin-drinkers would sink under." Another explanation of the origin of the name is that Harwood sent

round his men to his customers with the liquor, and that the men would
announce their arrival and their business by the cry of "Porter"—
meaning not the beer, but the bearer. Be this how it may, the embodiment
of Harwood's great idea had not attaained its majority before it was
known far and wide by its present name.

In *The Student* (1750) is thus related the first appearance of porter at
Oxford— ". . . Let us not derogate from the merits of porter—a liquor
entirely British—a liquor that pleases equally the mechanic and the peer—
a liquor which is the strength of our nation, the scourge of our enemies,
and which has given *immortality* to aldermen. 'Tis with the highest
satisfaction that we can inform our Oxford students that *Isis* herself has
taken this divine liquor into her protection, and that the *Muses* recommend
it to their votaries, as being far preferable to Hippocrene, Aganippe, the
Castalian spring, or any *poetical water* whatever. Know, then, that in the
middle of the High Street, at the sign of the King's Arms, opposite to its
opposite, Juggins's Coffee House, lives Captain Jolly; who *maugré* the
selfish opposition of his brother publicans, out of a pure affection to this
University, and regardless of private profit, reduc'd porter from its original
price of Sixpence, and in large golden characters generously informs us
that he sells

"London Porter
      At Fourpence a Quart."

Quoted in the same book a Professor Wilson relates how he switched
from ale to porter:

"From ale we naturally get to porter—porter—drink "fit for the gods,"
being, in fact, likely to be, now and then, *too potent* for mere mortals.
With porter we are less imbued than with ale; and this we hold to be one
of the great misfortunes of our life. We are early nurtured in love and
affection for good ale by our great aunt, with whom we were a young and
frequent visitant. Excellent old Aunt Patty! She was a Yorkshire woman,
and cousin (three times removed) to Mr. Wilberforce (the father). She
too hated *rum* as the devil's own brewage, but then she loved sound ale
in the same ratio. Thus it happened, as we derived our faith in malt liquor
from her, that we penetrated not the mysteries of porter until our elder
days. Our heresy was first effectually shaken by Charles Lamb, who, in his
admirable way, proved to us that, in a hot forenoon, a draught of Meux
or Barclay is beyond all cordial restoratives, and after a broiling
peregrination (the stages were all full) from Coleridge's lodgings at
Highgate to town, gave us a specimen of the inspiring powers of porter in a
perspiration, which we shall remember until the day of our death."
Lamb was known by all his friends to have an amiable weakness for porter,
and the poet, in "An Ode to Grog," thus commemorates the fact:—

The spruce Mr. Lamb ('pon my word it's no flam)
      With Whitbread's Entire makes his Pegasus jog;
I'll grant he's a poet, but then he don't show wit,
      In thinking that Porter is better than grog.

Burns was fond of porter, as of all other extracts of malt. He addressed the following lines to his friend Mr. Syme, along with a present of a dozen of bottled porter:—

> Oh, had the malt thy strength of mind,
> Or hops the flavour of thy wit,
> 'Twere drink for first of human kind,
> A gift that e'en for Syme were fit.

Before leaving our porters, one negative remark about this type of beer might be permissible:

> Much as porter's praises have been sung, one depreciatory remark is recorded to have been made by the late Judge Maule. "Why do you, brother Maule, drink so much stout?" he was asked by one of the judges. "To bring my intellect down to the level of the rest of the bench," was the not very flattering reply.

As can be seen from the first statement quoted from the *Curiosities* book the British once recognized ale as *separate from* and *not* a *type of* beer. Today, both terms are virtually synonymous. The British writer, Andrew Campbell, divides malted beverages into the following categories: mild beer (both dark and light), "Burton," brown ales and stouts. These divisions are generally based upon the specific gravity (weight compared with plain water) of the various types. However, there is no sharp division between categories. Thus, some superior mild beers show gravities of 1,037° to 1,039° (water has a specific gravity of 1,000), while ordinary stouts may begin at a gravity of 1,032°. Despite the failure to divide beer into firm types, each distinct from any other, based upon scientific rules, taste and flavor characteristics remain the drinker's best testing device. The British beer drinker will not likely confuse the soft, sweet flavor of a mild beer with a strongly hopped "Burton," nor again with the fuller-flavored, darker-colored stouts.

Bock Beer

This is the final major beer type. The following description of it was supplied by the Brewers Association of Canada:

> Traditionally brewed during winter for the spring market, the origins of the name *bock* are shrouded in the mists of history. For some reason it is associated with the symbol of a goat. The usual belief is that the name comes from the famous medieval brewing town of Einbeck in Germany. But curiously enough, a Mesopotamian seal of 2200 B.C. shows a queen and her nobles sipping beer through golden straws, and between them, a prancing goat. And the Hindustani word for goat is *bok*. In any event, it is a heavy, dark lager beer, full, rather sweet and hoppy in character. Its dark color is normally obtained through the use of high-colored malts.

ARTHUR GUINNESS SON & CO.

This stainless steel tun at the Guinness Brewery,
St. James's Gate, Dublin, is the largest fermenting
vessel in the world. At one brewing it can
ferment 8,000 bulk barrels (2,304,000 pints) of
stout. After each brewing the tun is hosed,
brushed, and sterilized with steam.

Bock beer is available in both light and dark varieties. Although sold throughout the year, light bock beer has its main selling period in late spring. In Bavaria, it is known as *Maibock* because of a promotional campaign in the Bavarian beer restaurants during the month of May. Dark bock beer is a typical Bavarian specialty that has made Munich beers famous the world over. It is generally considered more nutritious because of its distinct and aromatic taste of malt. In fact, as with all natural dark beers, the color comes from roasted cereals, and dark beers are of no greater nutritional value than light. In either case, bock beer is prized for its deep mahogany color and sweetish taste.

Malt Liquor

This variety of beer is essentially lager with a higher alcoholic content. Most states have laws which prohibit beer from containing more than a maximum of 5 percent alcohol by weight. If the malt beverage exceeds this alcohol percentage it must be sold as either malt liquor, ale, stout or porter. Thus, the origin of our domestic term malt liquor. While there is no

R. L. ZENTMAIER, PHOTO RESEARCHERS

At the Joseph Schlitz Brewery in Milwaukee, Wisconsin, quality-control personnel watch for imperfections in the beer, bottle, and label.

legal maximum on how strong a malt liquor may be, most domestics are in the 4 to 8 percent category. Carlsberg Elephant Malt Liquor contains nearly 9 percent alcohol, hence the reference to the largest of land mammals.

Champale Malt Liquor is unique in that it is a sparkling malted beverage, unlike any other. More like wine, or inexpensive champagne, this breed does not even taste like beer. It sparkles, pours and tastes like champagne, not even exhibiting a beerlike head.

Nonalcoholic Beers

A new entry into the huge beer marketplace are the nonalcoholic malt beverages. One of the best brewed examples is Birell from the Swiss brewers A. Hurlimann A/G. This beverage is not only rapidly taking its share of the market on the continent but even in Britain, a staunch beer-drinking nation.

This special type of lager beer is brewed like other alcohol-containing malt beverages. Birell conforms to German purity regulations, brewed exclusively from barley malt, hops and water. The only difference is that by a process exclusive to the brewers, the alcohol content is held to a level below 0.5 percent, by weight. (This constitutes the allowable alcoholic limit for orange and other fruit juices.)

All the valuable, components customary in beer, like vitamins PP, B_1, B_2, B_6, biotine, pantothenic acid, folic acid and inositol, are retained in this Swiss brew. It looks and tastes like a fine lager beer, has the same relaxing effects (due to the hops), and is brewed with the weight-conscious drinker in mind. Birell contains only about half the calories in the usual beer and even in diet beers.

Other groups besides the weight-conscious for whom this type of lager beer is recommended are drivers, mechanics, athletes, nursing mothers, patients with liver disease, alcoholics, ulcer victims and epileptics. However, the carbohydrate content is much higher than that of ordinary beer and therefore not recommended for diabetics. For this group, special diet beers are brewed.

Beer as Soda Pop

Americans developed their taste for sweet, light beer during prohibition when soda pop was the only legally available national beverage. According to Edmund Schorr, brewmaster of the Schlitz brewery in Tampa, Florida, beer brewed after prohibition was sweeter and lighter "to accommodate soda-pop tastes." There is no doubt that nearly all lager beer brewed in the United States is very much lighter and less hoppy than European lagers.

Lightness is not the only remarkable quality about domestic beers. The products of a few domestic brewers aside, our brews go directly from "barley to beer" (with adjuncts such as corn, rice and wheat as well as a slew of chemicals) in an average time of under five weeks. While two to three months is the regular production time for good European beers, some brewers take even more time and age their beer for four months. As mentioned earlier, one British beer, Russian Imperial Stout, is aged for up to two years.

If you believe in the concept of a free market as the truest testing place for a product's desirability, then foreign trade statistics are a fairly good index of consumers' taste preferences. In 1971 only 1 percent of all U.S. beer exported found a market in the combined nations of Europe. It seems the biggest fans of U.S. beer outside our national boundaries are the Caribbean people, who bought 46 percent of our total exported beer. The Asian market took 22 percent, the Australians 16 percent, Central America 6 percent, Canada and Mexico 6 percent, Africa 2 percent and South America just 1 percent. While it is true that the number of local beers available accounts in some part for the small amount of U.S. beer bought in each country, it must be pointed out that Australia, which has a great number of local beers, still accounted for 16 percent of the U.S. export market. They must like the taste of our beer. On the contrary, the Europeans are not impressed with our light, sweet lagers. But, perhaps the low import rate is really related to restrictive legislation.

Which countries seem to brew the beer Americans prefer? In 1974, Dutch beers accounted for the largest share of this market (nearly 7 million cases imported into the United States—mainly Heineken); next came the German beers (4.2 million cases—mainly Lowenbrau); next Canadian beer (3.9 million cases—Molson Ale and Labatt); then Mexican exports (Carta Blanca and Dos Equis—about 1.4 million cases); English and Scottish beer (about 700,000 cases—Whitbread, Bass and others); Norwegian (about 450,000 cases—Ringnes and Ski); Irish (about 360,000 cases of Guinness); Japanese beer (about 245,000 cases—Kirin and others); Philippine beer brought up the sizeable rear (San Miguel—about 229,000 cases.)

These figures, while handy, do not necessarily represent quality, flavor, superiority, etc. They may simply represent salesmanship, price or the desire for something with a foreign label. For example, Pilsner Urquell, the Czechoslovakian beer which is a large selling foreign beer in Germany, a nation of knowledgeable beer drinkers, accounted for only a small part of the beer imported into the United States, just 79,000 cases.

In an attempt to capitalize on the increasing American demand for imported beer (consumption of imported beer has risen at a faster rate than of domestic brews) the Carling Brewing Company is now producing a domestic version of the famous Danish Tuborg lager beer. Under special license from Tuborg Breweries, Ltd., it is made in three Carling breweries;

Brewing house at Heineken plant.

in Baltimore, Maryland; Frankenmuth, Michigan and Tacoma, Washington.

While this domestic Tuborg is definitely a good beer it is not quite the same as the Danish Tuborg. A little label-searching indicates that the U.S. version is "brewed light"—no doubt an attempt to entice the American lover of bland beer. While the Danes use only barley for their malt, their U.S. counterparts include corn (as do most domestic brewers). It must be remembered that even in Copenhagen all things are not perfect for brewing Tuborg beer. Access to high quality water is relatively easy in Denmark, but its calcium content must be lessened before brewing. In comparison, some of the adaptations necessary to make this Danish brew in the United States are relatively easy: European barley strains (two-row variety) are grown in North Dakota, Montana and Minnesota; hops are grown from European stock (some are imported); and the famous Tuborg yeast strain is domestically cultured. All are combined to produce a fine light lager brewed along traditional European lines. The thinking behind this venture is that the beer will cost less due to reduced shipping costs, and therefore be more competitive with medium-priced American beers. In addition, the beer will be *fresher,* an important factor for a product that is more perishable than butter. If these considerations prove to be right we can expect similar international brewing ventures in the future.*

CHANGING PATTERNS

While Americans continue to experiment with every new imported beer that comes their way (providing the quality is maintained) it should be pointed out that the German people too have been switching around in their beer-drinking choices.

For decades Germans have been drinking the bottom-fermented lager beers, but beginning in the late 1950's top-fermented beers began to rise in popularity. Once restricted to local markets, these tarter brews have increased in popularity at such a rate that in some regions they have taken over 80 percent of a market once dominated by lager beers.

Kölsch is the name of this type of light, top-fermented brew in Cologne. In Düsseldorf the top-fermented beer known as *Altbier* (old beer) or

---

*Löwenbräu is now brewed in the United States. It, too, is not the beer it is in its country of origin.

LÖWENBRÄU ZURICH

Fermenting cellar with a capacity of 7,000 barrels at the Löwenbräu Zurich plant.

Düssel is darker in color and richer in body. *Altbier* now accounts for over 80 percent of the market in Willich, a small town in the Lower Rhine Valley, which was once a strictly lager beer region.

The Hannen Brewery in Willich has had to triple its capacity in the past few years to keep up with demand, although the company discontinued all advertising in 1965. In a special interview with David Binder for the New York *Times* (April 27, 1967) Hannen's director, Günther Dicker, stated that the tremendous popularity for *Altbier* may have arisen due to "tavern rumors to the effect that top-fermented beer helped cure kidney stones and other ailments." While admitting the reasons are genuinely unclear, Mr. Dicker added, "We get a lot of orders from health clinics and hospitals."

As travel has increased, so has the taste for foreign products, including beer. On returning home from a trip abroad, there is nothing quite like a bottle of beer from a place visited to bring back pleasant memories. In addition to the souvenir aspect of changing beer tastes, both in America and abroad, there is the very real desire to drink a healthful brew and especially one not laced with adulterants.

THE BREWING PROCESS*

While no single scheme exists which applies to all breweries, the basics remain the same from plant to plant. Naturally, a giant brewery will differ from a small, local one, and individual preferences among brewers will determine the final taste of the beer. The following outline, provided by the Brewers Association of Canada, will serve as a typical brewing scheme.

Brewing is fundamentally a biochemical and biological process. The force which carries out the process is nature. The art and science of brewing is in using and controlling the process to convert natural food materials into a pure, pleasing beverage.

The Malt: The basic ingredient in beer is barley malt, which is barley that has been allowed to grow to a limited extent, then kiln-dried to halt further growth. This can be stated simply, but the malting process is actually a complicated one, requiring great skill and experience.

During the period of controlled growth in the malting plant the natural enzyme systems of the barley are released to break down the membranes of the starch cells, which make up most of the kernel. But these are internal changes only. Apart from a slight change in color the external characteristics remain essentially unchanged. When the malt leaves one of Canada's seven malting plants (in Calgary, Winnipeg, Fort William, Toronto and Montreal) it still looks like barley.

In the brewery the malt is screened and crushed before being mashed with water. It is crushed rather than ground to a flour in order to keep the grain husks as whole as possible. This not only prevents the extraction

*For additional brewing details, see pp. 191–196.

*One of Löwenbräu Zurich's two bottling plants
with a total capacity of 50,000 bottles an hour;
the filling-line on the right is for soft drinks;
the one on the left, for beer.*

of undesirable materials from the husks but also allows them to act as a
filter bed for separation of the liquid extract formed during mashing.

The Water: The all-important thing about the water used in brewing is
that it should be pure, to rigidly set standards. If it does not have the
proper calcium or acidic content for maximum activity of the enzyme
systems in the mash, it must be brought up to that standard.

Mashing: In the mashing process, the malt enzymes break down the
starch to sugar, and the complex proteins of the malt to simpler nitrogen
compounds. The mashing takes place in a large round tank called a "mash
mixer" or "mash tun," and requires careful temperature control. Sometime
at this point, depending on the type of beer desired, the malt is
supplemented by starch from other cereals such as corn, wheat or rice.

Lautering: When mashing is finished the mash is transferred to a
draining or "lautering" vessel, usually cylindrical, with a slotted false
bottom 2″ or 3″ above the true bottom. The liquid extract drains through
the false bottom and is run off to the brew kettle. Water is "sparged" or
sprayed through the grains to wash out as much of the extract as possible.

The "spent grains" are then removed and sold, for they are in great
demand by farmers for cattle feed. They are either dried and placed in
bags or sold wet.

Boiling and Hopping: The liquid in the brew kettle is called "wort." It
is not yet beer. The brew kettle, a huge cauldron holding up to 15,000 to
20,000 gallons and made of shiny copper or stainless steel, is probably the
most striking sight in a brewery. It is fitted with coils or a jacketed bottom
for steam heating and is designed to boil the wort under carefully
controlled conditions.

During the boil, which usually lasts about two hours, the green, aromatic hops are added. The hop resins contribute flavor, aroma and bitterness to the brew.

Boiling serves to concentrate the wort to the desired specific gravity, to sterilize it and to obtain the desired extract from the hops. Undesirable protein substances which have survived the journey from the mash tun are destroyed, leaving the wort pure and sterile.

Hop Separation and Cooling: After the beer has taken on the flavor of the hops they must be removed. The wort is passed through a "hop jack" or separator to remove both the hops and a large amount of the protein which was precipitated during the boil. This protein is known by the short and expressive name of "trub."

The wort itself proceeds from the hop jack to the "hot wort tank," where most of the remaining trub is removed by settling. The wort is then cooled, usually in a deceptively simple-looking apparatus called a "plate cooler." As the wort and a coolant flow past each other on opposite sides of stainless steel plates the temperature of the wort drops from boiling to about 50°F.—a drop of more than 150°F.—in a few seconds.

Fermentation: The wort is now moved to the fermenting vessels, and yeast, the jealously guarded central mystery of the ancient brewer's art, is added on the way. It is the yeast, these living, single-cell plants, which takes the sugar in the wort and breaks it down to carbon dioxide and alcohol.

There are many kinds of yeast, but that used in making beer is the *Saccharomyces Cerevisiae.* The brewer uses two types of this yeast, and depending on which is chosen, he produces ale or lager. One yeast type which rises to the top of the liquid at the completion of fermentation is used in brewing ale and stout. The other, which drops to the bottom of the brewing vessel, is used in brewing lager.

In all modern breweries, elaborate precautions are taken to ensure that the yeast remains pure and unchanged. Through the use of pure yeast culture plants a particular beer flavor can be maintained year after year.

During the fermentation, which usually lasts seven days, the yeast may multiply tenfold, and in the open tank fermenters used for brewing ale a creamy, frothy head may be seen on top of the brew. When the fermentation is over the yeast is removed—by skimming off when it is a top fermentation (ale) or by pumping off the beer when it is a bottom fermentation (lager). Now, for the first time, the liquid is called beer.

It is at the end of fermentation that the Canadian government makes its "excise dip" to determine the number of gallons on which taxes must be paid. The beer still has some weeks to go before it reaches the market, but the taxes must be paid immediately.

The Cellars: The beer now passes through a period of maturing and storage. After fermentation it is cooled and placed in primary storage at thirty-two degrees Fahrenheit for from one to three weeks. The beer is then filtered, cooled again to thirty-two degrees Fahrenheit and moved to the chilling storage.

After 10 to 14 days in this secondary storage the beer is "polished" by filtration, and transferred to tanks for bottling or "racking" into kegs. It is now finished beer.

Packaging: The bottleshop of a brewery is a vast, busy place with a

Rube Goldberg-like tangle of conveyors moving back and forth and from one floor to another. The returned empty bottles go through "soakers" in which they receive a thorough cleaning. After washing, the bottles are inspected both electronically and visually, and pass on to the rotary filler. Some of these whirling machines can fill up to 700 bottles per minute. A "crowning" machine, integrated with the filler, places caps on the bottles. The filled bottles then pass through a "tunnel" pasteurizer—often 75 feet from end to end and able to hold 15,000 bottles—where the temperature of the beer is raised to 140°F. for 10 minutes, then cooled to room temperature.

Emerging from the pasteurizer, the bottles are re-inspected, labeled, automatically placed in boxes, stacked on pallets by an automatic machine and carried by lift truck to the warehousing areas to wait for shipment.

Beer which is to be kegged and sold as "draught" goes a different route. Pasteurization adds to the "shelf life," or length of time beer may be kept. Since draught beer is sold immediately, it is not pasteurized, but placed in sterilized stainless steel or aluminum kegs (usually "half barrel" size, containing 12½ gallons), closed with a bung banged home by hand with a hammer, and it's ready to go.

—Brewing in Canada

Some Additional Brewing Details

Priming

Beer that has been brewed correctly and permitted to age adequately should be perfectly palatable when it is packaged. Brewers who wish to give their beer the "zing" of additional carbon dioxide, and those who aim for a sweeter brew, add a solution of invert sugar (lactose) or caramel at "racking" (after ageing—when the beer is passed into final storage kegs). Such "priming" encourages additional fermentation by any remaining yeast, which creates additional CO_2 and a sweeter taste. In Britain, the sweeter lactose is used for some milds and London stouts, and the caramel for drier pale ales and bitters. While priming is almost always practiced by home brewers, many traditional beer makers would never think of pepping their product in such a way. This is not a harmful practice in the sense of posing a threat to the health of the drinker; it is simply "not cricket" among those who value their craft. (It would be almost impossible to tell by taste alone if a beer has been primed. If a sediment remains in the bottom of the bottle it is probably yeast and the beer has probably been primed.)

Conditioning

Before the age of the so-called modern brewery, in the golden age of brewing, beers cleared by themselves. Solids such as proteins dropped during secondary fermentation without enzymes or other "finings." Particles which remained were not considered undesirable, and rightly not, for the stray particles were often rich in vitamins and proteins. Such solids have a tendency to coagulate when beer is refrigerated. Since American and continental lager drinkers prefer clear beer, several methods are employed to eliminate any cloudiness. Such cleared beer is less flavorful and less nutritious than the thicker, occasionally cloudy unfiltered or un-fined brews still made by some small breweries in Britain and Europe.

Beer is rendered brilliant by being filtered through such materials as asbestos, cellulose (pulp or paper), diatomaceous earth (also called *Kieselguhr* or silica) and felt. Some brewers, wishing to avoid the potential taste distortion caused by such filtering media, centrifuge their beer to remove undesirable particles. Other brewers utilize enzymes, such as papain, to digest proteinaceous particles. The most common clarifying agent used in Europe is made from isinglass, a very pure form of gelatin which comes from the swimming bladder of cod, ling, carp or sturgeon. This material arrives at the brewery as a very hard strip which is softened and made into a solution by the use of dilute tartaric or sulfuric acid. The clarifying acid solution is less than two parts per million (ppm) and completely harmless. Isinglass solution (some use pectin and other similar gelatinous compounds) acts by coagulating and trapping suspended particles, and carrying them to the bottom of the storage tanks.

According to Andrew Campbell caragheen moss is used by a few British brewers to coagulate solids and clear the brew. This traditional fining is gathered at low tide from rocks on the coast of Ireland. Caragheen moss is added while the wort is still boiling in the brew kettles, rather than to the storage tanks, as isinglass is.

The main problem with removing particles by artificial clarification is that a lasting head is often not possible unless foaming substances, such as those outlined under "additives," (Chapter 3) or extra CO_2 are added. A good, lasting head should result from the high nitrogen content of a good barley. Where "thinner" adjuncts such as corn, or rice are used, head-producing substances are almost always required.

Pasteurization

I strongly suspect that holding closed cans and bottles of beer at 140°F. for fifteen minutes to kill all bacteria does affect flavor characteristics. After all, what else is killed? The average drinker who simply knows that "draught beer tastes better" may not suspect the reason. It does "taste better," because it is unpasteurized, unfiltered and fresher. Coors is the only U.S. beer I know of that is unpasteurized, in kegs, cans or bottles. All are supposed to be kept refrigerated until the moment the beer is poured. Draught beer in cans and bottles is generally supposed to be more flavorful because the beer is unpasteurized. These brews are highly filtered with metal micropore filters (to remove unwanted, but nutritious solids) but should be kept refrigerated to be at their tastiest (38°F. to 40°F. is the best temperature).

Bottled or canned pasteurized beer should be enjoyed within two months and draught, unpasteurized beer within one week after leaving

RAND PUBLIC RELATIONS

The largest single shipment of canned beer to the United States—more than a million cans of Australian Foster's Lager—arrived in Port Jersey aboard the container ship Columbus America *during the summer of 1976.*

the brewery. Old beer is stale, and it might be appropriate to ask the brewers to date their products as other perishable foods are, such as milk, cream and butter.

Kegs, Bottles and Cans

As has been pointed out draught beer* tastes best because it is unpasteurized and fresher than "dead" canned or bottled beer. Glass containers affect taste characteristics little, if at all, while cans do have their effects on flavor. Unknown prior to 1935, beer cans now represent over 20 percent of the can industry's entire production. Each year, over twenty billion tin-coated steel cans and aluminum cans are used by beer drinkers in the United States alone. Bottles, being returnable in some places, are reused, therefore fewer are required—only eight *billion* each year!

Fortunately for our landscape, diminishing supplies and increasing costs of natural resources have forced some states to outlaw the use of nonreturnable containers. Thus brewers and other drink manufacturers have had to shift back to good old glass deposit bottles. This would not be very difficult to accomplish across America. According to a recent survey of packaged beer in the United States "the original throwaway bottle . . . confused consumers who could not understand why it should be thrown away." Some ignorant souls even committed such a stupid act as returning the bottles, without receiving a penny for their efforts. But, alas, these foolish conservationists were eventually educated into throwing away those useless bottles, becoming, no doubt, much better consumers in the mind of the bottle and can industries.

Would it be unpatriotic to suggest that all U.S. brewers be required to bottle their beer in standard bottles? Labels could, of course, be different, but this method would enable all brewers to accept each other's bottles being returned for deposit. The savings in resources would be enormous, as would the aesthetic saving of lands and waterways.

This system works beautifully in the United Kingdom where all domestic beers are bottled in standard ten ounce brown bottles. Labels are attached by glue rather than fired on, and are relatively easy to wash off in a hot-water bath.

Some will suggest that such an infringement of their right to choose bottle shape or color would be unconstitutional. I say SKOL! The British, who undeniably have a greater respect for individual differences, seem to do quite well with their standardized bottles—the beers, after all, are what matter, and on this account there is much greater variety of beer in the United Kingdom than in the United States. (The enterprising British are

---

*In Britain draught beer refers to that drawn from wooden barrels, while keg beer means that drawn from aluminum barrels.

such beer lovers that during World War II breweries were constructed on the largest of H.M. ships, to preserve valuable storage areas on cargo vessels and enable ships longer duty at sea. Desalinated sea water was "Burtonized" and combined with yeast, malt and hop concentrates.)

The "Church Key"

Before abandoning the subject of containers I may as well include *The Story of the "Quick and Easy" Opener* (the familiar "church key") as presented in a recent publication of the beer industry.*

> Flat top cans could not have been as readily accepted without the development and wide distribution of an inexpensive and effective can opener.
> The original opener developed by the American Can Company and later produced by the Vaughan Novelty Manufacturing Company was some five inches in length with a punch opener on one end and a bottle crown lifter on the other. These could be personalized with the brewer's name and were priced with discount at around a penny each.
> Initially, these were distributed through wholesalers and by insertion of one opener in each case of canned beer. . . .
> During the 1950's, as a means of conserving raw material, giveaway openers were reduced in length to about three inches.

But the can people were not to go unchallenged! The bottlers attempted to recapture the beer drinkers who were convinced that the beer can ". . . was unfriendly to beer flavor, and even after wide, brewer-subsidized distribution of punch-type openers, the container was considered to be somewhat difficult . . . to open." The one-way bottle was brought in, but to no avail. The aluminum, pull-top can became king!

But still the bottlers fought back—first with twist-off bottle caps (the average beer drinker doesn't like to worry about carrying an opener), and then by siding with ecologists who argued for returnable containers in friendly states.

Both groups may eventually lose out, however. I learned that one major brewery, a very progressive organization, is experimenting with varieties of an edible container! After drinking your beer you eat the container as a snack, satisfying both carnal and social instincts at once.

Becoming a Brewer

Attaching oneself to a master brewer and beginning in a lowly production position at a brewery is about the only route open to newcomers to the

---

*A *History of Packaged Beer and Its Market in the United States.* (Date, Author and Publisher unknown.)

field of commercial beer-making. If you are not the fourth generation of a famous Czechoslovakian brewing family, you will simply have to start at the bottom and learn the trade.

While in America there are no formal programs, (i.e. degree programs which automatically entitle you to claim entry into the field), there are two organizations which offer courses in brewing.

The Siebel Institute of Technology in Chicago offers a twelve-week course in Brewing Technology which is the only course of its type and intensity in the United States. Primarily intended to train brewery production personnel (two years of practical brewing experience is desirable), preference for admission is given to individuals who have the written endorsement of the master brewers under whom they have served.*

The United States Brewers' Academy, Mount Vernon, New York, offers a shorter but nonetheless intensive seminar in brewing, conducted annually, chiefly for new members of the brewing industry such as chemists, bacteriologists and engineers.**

For students who intend from the beginning of their careers as undergraduates to enter the brewing industry, a bachelor of science degree in brewing is offered by Heriot-Watt University in Edinburgh, Scotland. This course "covers the basic background scientific knowledge required of a brewer, including a course in actual malting and brewing sciences," according to Dr. Anna M. MacLeod.*** Students with a degree in a scientific subject who want to enter the industry may enroll in a nine-month postgraduate course, a one-year master of science course, or a three-year doctoral program in brewing science.

---

*For enrollment procedures, write to Mr. William R. Siebel, Siebel Institute of Technology, 4055 West Peterson Avenue, Chicago, Ill. 60646.

**For more information, write to Mr. J. Robert McDonald, Assistant Director, United States Brewers' Academy, 230 Washington Street, Mount Vernon, N.Y. 10551.

***Dr. Anna M. MacLeod, Reader in Brewing, Heriot-Watt University, Chambers Street, Edinburgh, Scotland.

5

Beers Around the World

ACCORDING to a recent United Nations report, the first new industry requested by developing nations is a brewery. Beer consumption is rising faster than production in many parts of the world, having doubled between 1950 and 1970, and is expected to double again by 1980.

Traditionally wine-drinking nations, such as Spain, Portugal, Italy and France, are seeing a great surge of popularity for this oldest of fermented drinks. It may be one effect of the establishment of the Common Market, where foreign things have become increasingly accessible. In an interview in *Business Week* (February 7, 1970), the manager of an English-style pub in Paris explained: "Beer is more expensive, snobbish, and better tasting than *vin ordinaire*. The kids love it." The free exchange of goods between European nations may also explain why many Europeans who once drank only their local, regional or national beers are now changing to brands of other nationalities.

As a result of this desire to experiment with something new and different, hundreds of small breweries have disappeared throughout Europe in the past ten years. "The last beer made by monks, Holland's *De Schaapskooi*, was acquired last year from the Trappists by Belgium's *Stella Artois*" (*Business Week*, February 7, 1970).

A prime force of persuasion in this new addiction to beer is given by campaigns against alcoholism. Intoxication from beer is a relatively slow process, due to its low alcoholic content of between 3 and 4 percent, as compared with 12 percent in table wines and 40 to 50 percent in hard drinks. The U.S.S.R. government officially supports beer drinking, to get people off the vodka wagon, while French campaigns against stronger beverages have had the same effect.

The United States is the freest beer market in the world; more brands of beer from more countries are available than in any other nation. There are approximately 600 brands available in the U.S. and this includes over 110 imported brands. Compare this free market with that of Germany, which has thousands of small breweries with as many brands but of which only twenty are imported. Great Britain, the third largest producer in the world after the U.S. and Germany, imports beers from Europe and Scandinavia, but does not have any beers from the United States. This is not snobbery; it is a purely economic barrier that prevents the sale of foreign labels.

The largest outlets for imported beers in America are New York (32 percent), Chicago (13 percent), Los Angeles (10 percent), San Francisco (5 percent), Boston (3 percent), Cleveland (3 percent), Washington, D.C. (2.7 percent), Philadelphia (2 percent), Detroit (2 percent) and Buffalo (2 percent).* Yet, even with tremendous interest in imported beers all imports sell to less than 1 percent of the U.S. beer market. The people who drink imported beers are mainly those who have traveled in or who were born or raised in another country. They might also be the culture snobs who do not want to order a local or regional beer.

In this chapter beers of the world are grouped according to the nation of origin with one exception: English and Scottish labels are combined under British beers.

Much of the historical background of each nation is reprinted here from *One Hundred Years of Brewing*, originally published in 1903 by H. S. Rich and Company, Chicago, and reproduced in 1973 by Sonja and Will Anderson of Newtown, Connecticut. Specific details of the history of brewing companies have been provided by the companies.

AUSTRALIA

Carlton and United

Foster's Lager, Victoria Bitter, Melbourne Bitter, Abbott's Lager, Crown Lager, Carlton Draught

In Australia, beer is closely intertwined with "manliness." Next to a "youngie" (i.e., a young girlfriend), the amount one can drink seems to be a veritable symbol of national identity. Now only third in per capita beer consumption worldwide (Czechs are first; Germans, second) the Aussies relish their frontier-busting image.

Little wonder then at the success of Carlton's overseas advertising campaign which has driven *Foster's Lager* into rapidly becoming the third largest nationally distributed imported beer in the United States. Can the browbeaten American male resist that smiling, tan, bush-suited, hairy-armed *macho*, with his cold, *big* (740 ml) can of beer? I myself drink Foster's Lager by the gallon while botanizing in Fiji, but I must admit it's more to avoid the headache that generally follows consumption of the local beer,

*Estimated for 1971 by All Brand Importers, Inc.

Herb Smith (left) *world champion boomerang thrower, offers some tips and a taste of Australia to Eugene Arnow* (right) *at the third annual Smithsonian Open Boomerang Tournament in Washington, D.C. Smith's talents failed to rub off on Arnow; he was awarded the Foster's Lager "No Return" Cup for his valiant and unsuccessful efforts to get his boomerang to return to his hand. Smith, of Sussex, England, holds the record for throwing a boomerang 109 yards in the air.*

Fiji Bitter, than it is to identify myself with the tan, smiling man from Down Under!

Consider this; the Czechs swallow an average of 40.3 U.S. gallons of beer per year, while the people of Darwin, the tropical northern Australian city, have set an unbelievable record of 62.4 gallons per person. Overall, the average Australian consumes only 22 gallons per annum.

Australian beers are largely lagers—light, sparkling and served too cold to be *touched* by the continental beer connoisseur. However, unlike American lagers, the Australian brews are *not* sweet, having the inviting tartness of some highly hopped British beers. Being more alcoholic than their American counterparts (over 4 percent) they also have a slightly stronger kick.

Tastewise, Foster's Lager is light in color, bouquet and body. It holds a strong head, is a bit dryer than other light lagers, and has a hoppy flavor.

Aftertaste is smooth and inviting. (Some on the tasting panel found it "weak," with "very little character.")

The ingredients of this beer were freely shared by the brewery, a good sign. I always suspect a beer when the brewer starts talking about the formula being a "trade secret . . . in the family for generations." By divulging the ingredients, a brewer does not teach the competition how to brew a particular flavor into a beer; that requires time and skill, something as vaporous as the head on yesterday's beer. Too many breweries simply withhold information from me (see Master List of the World) for me not to appreciate Carlton's integrity.

Foster's Lager is an all-barley malt beer; no other cereals are utilized. That's a plus, as is the fact that the hop extract is derived from hops grown at the world-renowned research station at Ringwood. Of course, pure hops are more desirable, in my opinion, but most average beers are brewed with extracts. The water supply at Melbourne requires no treatment, an unusual situation in a world of water too hard or too soft for most brewing. Fermentation runs for 100 to 120 hours, after which time the beer is run off into chillers and separated from "residual matter," a common practice which robs most modern beer of any significant nutritional value. After refrigerated storage for an undisclosed period, the new beer is filtered and pasteurized, and finally racked into casks or bottles.

Carlton's other national beers include *Victoria Bitter, Melbourne Bitter, Abbott's Lager, Crown Lager* and *Carlton Draught,* brands preferred by many Australian drinkers. The company now owns and operates ten breweries: five in Victoria (at Carlton, East Melbourne, Abbotsford, Geelong and Ballarat); four in Queensland (at Brisbane, Cairns, Rockhampton and Toowoomba); and one at Darwin (in the Northern Territory). In addition, a brewery in Fiji is jointly owned with W. R. Carpenter and Co., Ltd.

Carlton beers are available in over forty countries of the world and the company is Australia's largest exporter of beer. It is the largest brewer in the Southern hemisphere and is believed to be among the ten largest breweries in the world. Interestingly, the single largest shipment of beer ever made was an *entire* ocean-going freighter of Foster's Lager shipped to New York.

Tooheys, Limited

Tooheys Export Pilsener, Stag Lager, Old Draught, Miller Lager, Oatmeal Stout, Miller Stout, Flag Ale

Another label from New South Wales, *Tooheys Pilsener,* is a local favorite, eliciting fierce loyalty among serious drinkers. All Tooheys' labels are made from two-row barley, low-protein wheat, sugar syrup, Tasmanian "Ringwood" hops extract, a private strain of yeast and municipal water.

The pilsener and other Tooheys' lagers (*Stag Lager, Old Draught, Miller Lager, Oatmeal Stout* and *Miller Stout*) are bottom-fermented at 55°F. for seven days, then chilled to 32°F. and carbonated. Aged for an unspecified period at 32°F., these lagers are then filtered and carbonated again for filling. (The beers are *not* naturally krausened.)

Aside from slight alterations in formula, Tooheys *Flag Ale* is top-fermented at 70–75°F. for two to three days and then brewed like the lagers.

Tooheys, Ltd. operates five breweries—three in the city of Sydney and two in the country. The original brewery, known as the Albion Brewery, was founded in 1827. It was purchased in 1873 by the Toohey Brothers.

Other Australian Beers

In a land where "beer is a religion," we would expect many local breweries. Unfortunately, this is no longer true, corporatism having gobbled up the independents. About the only small brewery left in New South Wales is in Grafton, a small country town. Other brands in this segment of the continent are brewed by Tooth's, Resch's, and Miller's.

Foster's Lager was chug-a-lugged and sprayed on the audience at City Center Theatre, New York, by the Monty Python group portraying "the three Bruces," Aussies of a particularly aggressive and stereotypical nature.

A well-known draft beer is *Resch's Draft,* while *Resch's DA* (Dinner Ale) is a bit on the sweet, light side. The pilsener is bottled and widely distributed.

Western Australia is the home of *Swan Lager,* brewed at Perth. It is a very light beer, with light color, body and bouquet, as well as a nice light flavor. It is now quite popular in the United States since it tastes much like many domestic lagers. The aroma is fruity, the head weak, the flavor malty. Basically uninspiring.

South Australia offers *Cooper's Ale.* With above-average body and tartness and a hoppy bouquet, it is often compared to highly hopped English ales.

Queensland is a region where *Castlemaine Ale* and *Bulimba* are brewed. I've often enjoyed Castlemain in Fiji, where the tartness seemed just the thing to fight the alienation that rainy days seem to bring in Suva.

Tasmania, an island off the southeast coast of Australia, has a fine brewery at Hobart. The Cascade Brewery produces *Cascade Lager, Export Stout, Draught, Bitter Ale,* and *Sparkling Pale Ale.*

The barley and hops are grown on Tasmanian farms, where sugar is imported from Queensland. The intake of barley amounts to some 400,000 bushels a year, which is all malted by the brewery. While the quantity of Tasmanian-grown hops may vary, the consumption is in the vicinity of 300 bales a year. (There are 250 lbs. of hops to a bale.) A real plus is the fact that this brewery uses "nil" pesticides in growing their agricultural ingredients.

This picturesque brewery, with its mellowed freestone facade, sits beneath Mt. Wellington, a chief source of brewing water. The main water source is at the base of Strickland Falls, where Cascade obtains a constant supply of aerated, cascading mountain water. This cold stream carries the run-off from snow in winter and from summer rains, an enviable resource.

Peter Degraves, the founder, described his brew in 1832: "At this establishment publicans and private families can be supplied at all times with genuine beer from malt and hops, either in cask or bottle, and of very superior quality . . . fully equal to the best London manufacture." Today, the stout has a devout following on the mainland.

AUSTRIA

Beer was drunk in Vienna as early as 1340, but by the early part of the sixteenth century only officers of the Crown were allowed to brew. They could brew but they could not sell their product. By the seventeenth century these regulations and privileges were abolished and brewing was opened to all classes.

Bruder Reininghaus Brauerei, Graz

Reininghaus, Puntigam

The Austrian people at present support fourteen major breweries. The Bruder Reininghaus Brauerei in Graz, a southern city, has been a major producer for several centuries.

The earliest records indicate that a brewery existed in the Steinfeld area around 1697. In 1853 the facilities were purchased by the brothers Peter and Julius Reininghaus. The enterprising brothers introduced modern equipment and altered brewing techniques, making lager beer with bottom-fermenting yeast. In 1895 the aging Peter invented the *Wanderhaufen-mälzerei* ("shifting-heaps-malting") a method which is still in use (in updated form) and unchanged in principle.

The brewery has changed from a primitive stone-beer brewery (*Stein-bierbrauerei*) which produced a top-fermenting ale, to a highly mechanized lager facility, but the two principal brands *Reininghaus* and *Puntigam*, continue to be among the most respected in Austria.

CULVER PICTURES

Waiter in Vienna.

Both are made with barley malt as well as with cornmeal and rice adjuncts. All agricultural ingredients are grown in the moderate continental climate which has also proven ideal for brewing beer. Crops are principally fertilized "organically," that is with manure; however, they are occasionally treated with artificial fertilizer. Pesticide use is kept to an absolute minimum, utilized only when a crop failure is threatened and then only in small amounts. Harvesting of barley and hops is of course no longer done by hand. Grain is stored in large air-dried bins with no preservative chemicals. Water is drawn from a private, deep artesian well.

The complete brewing process, from raw materials to packaging, normally takes two months. A special beer, brewed once yearly and available locally, is aged for up to four months.

These two popular Austrian lagers are available in Yugoslavia, Hungary, Sweden, Portugal, Canada, United States, Guinea, Bahrein Islands, Israel, Pakistan and India. The brewery is very wisely tied to the brown 16-ounce "Euro-bottle" of standardized shape, color and volume, which makes it possible for European breweries using this bottle to accept each others' empties, thereby conserving resources and reducing the potential for litter.

Gosser Stifts Brau

Gosser Stifts Brau Dark Beer

Gosser Stifts Brau Dark Beer is an ochre-colored beer of above-average bouquet and hoppiness, with a high level of sweetness. The head is firm, the flavor strong; but if you like sweet, dark beers, Mackeson, a British stout, is unbeatable. Gosser Stifts is just *too* sweet.

Ottakringer

Gold Fassl

Gold Fassl must be one of Vienna's most outstanding lagers. This one *is* light, yet not without flavor. The head is natural, not lingering too long in the glass. This is reassuring in an export lager. Too many imports retain unduly tenacious heads, probably due to foam-extending chemicals. This beer, with its pronounced bouquet, has a superb flavor. Of medium body and with mildly euphoric aftertaste.

BELGIUM

Belgium has always been one of the highest beer-consuming countries in the world. The brewing industry is of ancient origin, beer having been manufactured in Brussels as early as the twelfth century. In the fifteenth, the varieties known as *walgbaert* and *hoppe* were white beers, made of a mixture of wheat and oats. There were also *roetbier* (red) and *zwartzbier* (black). All of these, with other varieties, were gradually replaced by the *lambic*, or strong beer, the *mais*, or small beer, and *faro*, a mixture of each.

At the beginning of this century definite types had become associated with localities: Antwerp had its *arge*, the Walloon provinces their *fortes-saisons* and Louvain its white, sparkling, summer beers. By the year 1910, 3,349 breweries were operating throughout Belgium. Following World War I, in 1920, 2,013 remained. By 1950, consolidations left only 663 in operation. As elsewhere, the number of breweries continues to decline, while overall beer consumption is rising. The pressures of the past decade have reduced the number of breweries from 414 in 1960 to 232 in 1970. In one year alone, 1971, another twenty-five had ceased operations. The more picturesque and quaint fell before the onslaught of modern business concepts, and perhaps decreasing consumer taste distinctions. A look at consumption figures over a forty-year span will show a remarkable fact: while per capita

CULVER PICTURES

"Good Bock Beer" by Edward Manet.

consumption dropped from 49.8 gallons in 1925 to 29.6 gallons in 1958, it rose by 1966 to 31.3 gallons, simply due to two contemporary marketing techniques.

The major Belgian brewers decided to bring beer into the daily life of the consumer in harmony with the nation's eating habits. By promoting home delivery, and through massive advertising, the amount of beer consumed with meals was dramatically doubled in about ten years. In 1958 beer was served with about 40 percent of all meals in Belgium; by 1968 it was included with 80 percent. Thus, advertising has had a direct impact on the life of a nation. Interestingly, foreign brewers, such as Amstel, Carlsberg, Whitbread and others, were the first to saturate the nation with beer promotion. Not unexpectedly the domestic brewers followed suit.

Brasserie Piedboeuf, Jupille

Jupiler

One exceptional lager—*Jupiler*—is brewed by Brasserie Piedboeuf in Jupille, near the eastern city of Liège. Quite popular throughout the continent, Jupiler is considered a fine import even among nationalistic Parisian beer drinkers. It is widely available, the company's 6,000 "tied" pubs accounting for major sales.

All malt used is derived from barley grown in Belgium and Bavaria. Hops are of Bavarian and Czechoslovakian origin, with local varieties used from time to time. The lager is fermented for about one week and then placed in a second fermentation storage process for ten to twelve weeks.

As consolidiations continue and fewer breweries remain, the Piedboeuf organization will be one of the few Belgian companies to survive this century. Jupiler signs at inns, pubs and food outlets may become synonymous with Belgian beer.

CANADA

BEER—A STAPLE IN NEW FRANCE*

In detailing the diet of a farm laborer in the little colony of New France, the Provincial of the Jesuits in Quebec writing in the Society's publication, *Relations* of 1636, mentions that in addition to their allowance of flour, lard, oil and vinegar, codfish, peas and so on, "they are given a chopine of cider a day, or a quart of beer."

There are numerous references in the *Relations* to the building of the home breweries which were considered a necessary adjunct of any large household or religious institution. In 1634, Father LeJeune, the first superior of the Jesuits in Canada, reported to France: "As for drinks, we shall have

---

Brewing in Canada, p. 12.

to make some beer; but we shall wait until we have built and a brewery is erected; these three articles are assured with time."

But even earlier, in 1633, when Champlain was making sagamite, a sort of stew for a Huron feast, he used a great kettle normally employed for brewing beer. And the position of the brewer is evident in a report of a religious celebration in Quebec in 1646, which lists the local crafts represented in the procession: "carpenters, masons, sailors, toolmakers, brewers and bakers."

When the capable Intendant Jean Talon decided to build a brewery in Quebec in 1668, his reasons were exactly the same as those which could be given today to indicate the necessity for maintaining a vigorous, healthy brewing industry in Canada:

"A brewery which M. Talon is having built will also contribute not only to the public welfare by forcing a decrease in the use of intoxicating drinks, which occasions a great lawlessness here; that can be obviated by using this other drink, which is very wholesome and not injurious. Moreover it will keep in the country the money which is now being sent out of it in purchase of so much liquor in France. It will also promote consumption of the super-abundance of grain which has sometimes been so great that the laborers can not find a market for it." So Father Francis LeMercier, S.J., wrote from Quebec to Father Etienne Des Champs, Provincial of the Jesuits in France.

There are at present fifty-two breweries operated by ten independent companies throughout each of Canada's ten provinces, except for Prince Edward Island, which does not have any form of tavern. The brewing industry is entirely Canadian; buying 97 percent of its raw materials in Canada and brewing nearly 100 percent of the beer Canadians drink. Majority ownership and control of the breweries is held by Canadians who comprise 95 percent of the 55,000 shareholders. While brewing is still thought of as a family business by the average person, all the major breweries in Canada are public companies.

In all, 119 brands of ale, lager, stout, porter and bock are brewed across the nation. Of this number about a dozen are so-called national brews, available from one coast to another. For the purposes of this guide two brewery companies and their labels will be examined—Molson, Ltd. and Moosehead, Ltd.

Molson Breweries, Ltd., Montreal, Quebec

Molson Ale, Molson Lager, Golden Ale, Canadian Lager Beer, Porter

Molson's is one of Canada's three largest brewery companies, and North America's oldest. Plants, which are located across the country from Vancouver to St. John's, produce well-known labels. The ale is especially popular in the United States, where many hunters and fishermen in the northern states seem to associate Canadian beers with such activities.

The founder of Molson's arrived in Canada from Lincolnshire, England, in 1782, at the age of eighteen. Within a few years he had acquired a small brewery on the banks of the St. Lawrence.

Beginning with ales and beer, and for a time spruce beer—popular for its medicinal properties—* Molson's production went from about 4,000 gallons in the first five-month season in 1786 to over 30,000 gallons by 1791. In 1972 over two million barrels (1 barrel = 31.5 gallons) were produced in nine plants.

Molson Ale is a good representative of what is generically known as Canadian sparkling ale. This is as typical as German lager or an English ale, and different from any other kind of beer. In fact experienced drinkers can often recognize it in unlabeled taste contests. It is hybrid in that it is brewed as an ale, with top-fermenting yeast, and cellared as a lager—yielding some characteristics of each. The result has become the largest-selling ale in North America.

Molson Lager is a typical light lager. With above-average body, an acidy flavor, meaty aroma and tart aftertaste, it is unexceptional overall.

---

*Spruce beer is due for a revival. With the current interest in herbal lore and the historical precedent for this North American beer, a wise brewing company looking for a new line is likely to produce this refreshing and healthful alternative. It is brewed like ale or lager with spruce needles (leaves) used in place of hops. These aromatic green spikes are rich in ascorbic acid and were popularly drunk in tea (and beer) for their healthful effects.

CULVER PICTURES

A nineteenth-century drinking saloon in Montreal; sketched by E. R. Morse.

All Molson beers are brewed with Canadian barley, hops from the only brewery-operated hop farm in the nation (blended with imported varieties) and a distinctive yeast strain. Molson's agriculturists assure me that Canada's cold climate reduces the danger of infections and infestations, which eliminates the need for fungicides and pesticides.

Natural carbonation is utilized in the brewing of all Molson products before storage. It is of interest that the storage vaults of the first Molson brewery (1786) still exist in the basement of the present-day Montreal plant.

Moosehead Breweries, Ltd., Dartmouth, Nova Scotia

Moosehead Ale, Ten Penny Ale, Alpine Lager, London Stout

Although not one of the giant national brewery companies, Moosehead produces in the Nova Scotia plant about 200,000 barrels annually, mainly of ale, with some lager. Very little stout is consumed in the Maritime Provinces.

Each of the Moosehead labels is made from western Canadian barley, U.S.-grown but Canadian-milled corn, hops of U.S., Yugoslavian and domestic origin, private strains of yeast, and pure lake water which is filtered through sand and carbon filters prior to use.

Beer is brewed in 260-barrel batches in a fully automated stainless-steel brewhouse. The process is semicontinuous to continuous, depending on demand. Standard modern equipment is used, including a mash mixer, lauter tun, kettle, hop separator, and a unique tangential-entry hot-wort tank. Storage tanks are glass-lined and the entire process, from barley to beer, takes approximately one month.

Other Canadian Beers

British Columbia happens to be blessed with a wide sample of "local" beers. On a recent visit to this province I purchased one bottle of each label and hand-carried two cartons through customs. The twenty-four bottles seemed to please the inspector who let me through without inspecting my other belongings. Apparently, beer drinkers are considered regular guys, certainly not the smuggling kind.

The following beers made it back to my sampling panel in California:

Heidelberg, brewed by the giant Carling, O'Keefe, is yellowish-gold in color with an indescribable odor and flavor. The aftertaste is fine if you need a strong purgative. Maybe this beer was spoiled.

Kokanee Pilsener is a product of Columbia Brewing. Pale amber in color, with a ratty aroma, sour flavor, miniscule head and weak body, this mixture has a surprisingly good aftertaste. Overall, it's not as bad as its features.

Kootenay Bière Pale Ale, another Columbia concoction, is a tangy light beer. With an aromatic bouquet, mild yellow color and average body, it is tart and decently flavored. Unfortunately, a sour aftertaste ruins the overall impression.

Kronenbrau, another label from Carling, O'Keefe, is slightly more amber than other Canadian beers sampled. With a weak head, mild aroma, and medium body, it imparts a lively sweet taste. A very drinkable, light beer.

Labatt's 50 Ale is brewed by the giant Canadian chain of regional breweries. Of average amber color, the head has strong holding qualities. The aroma is fruity and pronounced, the taste delicious. Most samplers agreed that drinking gallons of this brew is an inviting possibility. One of North America's best beers.

O'Keefe's Extra Old Stock Malt Liquor is strong and tart. With a winey bouquet, average body and flavor, a mild head and above-average dryness. Sharp aftertaste.

Old Blue Pilsener is rich and flavorful. One of a few labels from Uncle Ben's Breweries in Alberta, a productive independent, this one is delicious. It has above-average bouquet, body and flavor. The dry taste is attractive. Pungent and recommended.

Uncle Ben's Malt Liquor is a true light beer. With a thick body, strong head and more substance than average, this brand has an aged quality. It is a mellow, good beer, which was described by a sensitive, expecting wife as "a very pure beer." The soothing texture and inviting aftertaste make this my favorite Canadian beer.

CHINA

Trade with mainland China is bringing many interesting exports, among them *Yuchuan Beer,* from Peking. At first taste it is reminiscent of Kronenbourg, a superb Alsatian brew. As the drinking goes on, though, what tasted and smelled like that fine French beer slowly imparts a peculiar chemical aftertaste. I suspect that the "purest spring water of Peking's Yuchuan Hill" has been treated with chlorine before it hits the brewery. The Chinese have a fine tradition with wine; beer is a rather recent transplant. Prices being about equal, I'd recommend the Kronenbourg.

Tsingtao Beer is another disappointment. The color is average for a lager, the bouquet light. The neutral flavor and body did not prepare me for the heavy, overly dry finish.

CZECHOSLOVAKIA

Before looking at Czechoslovakia's famous Pilsner Urquell, a glance at the superior Saaz hops and the region in which they are cultivated is appropriate. Brewers of the most costly beers bid against one another for Saaz hops (from a production standpoint, cost is a reasonable index of quality).

The product is scarce, most of the crop being used by Czech brewers, and the price relative to hops of Bavaria or Kent, England, quite high.

BOHEMIAN HOPS*

The date of the first cultivation of hops in Bohemia has never been fixed; in fact, they are mentioned from the earliest historic times, and Saaz and Auscha, in Bohemia, have always been as noted for their hops as Kent, in England.

Saaz hops, if market prices are a criterion, are superior to those of Auscha.

The town of Saaz is about fifty miles south of Dresden and is almost as famous for its vines as for its hops. There are few localities in the world where the climate is more equable and it has the smallest rainfall of Bohemia, if not of all central Europe. Climate and soil combine to produce a fine variety of the plant, the region about Saaz being divided into three zones of hops—first, Saaz *Stadt* (city); second, Saaz *Bezirk* (district), and

One Hundred Years of Brewing, pp. 695–696.

A red-capped waiter fills mugs of beer
in Prague's U Flekŭ brewery, which has been
making beer since 1499.

third, Saaz *Kreis* (county). According to David G. Fairchild, of the United States Department of Agriculture, who has thoroughly investigated the subject, the best hops are produced upon a peculiar red clay loam called the *Rothliegende,* which lies along a small stream (the Goldbach), the waters of which are colored by the soil a warm, yellowish red. Two-thirds of the Saaz hops are grown along this stream. The distinguishing features of the Saaz hops are very compact, closed scales, a silky texture, abundance of fats and resins, a large amount of lupulin, a high polish, and, when properly dried, a bright greenish-yellow color.

The following is quoted verbatim from Mr. Fairchild's report (1900) to the United States Department of Agriculture:

In Saaz there are very few varieties of hops cultivated, the Auscha red hop being almost universally grown. The preference is given to this variety because of its great productiveness, although it is exceeded by the old Saaz variety in fineness of aroma and bitter flavor.

It is an interesting fact that every year thousands of cuttings of this Auscha red hop are imported into Saaz. Two-thirds of the hops cultivated are from these imported cuttings, and the yield from them, as compared with that from home-grown cuttings, is as thirteen to seven, and sometimes quite double. The average production from this variety is 110 pounds per 420 plants, but sometimes 240 plants produce a centner (110 pounds). The claim is made that the first and second years after their introduction into Saaz the plants grown from Auscha cuttings do not produce a hop that is equal to that from the old Saaz plants, but that gradually they become ameliorated by growth in the wonderful Saaz soil, and later yield a product quite up to the standard. The bearing capacity gradually decreases, however, and it is considered necessary with every new planting to import afresh the Auscha cuttings.

This Auscha red hop, above referred to, is known among Auscha hop growers as the Semsch hop, having been found in a garden near Auscha by a peasant of that name. In recognition of the value of his discovery the hop growers of Auscha, rather tardily it must be said, presented his son, now an old man, with a medal or diploma. No systematic attempts to breed new varieties of hops seem to have been made in these regions, notwithstanding this interesting discovery.

As the hop of commerce is the seedless flower cluster of the female plant, quite naturally only plants of this sex are cultivated in the gardens, although male plants are sometimes seen in cultivated fields. The greatest pains are taken to immediately root out any of the chance male plants which have come up from seed or have otherwise gotten into the garden. In Auscha there are old laws which enforce their immediate removal. Such male plants are called wild hops, and are most abundant in waste places about the gardens. A single male plant in a garden will fertilize enough females to materially injure the whole harvest by the formation of a high percentage of seeds in the otherwise seedless flowers. When the number of hops with seeds reaches more than two-tenths of one per cent they are rated in Bohemia as of second-grade quality.

Prazdroj Brewery, Pilsen

Pilsner Urquell

The Prazdroj brewery produces what many consider the best lager in the world. While taste is subjective, other parameters would tend to justify this opinion. *Pilsner Urquell* is the second largest selling import in Germany and the Germans are its biggest importers. Other traditional beer-consuming nations also import large quantities: Austria, Belgium, Hungary, Sweden and Switzerland. The Soviet Union also depends upon this Czech brewery for its finest beer.

But popularity by itself is never an assurance of quality. People are easily swayed by advertising. Looking at how this beer is made, "the best beer in the world" seems deserved as a claim. At least it is one of the six or so "best" beers of the world (depending on taste preferences the following seem to be the choices of experts: *Amstel, Carlsberg, Dortmunder, Guinness, Heineken, Löwenbräu, Stella Artois,* and *Tuborg*).

Beer from this Pilsen brewery has extraordinary properties and a quality resulting from both local conditions and raw materials, as well as from a brewing technology which is genuinely traditional. It is recommended for anyone liking the aroma of malt and hops.

Pilsner Urquell is probably the closest thing to an organic beer available. It is made without any artificial ingredients, either in the brewing or in the growing of the raw materials. In Bohemia and Moravia, where the barley and hops are grown, traditional farming methods are still employed with little use of pesticides or chemicals.

Hops come exclusively from the Zatec region, known among brewmasters for its rare agricultural products.

The water of Pilsen is the prototype for all lager brewers around the world. As we have seen, many brewers attempt to correct their waters by chemical means to obtain the qualities of Pilsen water, which is best described as low in total hardness and of constant composition.

Most of the malt is of Czech origin. The barley is prepared on the same floors that have been used since 1842. During the drying on double floor kilns, low colors are aimed at (to give a light beer) with high kilning temperatures, for a period of four hours.

The brewing kettles are heated by coal fires, which, according to Ivo Hlavacek, technical director of the brewery, creates an intensity of boiling not possible by electronic means. The classic three-mash process influences the quality of the wort, which has a high amount of dextrines and a low amount of nitrogenous substances.

The beer is fermented in giant 2,500-liter oak casks (without refrigeration) in six miles of cool limestone caves beneath the city. (The wood is said to impart a better flavor than the stainless steel, glass, or fiber-glass tanks of modern breweries.) Fermentation lasts twelve days.

The beer is then stored for three months at an average temperature of 1°C. in an unusual way. The tanks are left open for about three weeks after being filled with young beer. After this time the tanks are closed. Before bottling or barreling, the beer is filtered with *kieselguhr* or pulp filters.

Another factor which produces a consistent quality of finished beer, is the mixing of individual batches throughout all the liquid phases of the brewing process.

As a result of the popularity of Pilsner Urquell, especially in the export market, the brewery has recently undergone vast modernization. Reconstruction, however, has been conducted in accordance with the classic traditions of the brewery and is mainly in the area of final operations: bottling, racking and internal transport.

In an interview (*Playboy*, 1972) Mr. Hlavacek stated: "We spend two years studying each new brewing technique as it comes along—before rejecting it."

The recent expansion of production is the largest since 1842, when the many small breweries of Pilsen joined together. The beer had become popular soon after the foundation of the brewery. In 1856 it was exported to Vienna and later to Austria, Germany and Switzerland. In 1862 it was sent to London and Paris to meet the demand. In 1873 it was brought over to the United States, and by 1914 Americans were drinking more of it than any other imported beer. After two world wars and the resultant shifting political alliances, Pilsner Urquell got lost in the American marketplace. By expanding distribution and expending sums for advertising the owners have increased sales in America.

It is hoped the ad people will stick to the facts and not claim to be "the oldest beer in the world"—many English beers can trace their roots back further than 1292, when King Wenceslaus gave the people of Pilsen the right to make beer. The first mention of a Bohemian brewery is in 1086 in Prague. There is no denying that Bohemia (Czechoslovakia) is one of the most ancient centers of brewing in central Europe. One of the oldest of these breweries was established at Dobrau, near Pilsen, in 1378. This brewery is not directly related to the brewers of Pilsner Urquell, except that all beers of the region are of a similar character. Lighter in color than Bavarian beers the Pilseners also contain more alcohol. Bohemian brewing had an important influence on surrounding countries. The wheat beer of Bohemia was introduced into Bavaria in the sixteenth century and became so popular that at one time it threatened the wheat supply as a source of food. Consequently, the duke of Bavaria was obliged to forbid its use in the production of beer.

Of the 120 breweries in Czechoslovakia the Prazdroj company is by far the most famous. Czechs drink Pilsner Urquell under a Prazdroj label. Unlike many fine European beers which are brewed differently for the export market, Pilsner Urquell is the same brew that is sold in Europe. To many it is the finest in the world.

DENMARK

BEER OF THE NORSEMEN*

El, or ale—so it is gleaned from the early Norse writings—was long used by the people of modern Scandinavia as their chief national drink. At their three great winter festivals, especially, it was an effective means of lightening the gloom which seemed to be a characteristic of the typical Norseman.

Ale was drunk very new. A great brewing preceded, by a few days, the Yule gatherings and family feasts. Numerous references to this custom occur in the historical Sagas and popular stories. We are told, in the Orkney "Saga," for example, how Earl Rognwald (about 1050), a little before Christmas, went with a great following from Kirkwall to Papey, to fetch malt for the Yule brewing—an unlucky expedition, which ended in his death. The brewing was not forgotten even at sea. Eric the Red, who lived in Greenland, says of some countrymen who had arrived to spend the winter there: "I fear it will be said that never have you passed a worse Yule than Eric offered you in Greenland."

"Not so," answered the ship's captain, "for we have on board malt and meal and corn for Yule, which shall be sent to you, to make the feast your generosity requires."

A special brewer was often engaged before a private entertainment. We are told (A.D. 1253) that at the celebrated marriage feast given by Earl Gizur, which ended in fire and slaughter, the brewer engaged was a monk, and, therefore, probably his life was spared.

Such feasts generally lasted until the ale was finished, and then the guests went home. It was the custom of the Norwegian peasantry to brew strong ale just before Christmas and entertain the neighbors until it was consumed. Then probably no more ale was tasted until the following Christmas, or the next family festival.

But the Norsemen, or modern Scandinavians have, until late modern times, been more noted as consumers of distilled than of fermented liquors.

Barley Cultivation in Scandinavia and Iceland:

Notwithstanding the comparatively late period marking the rise of public brewing in Scandinavia, it is a fact that barley was cultivated both in Norway and Iceland at a very early day. The term corn was applied by the Norsemen to this grain from the earliest times, and as late as the eighteenth century the Norwegian laws mention the *kornskat,* or tax imposed upon land according to the corn which it was capable of producing. In one of the ancient Sagas mention is made of a barn in Helgeland, in latitude 65° north, in which corn was stored.

Barley was first cultivated in Iceland, at the time of its colonization in 870, and is said to have been raised there until 1400. Since that time what barley is used has been mostly imported from Denmark, Iceland

---

*One Hundred Years of Brewing, p. 707.

*With husbandly pride the groom offers his
bride her first sip of the beer brewed
especially for their wedding festivities.*

seeming to be the northern limit of its successful cultivation. Scientific
investigations go to show that barley cannot be grown, with certainty, in
Norway north of 60°, at more than from eighteen hundred to two thousand
feet above sea-level. In some of the valleys of Norway the grain may, in
favorable seasons, be cut eight or nine weeks after sowing and thus two
crops reaped in one summer.

In Sweden the polar limit is fixed at about 66°, but there, as in Finland,
night frosts prove very destructive to young barley.

At the Beginning of the Nineteenth Century:

The production and consumption of distilled spirits in the Scandinavian
countries, at the beginning of the nineteenth century, were of so much
importance that malted liquors were scarcely mentioned; in fact, as articles
of home manufacture, except in Sweden, they scarcely existed. Denmark
imported vast quantities of brandies from France, and in 1800 the distillers
of Copenhagen alone numbered more than 300.

Norway, in fact, until the century was well advanced, had made little
progress even in distilling. Ale from Great Britain was imported to a
considerable extent, but only used freely upon such special occasions as
weddings, christenings and festivals. For stronger drink the Norwegians
depended upon the Danes, Dutch and French. The Dutch, in return for
their gin, received larger quantities of juniper berries, which they used in
its distillation. At this time the only beverage made in Norway was
procured by adding sugar to the juice of the birch tree, boiling and
fermenting it.

Only a small proportion of the spirits consumed in Sweden was manufactured in the country, and thinness was noted as a characteristic of the people, being attributed to their constant use of highly alcoholic drinks. At the beginning of the 19th century, however, Sweden had made considerable progress in brewing and it is recorded that in 1809 there were 159 registered breweries in the country, and that as early as 1790 they were able to export 169 barrels from Stockholm. At this time large quantities of French wines were also imported.

Carlsberg/Tuborg Breweries, Copenhagen

Carlsberg Beer, Carlsberg Special Dark Lager

There are at present five major brewery companies in Denmark. By far the largest, and best-known, both within the country and abroad, are Carlsberg and Tuborg. Once independent operations, the two giants were merged in 1969, but remained competitive in the international-brewing marketplace.

Carlsberg beers are made from Danish barley and hops, both developed on experimental farms run by the brewery. The company produces its own malt every day in the Copenhagen plant.

In the brewhouse the finished malt is ground and mixed with water to form a mash. When the mash has been heated in stages to a temperature of 76°C. in the mash kettles, it is filtered through mash filters or straining vats, which retain the insoluble husks. This residue forms as we know a valuable cattle food.

After filtration, the beer wort is conveyed to the coppers where it is boiled with hops. After the hops have been strained off, the beer wort is cooled down before being transferred to the fermenting vats.

The method for the pure cultivation of yeast was developed in 1883 by Professor Emil C. Hansen, who was then head of the Carlsberg Laboratory. Briefly, a single yeast cell is chosen under a microscope and allowed to multiply in sterile wort. This yeast culture is then transferred to a cultivation unit, from which the pure yeast is taken for use in the brewery.

Fermentation, which had hitherto been a matter of chance, was thus brought under control—a step of revolutionary significance to the brewing industry. In keeping with the statutes of the Laboratory, the results of this research were placed completely without charge at the disposal of everyone. Today, the method is used the world over.

By adding only a very small quantity of the pure cultivated yeast, a part of the wort-extract content—the sugar—is broken down to equal parts of alcohol and carbon dioxide. Fermentation lasts for eight to nine days.

After fermentation, the beer is stored at a temperature of approximately 0°C. in modern aluminum, enameled or stainless-steel tanks. These are distributed among 140 storage vaults covering an area of approximately nine acres. There are 1,300 tanks with a total capacity of something like 620,000 hectoliters—corresponding to 187 million bottles of beer.

The storage vaults were previously below ground, where refrigeration was supplied from separate cold-storage rooms filled with cargoes of ice shipped from Norway during the winter. Modern refrigeration and insulation techniques make it possible for Carlsberg to have storage vaults five stories above the ground. During storage the yeast settles, and the beer matures in taste, while becoming clear and saturated with carbon dioxide. The period of storage varies from two to three months for the normal types of beer and from three to five months for the more potent varieties.

After storage the beer is clarified in the filtering room, either by centrifugation, with ensuing fine filtration through sterile cotton filters, or by a process of diatomite filtration. The beer, now clear and ready for bottling, is drawn off into enameled steel pressure tanks. All bottled beer is pasteurized.

Carlsberg Beer is one of the world's top lagers. The bouquet is light, as is the body; but the aroma of hops is not vague. The color represents the amount of barley used in brewing, not the skills of a color chemist. It is a light, dry, fully flavored beer that finishes well.

Carlsberg Special Dark Lager is a good contender for the dark-beer crown. Dark without being heavy or sweet, it nevertheless is well flavored. What more need be said?

Both Carlsberg and Tuborg breweries produce beer of the highest standards in the industry. As with all beers the best way to form a correct opinion is to sample the beer, on draught, at the brewery. When in Denmark, visit Tuborg from 8:30 A. M. to 2:30 P.M., Mondays through Fridays. Guides will answer questions in over six languages and, unlike in some breweries, there is no limit to the quantity you can drink in the warm, wood-paneled tasting-room.

Another Danish Beer

Another Danish beer available in export and gaining in popularity is *Ceres Red Eric*, which is a lager and only marked "malt liquor" to satisfy the nutty requirements of various state liquor boards in the United States. It is heavy and bitter.

ENGLAND AND SCOTLAND

BEER OF THE ANCIENT BRITONS*

The population of the southern coast had been in contact with the Phoenicians, and there we find the first traces of their civilization. In this part of the country spirituous beverages made from grain or fruit, especially

---

One Hundred Years of Brewing.

meth, were known, and with the extension of agriculture, favored by the character of the soil, the brewing of ale became general. The first description of the production of such liquors corresponds literally with the description of beer-brewing in the Iberian peninsula, Spain.

Wine was first brought to Britain by the Romans, and when Emperor Probus repealed the edict of Domitian, at the end of the second century, grapes were planted in the southern part of the British island, and were successfully cultivated for several centuries. It appears, indeed, that the consumption of wine at that period by far exceeded that of *meth*. Ale-houses and wine-houses were established and the first tavern signs, "whether an advantage or otherwise, we undoubtedly owe to the Romans," says French, in *Nineteen Centuries of Drink in England*, together with the Roman civilization. Excessive drinking, even at that early period, prevailed in England, and more than in other countries that island has experienced periods when inebriety has been a general vice rising to the extreme of excess.

The English pub has long been viewed as a "home away from home." Not thought of as a place of escape (as are American bars), the pub is seen as an integral part of socializing—a place for quiet conversation rather than an arena for boisterous rituals of courtship.

While beer drinking continues to rise in Britain, home consumption represents a far smaller share of the market than in the United States, where packaged sales outnumber bar sales. Most pubs are "tied houses," that is, they are owned by large brewers who operate chains. However, some of the brewery-owned pubs are very careful to offer many brands of beer, so as not to polarize the drinkers into brand-loyal groups. Like the interchangeable British beer bottles, pubs stand on their own intrinsic merits rather than on their appearance, which seems to be more important to the newcomer or the foreign traveler.

Most British beers are top-fermented—lager representing about 5 percent of production. The trend is from dark to paler beers and large brewing conglomerates are trying to capture the strength of regional beers in local markets.

Allied Breweries (UK) Ltd., London

Double Diamond, Long Life, Skol

Allied is the second largest beer producer in the United Kingdom. It owns 8,000 pubs and 1,500 licensed shops and its range of beers includes twenty-five different qualities of draught and thirty of bottled and canned beers.

Its three most popular national brands are *Double Diamond* (Britain's top-selling ale), *Long Life* (the largest selling canned beer in Britain) and *Skol* (an international brand brewed or sold in fifty-five countries—the largest-selling international lager).

In 1968 and 1969 Allied acquired two old-established Dutch brewing companies, D'Oranjeboom and Breda, which gave it 20 percent of the Dutch beer market and an entry into Europe.

Founded in 1961 through the merger of three brewing companies—Ind Coope, Tetley Walker and Ansells—the giant conglomerate came originally from the fourteenth-century Burton Abbey monks. It was then, at Burton-on-Trent, that the monks discovered the water was perfect for brewing. (The gypsum-laden soil of the Trent Valley gives it qualities which impart a distinctive flavor to the beer.) By 1700 some twenty breweries were operating in the town. Today, Allied still draws its water for Double Diamond from artesian wells in the area.

But the story of Double Diamond itself really begins at the start of the nineteenth century. In the words of the brewery:

> It was then that Napoleon Bonaparte closed continental ports to British trade, severing the firm's vital export business.
>
> Having depended so much on exports for almost 100 years, it was a tremendous financial blow and the company looked for various ways to build up sales in the home market to compensate.
>
> It wasn't until 1822 that a development came which really put the company back on its feet . . . the brewing of the first India Pale Ale, the forerunner of Double Diamond.
>
> So the story goes, Samuel Allsopp was given a bottle of beer which had acquired a unique flavour having been to India and back. He was told that if he could copy its flavour he would make his fortune.
>
> After hours of trial and error, the company's veteran maltster Job Goodhead brewed the first Burton IPA in a teapot. In four years its success was established and the beer originally intended for export became as popular in England as it did in India.
>
> How this beer evolved to become Allied's leading brand is a fascinating story in its own right. . . .
>
> Allsopps prospered steadily over the years, growing through acquisitions and mergers and surviving the slump of the 20's which spelled disaster for many less efficient concerns.
>
> In 1934 it finally merged with another Burton brewery, Ind Coope Ltd., a company with roots going back to 1799 and a name (whichever way you pronounce it) much respected for good beer and pubs, particularly in the South of England. As a joint force they occupied a leading position in the industry and both sides found the "marriage" gave them a springboard for the future.
>
> They set their sights on growth and the potential was heavily underlined in the 50's when Ind Coope (the name Allsopp was dropped) acquired over 2,000 more pubs and off-licences in the South by acquiring Benskins brewery in Watford and the Taylor-Walker concern of London and Essex.
>
> In April 1961 the most far-reaching development in the company's history was announced—the merger between Ind Coope, Tetley Walker of Leeds and Warrington and Ansells of Birmingham to form the foundations of Allied Breweries. At the time the link-up was described as a "commonwealth concept" of the brewing industry.

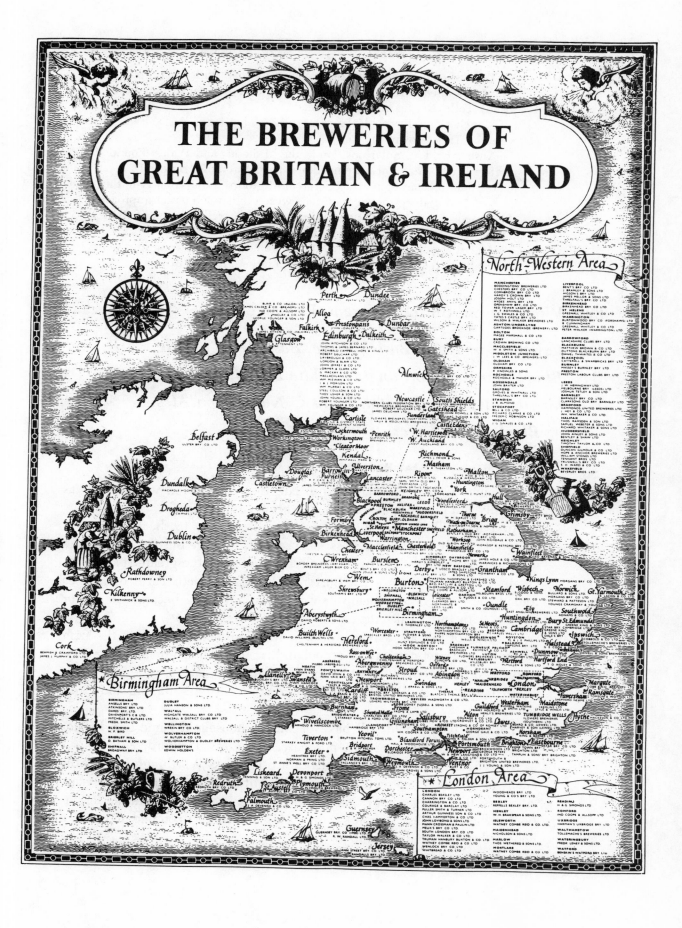

THE BREWERIES OF GREAT BRITAIN & IRELAND

Tetleys—the "Beer at Its Best" company—had built up a reputation for quality unequalled in the North of England ever since 1822 when Joshua Tetley set up business in Leeds.

Manchester, Liverpool, the great industrial cities of Yorkshire . . . these were the Tetley towns.

Ansells held a similar position in the Midlands and Wales. Founded in 1857 it had grown at a tremendous speed through a series of acquisitions, becoming one of the foremost groups in the country in the 30's.

Combining deep-rooted traditions with a dynamic market approach, the Ansells reputation for good beer and pubs paralleled that of its new partners.

Added together the three made a huge new group, strong in resources and skills, and serving all the major population areas of Britain.

Bass Worthington, Burton-on-Trent, England

Bass Export, Bass No. 1 Barley Wine, Bass Red Triangle, Bass Blue Triangle, Worthington White Shield, Worthington "E," Worthington Light & Nut Brown Ales, Carling Black Label Lager

THE HISTORY OF BASS WORTHINGTON

Monks, who were the first to appreciate that the Burton well-water was especially suitable for pale ales, began brewing in 1004.

In 1744 William Worthington set up his brewery in the High Street, followed closely by William Bass, who sold his haulage business to become a brewer. Both sold their beers locally but exported the greater part, principally to Russia where "Piva Burtonski" was acclaimed. Tariff difficulties forced the brewers to develop new markets and India became the major target—with India Pale Ale.

A cargo of this ale, salvaged from a wrecked merchantman in the Irish Channel, was auctioned at Liverpool and created a home demand for Bass leading to its acceptance as the national beer.

In 1926 Bass and Worthington merged to form Bass, Ratcliff and Gretton Ltd.

Perhaps Bass would still have become a household name had he not sold his haulage business—the purchaser was a Mr. Pickford.

In 1961 the two great Midlands breweries, Bass Worthington and Mitchells and Butlers, merged to form Bass, Mitchells and Butlers. Six years later a further merger with Charrington United Breweries led to the formation of the Bass Charrington Group with more than 11,500 licensed public houses throughout the country.

Interestingly, the Bass red triangle, originally a shipping mark, is the oldest registered trade mark in the world. When registration became compulsory under the Trade Marks Act of 1875, a member of the Bass staff spent the night on the steps of the registrar's office to ensure that the triangle would be the first.

RAW MATERIALS OF BASS BEER

The best quality barley used by the breweries is grown in East Anglia. Hops are grown exclusively for the brewing industry in southeast England and the West Midlands. Hop-picking by hand, once the traditional working holiday for thousands of people from industrial areas, has now been largely replaced by machine picking. The sugar used comes from plantations in the former Commonwealth countries and is specially blended and processed for use by the brewers.

Water, sometimes referred to in the brewing industry as liquor, comes from the brewery's own wells at Burton-on-Trent. These world-famous brewing waters are rich in gypsum, which makes them suitable for the brewing of fine, pale, well-hopped ales. Bass Worthington's brewing water is principally drawn from wells situated in the gravel beds on the company's farmland at the south end of the town.

TYPES OF BASS BEER

Cask Beer. Beers drawn from wooden casks in the traditional way still have a large following. Among the cask beers brewed at Burton-on-Trent are Draught Bass and Worthington "E." Both are unpasteurized.

HENRI CARTIER-BRESSON, MAGNUM

Restaurant and bar in Throgmorton Street.

Keg Beer. These, served under pressure after careful pasteurization, include Bass and Worthington "E." The method of filtration and serving ensures good quality. Carling Black Label Lager is also available in keg as well as in bottle in Bass Worthington public houses.

Bulk Beer. Bulk beers are drawn from large stainless steel tanks. This type of installation is ideal for outlets with a large and regular demand. Bass, Worthington "E" and "B.B." are supplied in this way.

Canned Beer. Ease of handling and transport recommends canned beers which are also sold on airlines, railways and on board ship. Ring-pull opening is now almost universal. Bumper cans in four-pint and seven-pint sizes are gaining in popularity for parties, picnics, camping and fishing excursions.

Bottled Beer. Many qualities of Midlands beers are sold in the familiar bottle in pub or off-license. Bass Red Triangle and Worthington White Shield are traditional Burton-brewed beers which mature in bottle. Other bottled beers are Bass Blue Triangle, Worthington "E,'" Bass Export, Worthington Light and Nut Brown Ales, Carling Black Label Lager and Bass No. 1 Barley Wine.

BASS PALE ALE

A fine golden color, with above average bouquet and head, introduces one's palate to one of the world's finest ales. The body is in the medium to full range, while the flavor is full, rich with hops and a faint trace of malt. Not negatively "bitter" as described by some tasters, used to tasteless lagers, but just plain tart, as an ale should be. Highly recommended.

Courage Ltd., London, England

Russian Imperial Stout

Perhaps the most unusual commercially produced beer, *Russian Imperial Stout,* is also among the strongest in the world. First brewed by Barclay Perkins—a London brewery—this rare label is now under the corporate banner of the Courage group.

The following tale *Cyril Ray Cracks a Bottle of 1948 Russian Stout* first appeared in *Queen* magazine, London:

> The old London brewing firm of Courage and Barclay has decided, after all, to resume the brewing of its Russian Imperial Stout, a noble product that had been under sentence of death as being too expensive to make and not in wide enough demand. Indeed, brewing was suspended throughout 1964 and 1965, although this beer in the past had been brewed each year, just before Christmas. The directors have now come to the conclusion that they owe something to tradition, and in the summer of 1966 a beer that was first brewed in the late eighteenth century will be brewed

Darts and beer in an English pub.

again. On hearing of the reprieve I went along to what are still called "the Russian cellars," at the Courage and Barclay headquarters by Southwark Bridge to sink a celebratory bottle.

Russian Imperial Stout is so called because, as long ago as 1795, Catherine the Great, according to one of her contemporaries, "ordered repeatedly very large quantities for her own drinking and that of her Court." The beer was brewed in recent years at the Courage brewery in Horselydown Lane and matured in the Russian cellars for two months in cask, before being given another year in bottle.

The firm's visitors' bar stood me a bottle of the 1962 Russian Stout. This is not the latest brew, but it is the one that most pubs would have that stock it at all. The 1963, bottled in 1964, is barely ready yet, and those publicans who buy it will be giving it a little more bottle-age than the minimum of a year that it gets in the Russian cellars. Russian Stout is sold in "nip" bottles that hold about one-third of a pint, as against the half-pint of a standard beer bottle—quite enough to be going on with, for Russian Stout is about twice as strong as Guinness, half as strong again as Bass Barley Wine, and the nip is said to pack the same alcoholic punch as four whiskies. Nobody, my expert hosts told me, could floor more than four at one go and not show the effects.

A smooth, rich, velvety depth-charge of a drink—sweet, but with the sweetness only of the malt, for there is no added sugar, and yet with the bitter tang of hops. "Not quite so great a brew as the 1951," said one of my companions, going on to explain that slight differences of temperature and humidity during the brewing and the bottling can affect the quality of a fine beer, and that the year's climate can influence the quality of the malt.

This led him to invite me down to the Russian cellars to taste one or two that had been specially bottled and long matured. First the 1957, poured from a pint champagne bottle that had been corked and wired, exactly like champagne, and matured lying on its side. (Beer which is crown-corked—that is, with a metal closure—must stand up; if it has an

"*Long live the Watney's Red Revolution!*"

ordinary cork, it must lie down like wine.) The cork came out with a pop, and the beer frothed creamily into the glass, dark and rich. Smoother still than the 1962, I thought, but it was surpassed by the 1948 which came from a full-sized champagne bottle, smelled like a burgundy and drank like liquid silk.

My brewer friends told me that they could not always be sure that a bottle as old as this would be as good, but that Russian Stout had a great capacity for ageing. (In 1796, Farington recorded in his diary that he drank some of the Porter from Thrale's Brewhouse—the same beer—and that "it was specially brewed for the Empress of Russia and would keep seven years.") Clearly, it is capable of keeping—and improving—over a much longer period, and I asked whether these champagne bottles of Russian Stout were generally available for laying down like claret. Alas, no, but the ordinary nips keep quite well—I have already recorded in these columns how, earlier this year, I took a nip of the 1958 Russian Stout and one of the 1961 over to Dublin, to drink with Bryan Guinness. We found the 1958 in better condition, with more life and sparkle, but the 1961 had more style and a cleaner finish.

The authorities in Courage and Barclay's Russian cellar told me how to make extra sure that the nips would keep really well. This is done by covering the crown cork with ordinary sealing wax, to make the bottle really airtight, making sure to get it under the skirts—if you will pardon the expression—of the cork.

The Courage group also markets a wide range of draught beer which varies in different parts of Britain depending upon local tastes. Included are Courage *Tavern*, a premium bitter, *Best Bitter, John Smith's Bitter, Barnsley Bitter* and *Directors Bitter*, a strong traditional cask beer.

In addition to *Russian Imperial Stout* the group produces several other canned and bottled beers. Brands are *Courage Light Ale*, a brand leader in southern England, *John Courage* and *Magnet Pale Ale*, two well-known premium beers, specialty beers such as *Velvet Stout* and *Barley Wine* and the very strong bottled beers, *Bulldog* and *Magnet Old*.

Harp Lager is brewed by Courage in association with the Guinness organization and Scottish and Newcastle Breweries Ltd. Britain's most popular lager was developed as late as 1960 and became the brand leader through massive advertising, which tells the drinker that this British lager is brewed of the best raw materials by traditional continental methods. A taste for the lighter lager beer is even overtaking England, the land of heavier, stronger brews. Harp is a medium amber colored beer, with strong bouquet and body. The flavor is dry and well balanced. Recommended.

Donnington Brewery

Donnington Draught, Bitter, Double D

The general manager of Cascade Brewery in Tasmania, Mr. H. J. Gray, suggested I include reference to "a most picturesque brewery in the Cotswold area." Apparently it is one of the smallest commercial breweries in the world. The power used for the pumps and for driving a malt mill is derived from a water wheel, all in a picturesque setting. A small brochure released by Donnington describes the history of this old-world brewhouse and some of its products:

THE HISTORY OF DONNINGTON BREWERY

Donnington Mill was perhaps one of the Mills of Broadwell Manor, which dated back to 1291. In the 16th century it was used as a Cloth Mill which the Lord of the Manor of Donnington rebuilt and converted into two Corn Mills *circa* 1580.

However, early in the 17th century, the Mill became a separate freehold estate, and in 1827 the buildings were bought by Thomas Arkell, whose descendant Richard Arkell started a Brewery there in 1865. The Brewery flourishes today; has been owned and run by the Arkell family ever since and today is managed by the grandson of the founder.

Much of the neighbouring land is owned by the family and, until the mid-1960s, it provided barley for use in the brewing process; however, since that time malt has been supplied by a Cirencester maltings, together with hops obtained locally from Worcestershire. In fact, the small quantity of sugar required is the only imported ingredient.

Today the Millhouse is still there in splendid condition, and operates as part of the Brewery. Even the mill wheel is still used to drive small pumps and machines.

The end product, Donnington's traditional beers, are still produced by much the same recipe that has always been in use; the basic requirement, that is water or, in brewing terms "liquor," is drawn from a strong spring beside the mill pond and has proved to be satisfactory for use in the brewing process in its natural state.

Three draught beers ar brewed, two bitters and a mild, as well as three bottled beers; Light, Brown and Double D which is simply referred to as a "little stronger." However, they defy words, and the only way to identify them is to try them.

Of the Brewery itself, the setting and the architecture can only be described as idyllic, with beautiful Cotswold buildings, carefully tended lawns and paths leading down to the mill pond, which is the domicile of much bird life.

Unfortunately, the brewery process is not a subject that lends itself to the spectator, and Donnington would soon become over-run if it were open to the public, so very reluctantly Mr. Arkell cannot entertain visitors, but the Inns certainly can!

Finally, it is only fitting that Mr. Arkell should have the last words about this unique enterprise: "Certainly we have a piece of English history here at Donnington, and it would still not survive today without the hard work and loyalty of our staff over the years. However, let it not be forgotten that we can only continue to brew so long as our Houses sell the beer we produce: and this is where I can pay public tribute to the landlords and their wives for the way in which they run their Houses, which are so popular with their customers, whether it is with darts, skittles or food and for the support they give me personally."

Greene, King and Sons, Ltd., Suffolk, England

St. Edmund Ale

St. Edmund Ale is a relatively young label, first brewed in 1953 as a Coronation ale to mark the anniversary of Queen Elizabeth II's accession to the throne. The formula was revived in 1970 when the Borough of Bury St. Edmunds celebrated the eleven-hundredth anniversary of the martyrdom of Edmund, King of the Angles, from whom the town takes its name. To mark the occasion Greene, King and Sons were asked if they would produce a special beer, and early in 1970 the Mayor duly initiated the first brew.

Originally only twelve brews were planned for St. Edmund, but it was so well received that the brewers decided to include the beer as a permanent brand. The design of the label incorporates the symbol adopted by the Borough as the theme of St. Edmunds anniversary.

St. Edmund Ale combines a pale gold color with a unique full malty flavor. This results from the use of crystal malts produced on the brewery site, with flaked maize and invert sugar. East Kent Goldings hops are the type selected. The controlled fermentation process yields a high alcoholic content (about 6 percent). The ale is aged four weeks before bottling,

Stout for strength.

which accounts for its full flavor. It is unlikely that this rare brew will receive wide distribution, however; therefore, a visit to England may call for a detour to Bury St. Edmunds, just to sample the local ale.

Scottish and Newcastle, Edinburgh

MacEwan's Edinburgh Ale, MacEwan's Tartan Ale, MacEwan's Scotch Ale, Newcastle Brown Ale

Scottish and Newcastle of Edinburgh brew four fine ales worth looking for. Held up to the sunlight, *MacEwan's Edinburgh Ale* transmits a creamy brown color. A full, rich, malty bouquet is followed by a too rapidly dissipated head, but the flavor of this dark ale more than compensates. It is highly carbonated, strong and rich. Recommended.

MacEwan's Tartan Ale is also creamy and dark brown and also loses its head almost on pouring. But the above average malty bouquet and slightly sweeter taste leaves the drinker with a smooth, pleasant after-taste. Definitely less dramatic in taste than Guinness Stout or Mackeson Stout, it must be remembered that this label is dark ale, not stout. Recommended.

MacEwan's Scotch Ale is the kind of brew that makes beer drinking an art form. The honey-amber color and creamy head, aided by a mildly sharp bouquet, prepares your palate for a solidly tasty beer. The aftertaste is delicious. Highly recommended.

Serving as chief taster and quality controller for a brewery is not exactly an Anglican churchman's province, but for Bishop George E. Reindorp of Salisbury, England, it is "going down" quite well, like the strong new beer named for him. "Lovely stuff," was the bishop's description of Bishop's Tipple, which is produced by a local brewery. Bishop Reindorp dispensed the potent brew—closer to ale than beer—to forty parishioners in the picturesque gardens of his house in Salisbury.

Newcastle Brown Ale is full-bodied and tangy. Dark amber in color, with a solid head and nut-like aroma, it is captivating with an inviting aftertaste. Overall it tastes like a mixture of light and dark lagers. One of my favorite blends. Highly recommended.

Tennent Caledonian Breweries, Ltd., Glasgow, Scotland

Tennent's Lager

HISTORY AND ORIGIN OF THE BEER

Although the early history of J. and R. Tennent Limited, the original owners of Wellpark, is only sketchily outlined in company documents because the official records were destroyed by two fires at the brewery, there are papers which trace its brewing activities back to 1556, when Mary Queen of Scots was a mere lass of fourteen and Glasgow was no bigger than a hamlet. The next reference to Tennent is found in the Chronicles of the Maltmen Craft when the Incorporation of Maltmen was formed in 1605. In 1745, another reference introduces a romantic fragment of Scottish history. In records relating to the visit of Prince Charles Edward—Bonnie Prince Charlie—to Glasgow, appears the phrase: "Each and every man was refreshed and heartened by the brew at Wellpark." Another strong link with old Glasgow is recorded ten years later when Robert Tennent erected the Saracen's Head Hotel, which was to become one of the city's most famous taverns. The Lords of Justiciary stayed there, and in 1773 Dr. Samuel Johnson and his biographer James Boswell were among its guests. Reference to the hotel can be found in several publications of the period. The opening announcement on November 17, 1755, read: "Robert Tennent, who formerly kept the White Hart Inn without the Gallowgate, is removed to the Saracen's Head where the Port formerly stood." In the first Glasgow *Directory*, published in 1783, there is an entry referring to John and Robert Tennent, Brewers and Malsters, of the Drygate. By that time Tennent's was fully established and in the process of building an export trade which today covers some 100 markets through the world. In 1963 Tennent's joined the Charrington United Breweries Group. The original company of J. and R. Tennent thereafter became part of Tennent Caledonian Breweries Limited, the Scottish unit of the Group. In 1966 Charrington United Breweries linked their interest with Bass, Mitchell and Butler to become Bass Charrington, the biggest brewery organization in the country with over 12,000 tied public houses. Wellpark Brewery is the oldest brewery in Scotland, if not in Great Britain.

Tennent Caledonian Breweries Limited brew and distribute Lager Beer, Ale and Stout, and are producing in increasing volume both at Wellpark Brewery and at Heriot Brewery, Edinburgh.

Lunch break for shipyard workers in Glasgow.

This lager is unique to Scotland, a traditional ale nation. It is made of Scottish barley malted at Alloa, a blend of English and Continental hops and water from Loch Katrine, in the Trossachs. While Tennent's has been available in the past in many specialized establishments throughout the world, local demands and shipping difficulties have dried-up the foreign outlet. A recent round at Tommy's Joynt in San Francisco, a great place for sampling beer from around the world, found Tennent's Stout and Lager crossed off the list.

Whitbread and Company, Ltd., London

Whitbread Pale Ale, Mackeson Stout, Brewmaster Beer, Final Selection Malt Liquor, Gold Label Malt Liquor

The Chiswell Street brewery, which is 250 years old, is the only brewery in the old square-mile city of London. It has the privilege of supplying the horses and draymen to pull the Lord Mayor's Coach at the annual opening of Parliament, and on special occasions such as coronations, royal weddings, etc. Louis Pasteur studied the fermentation of beer at this brewery between 1871 and 1872 and James Watt, inventor of the steam engine gave them one of his early beam engines in 1875. (This engine is now in the Science Museum in Sydney, Australia.)

The odyssey of the development of one of England's largest brewing companies is so perfectly treated by Samuel Whitbread, who was sent to London at the age of fourteen to be apprenticed to a brewer by his widowed mother, in *The Story of Whitbread's*, as to render an abridged version undesirable. Space does not permit reproduction of this fifty-four-page book, which is available from the brewery. We will look instead at the brewing of their beers.

While each formula is different, depending on the type produced (ale, stout, lager, malt liquor), all Whitbread brands are made from malts of British origin, and hops from the United Kingdom, supplemented by blossoms from Germany, Yugoslavia and Czechoslovakia. Yeasts for each type of beer are, of course, cultivated by the company. Water is drawn from artesian wells; however, auxillary breweries condition the available supplies to maintain a standardized taste quality, regardless of the area of production.

All brands are produced by the single-mash infusion method, in batches of 350 imperial barrels (one imperial barrel equals thirty-six imperial gallons). Production units are equipped with strain-masters, whirlpool separators and conical fermentation vessels.

While brown bottles are used in the export trade (to reduce the effect of light on the beer) labels in these markets vary from place to place according to state liquor regulations. A standard body label is generally maintained worldwide and all the requisite liquor authority requirements contained on a supplementary neck slip.

Whitbread's is not new to America. The brand was brought to the New World in 1759 and was even sold in California during the Gold Rush.

Whitbread Pale Ale exhibits one of the finest hues of amber, topped by a firm, thick, natural head. Does burnished copper adequately describe the color of this fine bodied ale? While delivering a rich molasseslike taste this brew is not burdened with an overly dense body or flavor. Quite expensive in the export version, this ale is nevertheless very worthwhile and sure to please knowledgeable drinkers. Recommended.

Mackeson Stout is for connoisseurs and committed, but unschooled, lovers of rich, dark beers. The color is so black that it is impervious to light (I tried a 75 watt lamp at three inches; the brew was not even translucent!) As lovers of stouts will tell you, the darker the better, providing the color is natural. The head is about the most stable and thick of all those tasted; the bouquet is very full. (This heavy-bodied beer *has* to be good for you!) I'd recommend it to those who like Guinness Stout but find it a bit too dry. Mackeson is the best-balanced dark beer tasted and a very satisfying change. The standard for dark beers. Recommended.

Brewmaster Beer. This fine lager is highly recommended. It has a delicate pale amber color and a light hoppy bouquet. The flavor and body are well balanced, while the aftertaste is good and dry. Brewmaster is so good that changing drinking tastes in Britain are making this lager the beer of choice.

Whitbread Gold Label Malt Liquor is now available in 6.4 ounce bottles. This small size is more than compensated for by the powerful, delicious brew. Twirl the bottle slightly; you'll notice the filaments of yeast in the honey amber liquid. A fine sign; for that's an unfiltered beer, richer in nutrients than your typical filtered, sterile lager. If you favor a *strong,* tart beer, of mild aromatic qualities with a pronounced malt flavor, this label is worth looking for. Recommended.

Young and Company's Brewery, Ltd., London

Young's Stout, Pale Ale, Special Bitter, Mild, Mellow Sweet Stout, Celebration Ale, Brown Ale, Export Pale Ale

Beer has probably been brewed at the Ram Brewery for over 300 years, though it was not until 1831 that the Young family bought their interest in the brewery. Power required for the various processes in the brewery is still supplied by two ancient but efficient beam engines. The oldest, of "twelve horses power," was installed in 1835. The younger engine, of "twenty horses power," was added in 1867. The engines operate through gearing fitted with hornbeam teeth. Besides four pumps they also drive a vertical shaft from which power is taken on the various floors for milling and mashing. Only one engine is used at a time, the other being kept for standby. The stint for the "duty" engine is twelve hours daily virtually nonstop.

Young's beers are all made from high quality, low nitrogen barley, Fuggles and Goldings hops grown in English gardens, private yeast strains and London municipal water. The beer is conditioned in traditional wooden casks.

Young's eight labels are popular in London and the surrounding counties; however, none are yet available in America.

A strongly tradition-oriented company, the brewery still keeps twenty-two working geldings, only three less than were used thirty-six years ago, and all shire horses. The history of the shire horse goes back hundreds of years: in the days when a man and his armor weighed upwards of 400 pounds they were used to carry knights into battle.

These beautiful horses make three trips daily within a three-mile radius of the brewery, delivering an average of 10,000 tons of beer per year. (Trucks are also employed.)

GERMANY

Thanks perhaps to punishments in the early 1500's, of "rod-beatings, banishment and death" for selling bad beer the German people still—nearly five hundred years later—enjoy the purest beer in the world.

The purity decree, passed by Wilhelm IV, Duke of Bavaria, in 1516, is still valid. It was soon adopted by other German states and all breweries in the Federal Republic today still abide by it, as do breweries in Luxemburg and Switzerland.

This decree may be the oldest law still in effect which deals with the production of food and drink. In addition to setting the price that could be charged (since changed unfortunately), it was decreed that beer can be brewed only from barley malt, hops, water and yeast.

A translation of the Bavarian Pledge of Purity (*das Reinheitsgebot*) appears on the following page.

Just as the present state of the brewing art is based on a past of five hundred years ago, so was the brewing art of the fifteenth century based upon an earlier time. Since the history of brewing in Germany is in a sense the history of beer-making throughout much of the modern world, a brief look at the chief developments may be worthwhile.

WE hereby proclaim and decree, by Authority of our Province, that henceforth in the Duchy of Bavaria, in the country as well as in the cities and marketplaces, the following rules apply to the sale of beer:

From Michaelmas to Georgi, the price for one *Mass* [Bavarian Liter 1,069] or one *Kopf* [bowl-shaped container for fluids, not quite one *Mass*], is not to exceed one *Pfennig* Munich value, and

From Georgi to Michaelmas, the *Mass* shall not be sold for more than two *Pfennig* of the same value, the *Kopf* not more than three *Heller* [*Heller* usually one-half *Pfennig*].

If this is not adhered to, the punishment stated below shall be administered.

Should any person brew, or otherwise have, other beer than March beer, it is not to be sold any higher than one *Pfennig* per *Mass*.

Furthermore, we wish to emphasize that in future in all cities, markets and in the country, the only ingredients used for the brewing of beer must be Barley, Hops and Water. Whosoever knowingly disregards or transgresses upon this ordinance, shall be punished by the Court Authorities' confiscating such barrels of beer, without fail.

Should, however, an Innkeeper in the country, city or markets buy two or three pails of beer [containing 60 *Mass*] and sell it again to the common peasantry, he alone shall be permitted to charge one *Heller* more for the *Mass* or the *Kopf*, than mentioned above. Furthermore, should there arise a scarcity and subsequent price increase of the barley (also considering that the times of harvest differ, due to the location), WE, the Bavarian Duchy, shall have the right to order curtailments for the good of all concerned.

BEER OF THE ANCIENT TEUTONS*

The Roman historian Tacitus [born about 54 A.D.] in his work, *Germania*, written about 99 A.D., gives us the first information about the people of Germany, their habits and customs. Though probably not based upon personal knowledge, this work contains the most valuable descriptions of popular life in Germany, "Straight from sleep (Tacitus relates), which, as a rule, lasts until late into the day, a bath is taken, mostly warm, and naturally, in a climate where winter weather is so predominating. The bath is succeeded by a repast; each one has a special seat and his own table. Then they go to their business, or else just as often, to the drinking bout, always carrying their arms. There is nothing reprehensible to them in drinking day and night. The natural consequences of such drinking habits are frequent quarrels, and seldom these remain confined to words, but as a rule they wind up with wounding and killing. The conciliation of enemies, the tying of marital knots, the election of chiefs, even war and peace, are usually resolved and acted upon while drinking.

"Their beverage they prepare from barley or wheat, a brew which slightly resembles an inferior quality of wine. Their food is plain—wild fruit, fresh game or sour milk; without luxury, without delicacies, they are satisfied to appease their hunger. But their temperance is not proof against thirst; whoever plays upon this weakness of the German and supplies him with drink to his heart's content, will be able in future days to subdue him by his own vices with the same ease as by force of arms."

From the time of Tacitus up to the days of the Carlovingians, historical sources are exceedingly scant as to information about brewing. Fortunately, however, we possess . . . that great book of Northern mythology, the *Edda*. Though this collection of legends was not written down until the ninth century, it contains the popular traditions of centuries.

The beverages in the heaven populated by the Northern gods naturally played as important a part as they did in the daily life of the people whose mind had invented that heaven. "On *wine* alone does Odin, adorned in armor, subsist at all times. With *meth* and game the gods of victory feast. Beer or *oil*, also called *aul*, the Einherians drink. The goat Heindrun supplies milk, that all Einherians may become thoroughly intoxicated. This milk, which was strong enough to intoxicate the Einherians, must have been in a state of alcoholic fermentation, like those beverages known as *kumyss* and *kefyr*," as Kobert tells us in his work, *The History of Beer*.

Meth, the oldest intoxicating beverage, was made from honey and water, those having been the ingredients since the remotest days, first in Asia, and afterward in all European countries, long before the production of grain, wine or beer was known. The name is known to every language, in Sanskrit, *mathu;* Greek, *methey* and *mely;* Latin, *mel;* Saxon, *medo, medu;* Welsh, *meddyglyn;* English, *metheglin, mydromel, mead;* Danish, *miod;* German, *meth.*

At the meetings and feasting of the old Germans, a certain ceremonial in drinking was developed, customs which originated in the most ancient times and were preserved during the Middle Ages, being in practice even now, as they were two thousand years ago. We are met by the same

---

*From *One Hundred Years of Brewing.*

customs in Gaul, but more especially in Britain. Their origin can be traced back to the same usages found to have prevailed many years before in the heart of Asia, and which probably rose at a period when our branch of the human family was nearer to the original home, and the members were still in closer connection with each other. In China we have already met the drinking horn making the rounds, and the toast; in Persia we have seen the people deliberate under the influence of intoxicating drink, and the worshiping of the gods by drunken revelries and offerings of intoxicating beverages.

The Germans, referring again to the *Edda,* had their beer conventionals. Whoever acted in violation of the latter had to empty the penal horn in one draught. Only a weakling required three draughts to atone for his offense. Blood friendship was formed in such manner that the two men inflicted a slight wound upon each other, from which the blood trickled into a full goblet, which then was emptied by them together. When they took the dram of love (*minnetrank*) the men met in front of the altar of the gods, drinking love (*minne*) to each other, which was supposed to receive the blessing of the gods.

In order to prevent intoxication or injury when they drank to each other, or as an assurance that the goblet did not contain a poisonous drink, beer runes were scratched into the drink horn, also in the back of the hand or in the fingernails, which were supposed to protect the drinker against such dangers. Rune sticks thrown into the drink horn gave magical power, strength and glory. As the Greeks threw leek into the goblet to avert a charm, so the Germans were accustomed to break a charm by the same herb. "The goblet bless, to ban mishap thrown into the dram of cheer, leek; then I do not fear that harmful things are mixed into thy *meth* by an enemy."

The brewing of beer was left to the woman, and remained her task until within the Middle Ages, when brewhouses were established in monasteries and villages. In very old laws we find the principle laid down that the vessels and kettles used in beer-brewing always were the personal property of the housewife.

During the Middle Ages the art of beer-making reached its highest levels in breweries attached to monasteries.

Soon afterwards the chief brewing cities of Germany recognized the importance of regulating the industry in the interest of public hygiene; but some of the extreme measures which they adopted seemed to far exceed the danger of the situation. In 1155, for instance, Augsburg passed laws imposing heavy penalties upon those who manufactured bad beer or used false measures. One of the first to enforce an excise law was Ulm, in 1255. During the last portion of the fifteenth and the first of the sixteenth century, Augsburg and other Bavarian towns went even further in their "regulations," and, with rod-beatings, banishment and death, punished the selling of bad beer as "a crime against Christian love." In fact, every effort was made, both by the severity of municipal laws and through the public prints, to raise the grade of malt liquors placed upon the market for the consumption of the burghers. The estimation in which the industry was held in the sixteenth century is well illustrated by the title of a publication issued from Erfurt, in 1575: "The Five Books of the Divine and Noble Gift of the Philosophical, Highly Honorable and Wonderful Art of Brewing."

BEERS OF THE PRESENT

In a nation where beer is king, as you would expect, a wide variety of brands exist. West Germany's nearly 2,200 breweries produce more than 6,000 local beers, a number so fantastic as to make a section like this practically impossible.

Nevertheless, the current picture of some of Germany's breweries, including one of the largest, and some of the smallest is presented. It is best to remember that an adequate sampling of even 10 percent of the nation's breweries would fill several volumes. What follows is a mere taste.

Beck and Company, Bremen

Beck's Beer

The Hanseatic city of Bremen, situated in northern Germany a few miles inland from the sea, is the home of *Beck's Beer*. With its thousand years of history it is one of the oldest towns in Germany.

Contrary to the general opinion that German beer originated in Bavaria, the city of Bremen was already well-known for the excellent quality of beers brewed there in the very early centuries. Chronicles from the thir-

Beer and love.

HENRI CARTIER-BRESSON, MAGNUM

"Oktoberfest," a caricature by Hans-Georg Rauch.

teenth century report that Bremen beer was appreciated not only in the German states but in Scandinavia, Holland and England. At this time the brewers of Bremen founded the Brewing Society of Bremen. The Society's first constitution belongs to the year 1489 and shows that it is the oldest guild of the brewing trade in Germany. Another important year in the Bremen brewing industry would appear to be 1553, the year to which the brewery Beck and Company traces its origin.

In Germany Beck's enjoys prestige among the premium beers. It has a unique character which does not allow classification as a lager, export, Pilsner or other type of beer. According to the brewer Beck's is a type of its own. It is recognized as one of the national beers of Germany.

Beck's is brewed of barley malt, German hops, a private yeast strain and water from the Harz Mountains.

While the actual brewing process is something of a secret, we learned that the beer is brewed in a conventional brewhouse, is fermented at a very low temperature over a longer than average time, and is stored in chilled steel tanks for several months. In the author's opinion, the result is a beer of medium-light amber with above-average flavor and bouquet. The head is firm while the body is average. It is a dry beer but quite salty, with a sharp aftertaste.

Dortmunder Hansa, Dortmund

Alt Seidelbrau, Dortmunder Hansa

These two exceptional lager beers are brewed by the DAB/Hansa-Brewing Group, a recently merged organization of two famous Dortmund brewing companies.

The older brewery, Dortmund *Actien* (DAB) was founded in 1868, three years before the foundation of the German Empire. The Hansa brewery was founded in 1901. In 1971 the two companies merged, maintaining separate facilities.

Alt Seidelbrau and Dortmunder Hansa are nearly identical lagers. Both are brewed from barley malt purchased from German, Belgian, and French suppliers. Only certain varieties of hops are used; medium-early Hallertau, Hallertau-Nordbrauer, Hallertau-Goldbrauer and Tettnang (all are grown in Germany).

A standard two-mash system supplies the wort, which is fermented for seven to eight days. The young beer is filtered and fined with *kieselguhr*. Apparently, all canned and bottled beer is pasteurized after three to four months of ageing in steel tanks.

Dortmunder Union Brewery, Dortmund

Dortmunder Union

This brand is another famous lager from the town of Dortmund, the largest beer-brewing center in Europe. While beer has been brewed here for almost 700 years, Dortmunder Union was founded over 100 years ago, in 1873, as an amalgamation of many small breweries.

After its merger with Schultheiss, Berlin, in 1972, this became one of the largest brewing groups in Germany and the world.

Dortmunder Union is made of the same basic ingredients as other German beers; barley malt, natural hops, yeast and water. After brewing by the standard two-mash process the beer is stored for a minimum of three months.

This is another of Germany's national beers and has been awarded important prizes worldwide. At international exhibitions, such as Vienna in 1873, Philadelphia 1876, Brussels 1891, The Hague 1892, and Antwerp 1894, Dortmunder Union beer received its first important awards. In 1880 the brewery was awarded the Prussian State medal.

Löwenbräu, Munich

Löwenbräu-Munich, Oktoberfest Malt Liquor

Löwenbräu is the largest-selling German beer in the United States. It owes its popularity not only to its fine quality (as we know, all German beers are brewed by the same high standards) but to the determination of the agency that made it one of the first to be imported after the repeal of Prohibition.

A book prepared by the brewery describes in detail the making of Löwenbräu. Their process follows:

The special type of barley which is used for brewing grows locally in large quantities. Its quality is the result of decades of cultivation and research.

Hops also contribute much to the characteristic flavor of the beer. Over the centuries, the cultivation of hop gardens has become one of the most lucrative offshoots of farming in southern Germany. The official seals of several places testify to the renown which this so-called "green gold" has brought them.

The water used for brewing comes from the clear and sparkling streams and brooks which tumble down from the Alpine foothills. Its freshness and purity contribute in no small way to the essential characteristics of a full-bodied beer.

"Malt is the soul of beer" goes an old brewer's saying. Löwenbräu therefore places great emphasis on the production of its own malt. Barley provides malt and it is only in the form of malt that its activating and taste-giving properties are developed. Malting barley must be of a special type: even in size, with plump grains; short on water and proteins; mealy, or rich in starch and therefore in extract.

Shortly after harvesting, the barley is brought to the brewery to be checked for foreign bodies like small stones, weeds or barley beard. It is then sifted and stored in the silo, where it is kept moving and aerated, and where after several weeks' dormancy, it is ready to be malted. The tall silo, a local landmark, is used to store barley and malt and can take up to 10,000 tons, at present about half Löwenbräu's yearly consumption.

Automatic equipment facilitates the daily unloading of up to twenty trucks of barley, which can then be conveyed to the various silo elements by means of a centralized switching system.

The barley is steeped in water in large cylindrical drums, where it is kept aerated and humidified. It is then put into large rectangular boxes, or spread in flattish heaps on the malting floor. The swollen grain now begins to germinate, to "grow" as the malster says, just as it would outside in a damp field. If in boxes, it is mechanically turned and aerated at regu-

HENRI CARTIER-BRESSON, MAGNUM

Löwenbräu and love.

lated temperatures, or turned with shovels if on the malting floor. During the "growing" period, the enzymes develop; these natural substances are of paramount importance in the later brewing process. "Growing" lasts hardly a week and no further changes should take place inside the "green malt." It next goes into the kiln, a wire frame or grille through which hot air is circulated, where it is dried out at temperatures slowly increasing to 100°C., and the malting process comes to an end. After the removal of its rootlets by "screening," the malt is stored in the silo to await processing.

In the brewhouse, the heart of the brewery, the first process is that of mashing. Bruised malt or grist is mixed with water in the mash tub. The insoluble starch contained in the barley's endosperm is converted in the mash pans into soluble maltose and dextrins by the enzymes developed during malting. The mash thus obtained is separated in the lauter tubs,

Lager beer saloon, Berlin, 1856.

the wort or sugar solution filtering into the wort kettles through the husks which remain behind. The wort is now boiled for some hours and this is the stage at which the hops are gradually added. After boiling, the wort is fed into the "cool ship," where it is cooled down.

From the coolers, the wort is taken to the fermentation cellars. Löwenbräu has over one hundred fermentation tanks with a total capacity of 40,000 hectoliters standing in these rooms, which are well isolated and kept supplied with a continuous flow of cooled, bacteria-free air. Pure homemade yeast culture is now mixed with the wort, a process known in the trade as "pitching." The temperature is controlled by means of special equipment and is kept between 5° and 8°C. The yeast causes the wort to ferment so quickly, that the process is actually visible to the eye. Yeast is rich in enzymes and vitamins, and converts the sugar in the wort into alcohol and carbon dioxide. The tanks are soon covered with high white heads known as "cauliflowers," showing that fermentation is well under way. After seven to nine days, the process is at an end.

The clear "green beer" is now piped through copper tubes to the storage cellars, where it undergoes secondary fermentation at below 0°C. Carefully supervised by the cellarmen, the ageing process may take two to three months before the beer develops its full flavor, and with stronger beers even longer. Clarified and richer in carbon dioxide due to this lagering period, the beer is at last ready for tapping. Sparkling clear, it is again tasted by experts and then filled into kegs, bottles or cans.

Löwenbräu is now being brewed in the United States and is no longer the same as brewed in Germany. The only way to determine whether the bottled Löwenbräu you drink is domestic or imported is to read the label. In the smallest lettering possible you will find either "Brewed by Miller" or "Imported by Miller . . ." No matter how good the craftsmanship, a grain-malt beer is not the same as a 100 percent barley malt beer. Nevertheless, I'll guess that most American beer drinkers, in a blind taste test, would give the American version of this fine lager a higher score than the German brew. I've seen descriptions such as "heavy nose," and "full of malt" applied to the German variety (in blind tests) and suspect that too many beer drinkers in the United States actually prefer overly light, weak-bodied beers. Ah, well, as I've said earlier, taste is a highly subjective phenomenon and in the case of beer, one man's mead is another's poison.

Schultheiss Brewery, Berlin

Berliner Weisse

> Berliners are in the habit of saying dryly "Thirst is worse than homesickness." And when the mercury outdoors climbs to over 20°C, one can hear—in the fashionable garden bars in the outskirts of Berlin—the nearly desperate shout coming out of a dried out throat: "Waiter! A Weisse . . ." and the waiter balancing his tray, loaded to the breaking point, like a circus performer, over the heads of the guests, asks "With or without?" Whereupon the impatient guest calls "It's all the same. Bring it without—but bring it with you!"
>
> *(From a brewery brochure.*
> *Translated by Paula Szilard)*

Berliner Weisse is a top-fermented beverage that differs from other beers in that fermentation takes place in the bottle. The yeast is left inside and gradually settles to the bottom. The natural cloudiness that results should not be regarded with distaste. The yeast contains numerous vitamins, especially of the B-complex group. According to some experts the special bouquet of Berliner Weisse results from acids formed during the ripening process. Some like to add raspberry syrup or a sweet cordial to balance the tartness.

This is not a white beer, in the usual sense, as it is brewed from a mixture of wheat and barley malt, hops, yeast and water.

In handling, the brewery recommends the following:

1. Store bottles in an upright position at 8°–10°C.

2. Do not vibrate or shake the bottles as this will send the yeast up from the bottom. If yeast does get into your glass—drink it. It is vitamin rich.

3. Wash and dry glasses thoroughly. Fat or grease on the glass will destroy the head.

Wurzburger Hofbrau, Wurzburg, Bavaria

Wurzburger Light and Dark Beer

HISTORY

Wurzburger Hofbrau Beer gets its name from the ancient city of Wurzburg, which is situated in Northern Bavaria in the pleasant valley of the river Main, one of the chief tributaries of the Rhine. It is both a picturesque and a fertile valley, which grows excellent barley, vines and fruit.

A large former settlement on the site of the present city of Wurzburg can be traced back to the seventh century, at the end of which an Irish missionary named Kilian, together with two Irish priests, came to visit Duke Gosbert, ruler of the Wurzburg region. Kilian chose the Wurzburg settlement as a center for his missionary work, and there he died a martyr's death 689 A.D. The seed of Christianity sowed by St. Kilian was, however, so fruitful that during the following century—around 740 A.D.—Wurzburg, although a comparatively small community, was elevated by St. Boniface to a bishopric. St. Boniface appointed as its first bishop St. Burkhard, whose memory, together with that of St. Kilian, is still held in high esteem by the local population.

Thousands of pilgrims from all parts of the Main valley would visit the shrine of St. Kilian which gave the growth of Wurzburg an impetus, not only as a religious center, but as a trading and political center. Spiritual and secular power came more and more into the hands of the bishops of Wurzburg and they were to exert a decisive influence in the cultural and the economic development of the city. It was one of them, the Prince-Bishop Johann Philipp von Schonborn, who in 1643 decided to erect a court brewery to supply not only his own court (in German *Hof*, hence the name *Hofbrau* or the court brewery) but the whole population of Wurzburg and its visitors with beer. Originally, Wurzburg was a wine-producing center, and it was not until toward the end of the devastating Thirty Years War that the building of a brewery was decided upon for a very practical reason: the warring Swedish and Imperial Troops had drunk the city wine cellars dry.

Little did the worthy Bishop Johann Philipp know that by this emergency measure he had laid foundation for a prosperous industry, destined to spread the name of Wurzburg wider even than the cherished wine industry had.

Under Napoleon's occupation, the secular rule of the bishops was abolished and the Royal Bavarian Government assumed political power. With this change the brewery also changed hands: it became the court brewery of the Bavarian kings.

It is from this early period of its existence that the brewery bears on its

*University students in Munster, clad in the
uniform of their student association, gather at
Pinkus Müller's tavern for a* Dämmerschoppen, *or
drink, at twilight, singing and drinking beer from
a traditional glass boot. The beer is Müller's famous*
Altbier, *from the tavern's own 150-year-old brewery.*

crest the insignia of the ancient sovereigns—the star and the crown. In its
advertisements Wurzburger Hofbrau also uses a picture of the old castle of
Marienberg. Originally a residence of the prince-bishops, it was reduced
to a mere citadel in the eighteenth century. The brewery is situated right
below the castle, on the flank of the Marienberg Hill.

The brewery did not, however, remain king's property for long. In
1863 it passed into private hands and in 1874 it was acquired by one Henry
Theodore Boettinger from the famous English beer town of Burton-on-
Trent. The new owner completely rebuilt the brewery and in 1882 turned
it into a public company. Thanks to its unsurpassed quality Wurzburger

Cabby toasting his horse with a goblet of beer in Berlin, 1920.

Hofbrau beer soon found ardent friends and admirers abroad. Except during the Prohibition period it has been steadily imported in the United States of America since 1882.

In the United States the biggest boost to business came after 1887 when the brewery began to supply Lüchow's Restaurant in New York. Wurzburger on draught caught on and word spread fast across the nation.

Production and Properties of Wurzburger Hofbrau. It would be more correct to use the word brewing than production, for Wurzburger Hofbrau is by no means mechanically produced, like so many consumer goods, but brewed, matured and nursed with the same care and skill with which a loving wife and mother prepares the Sunday dinner. Of course, in doing so, the Wurzburg brewery makes ample use of all up-to-date scientific and technical improvements; their purpose, however, is not to simplify, mechanize, or render less expensive, the process, but to make the brewer's task more precise and less dependent on chance and nature.

Wurzburger Hofbrau is brewed from pure barley malt and hops of the finest available quality. The law prevents the brewer from using any raw materials but these two, apart from yeast and water. There is no room for any substitute materials like rice, sugar or corn flakes, so extensively used in other countries.

Furthermore, Wurzburger Hofbrau is fermented and matured slowly, for months on end. There is no question of speeding up the production if the demand suddenly increases. It is one of the most difficult jobs of the Wurzburg master brewer to forecast correctly the demand perhaps some four to six months ahead. The fermentation and maturing of the Wurzburg beer must be allowed to take their course fully, without any shortcuts, bypasses or, for that matter, slowdowns.

These are the chief reasons that make Wurzburger Hofbrau a beer of such a distinctive character.

Wurzburger Hofbrau is available in export in four different types—the light *Edelquell,* the amber *Marzen,* the dark *Export* and the *Special Bock.* Naturally enough, the four types of Wurzburger do not all taste alike; the light Edelquell is not only light in color but also in body, distinguished by a crisp, refreshing, hoppy flavor; the amber Marzen is for those who prefer a satisfying, full-bodied drink; the dark Export is a tasty, mellow and hearty old Bavarian beer; the Special Bock, a rich and delightful drink, is featured mainly during the cooler season, from October to May.

Other German Beers

In the future I hope to devote an entire book to the beers of Germany but for now the reader will have to content himself with those here outlined, and taste what is available in his neighborhood perhaps using the beer-profile form provided in chapter one.

On your next trip to Germany try to find a smoked beer such as *Rauchbier* which is brewed in Bamberg, mostly for consumption in taverns. Smoked beer developed in the 1500's because there were no kilns in the region for heating the barley during the malting process. To compensate for a kiln local beer makers decided to smoke the barley over beechwood fires to arrest germination and produce the finished malt. This gives the beer a special smoke-cured flavor that is very popular in Bamberg. Naturally, beer brewed for such a local market is unpasteurized and therefore more flavorful and nutritious. Incidentally, the Bavarians of Bamberg consume more beer per capita than any people in the world. While the 70,000 inhabitants imbibe an average fifty gallons of beer each year, the average for all of Germany is only twenty-eight gallons.

Another beer worth looking for is the original *Budvar Budweiser* brewed in Budweis, South Bohemia. This beer is imported into the United States but with a *Moldaubrau* label. An agreement between the Budvar Budweiser brewery and the Anheuser-Busch Company states that the American brewer will not sell Budweiser in Europe if the German brewer does not sell its label in the United States.

Things are changing in Germany. Even the devout Bavarians are now buying increasing quantities of packaged beer in supermarkets and often choosing that which costs the least.

There has even been an attempt over the past few years to produce a national beer according to a common formula, in an attempt to decrease inefficiency. Several groups of small brewers have already joined to produce and market a nationally distributed beer.

One such group, an association of twenty-two independent breweries coordinated by the Scheuermann Marketing Corporation of Hamburg, is producing *Co-Brau* from a common formula, in addition to their own labels.

Another new entry into the national beer race is *Deutsches Stern Pils* produced by forty breweries brought together by the Stern Brewery of Essen.

If these beers become popular throughout Germany (as even the most successful of German beers have not been able to do—notably *Beck's, Dortmunder Union* and *Löwenbräu*) the leadership for the world of the German brewers will eventually decline.

Astra Ale, brewed by the St. Pauli Brauerei in Hamburg, is highly recommended. The bouquet is of "ale" (which means it's hoppy), the color pale amber, the head lasting. A distinct malt flavor is balanced by a tartness which leads to a very satisfying finish.

Berliner Kindl (Weisse) was immediately rejected for its celerylike flavor, and almost sweet aftertaste. Definitely *not* appropriate for those who like a tart, hoppy lager beer. (If you like Dr. Brown's Celery Tonic you might try this beer.)

Bock Dark Malt Liquor, by St. Pauli Brauerei, Hamburg, is another mild German dark beer. Slightly more tart than *Kulmbacher,* this beer loses its head almost on pouring. Of average body and bouquet, it lacks any special characteristics. Stick to Mackeson or Guinness.

Dinkelacker Bock Extra. The high yeasty character imparts a flavor described as "very fresh" or "home brewed." The color is a fine light amber, the head small but lasting, the bouquet above average. Neither dry nor sweet, but a pleasant, balanced brew. A very subtle beer.

Dinkelacker Malt Liquor. Golden amber color, strong head, well carbonated. With a full body and bouquet, it has a marvelous taste that is sweet at first but good and tart in the aftertaste.

Dortmunder Kronen Malt Liquor. A pale (almost blonde) lager, of average bouquet intensity, it has above average body and flavor, and average dryness. It finishes with some hoppiness, which is desirable and makes for a very pleasant drink. Recommended.

Dressler's Export Beer, like Beck's, is too salty and too bitter for my taste. It must be something about this northern geography that has imbued the local beers with such pointed qualities. I've got it! The red ship's life float on Dressler's label tells me that the seamen have had their influence on

They also drink who only stand and wait.

the brewers of Bremen. Is it something about a life at sea that demands a tart and bitter brew? Who knows? At this point my anthropo-physiological questioning begins to sound quite fishy and I abandon this bitter Bremen brew for flavors more amenable.

Henninger. In a country where beer is always good, and frequently excellent, a truly superb beer may easily go unnoticed by visitors for decades. This is the case with Henninger lager. Crafted by Frankfurt's largest brewery, it's been a local favorite for a long while and only recently entered the international marketplace. With adequate promotion this fine lager could easily gain a major share of drinkers outside Germany. Henninger comes on tart, as beer should, and is accompanied with a bright, lasting head. It is a fine light amber. The bouquet is delicate, body and flavor medium. Aftertaste is easy to live with, as it is dry *without* meddlesome additives. Overall, one of the best lager beers sampled. Highly recommended.

Jever German Pilsener. Pale yellow lager. Very mild bouquet. Very bitter. Harsh aftertaste. Not recommended.

Kulmbacher Monkshof Dark Beer. Of reddish amber color, with strong bouquet, lasting head and average body, this beer is not to be compared with Mackeson or Guinness. It is very different, for a different taste; more likely to please the light beer drinker who occasionally takes a dark. This one is not sweet, but highly malty with a full flavor profile and pleasant aftertaste.

Alligators or crocodiles in Bavaria? I cannot tell which of the above crocodilians appears on the export label of *Lederer-Brau,* but I must admit it is another fine Bavarian lager. "As traditionally brewed . . . in Germany since 1468" also appears on this label. These statements are probably not misleading. Lederer-Brau is one of Nuremberg's two largest breweries, but quality is still enforced by master brewers Schenleim and Jakob. I like this Bavarian lager for several reasons—it's delightfully tart, without additives and a fine alternative to the hubris of Löwenbräu which has dominated the export market for thirty years, primarily due to aggressive marketing. Recommended.

Optimator Doppelspaten, by Spaten-Brau of Munich, has a reddish color and above average bouquet. Above average body and flavor with medium sweetness. Nothing special about it.

Spaten Munich Light by Spaten Brau, Munich is one of the lightest colored beers tasted. Strong body, very sweet flavor. A good, sweet lager.

GREECE

Amber-yellow in color, with a good, sharp taste, *Fix Beer* compares favorably with some excellent Central European lagers. Somehow, I even prefer the Fix export. It has a particular flavor that must reflect the combination of local Athens water with good barley malt and a fine yeast strain. It could be that I was more thirsty when I sampled this Greek beer, but I truly believe the statement embossed on its red, white and blue label, "36 Gold and Prize Medals." Definitely worth looking for. Recommended.

HOLLAND

The brewing of ale and beer has been a part of life in Holland since early times. In the thirteenth century the Dutch scholars Isaac and John Hollandus wrote on fermentation and brewing. Delft was once as famous for its beer as for its ceramics, and by 1480 even a small town like Gouda had as many as 350 breweries. By the seventeenth century the average Dutchman was drinking about eighty gallons of beer per year, and children under eight years of age consumed an average of forty. A contemporary Dutch brewery has pointed out that the very poor water of those days is, in part, an explanation for those high rates of consumption.

There are at present five major breweries in Holland. Of these, Heineken supplies nearly 40 percent of all beer consumed in the Netherlands.

CULVER PICTURES

Politicians enjoying a congenial mug;
from a painting by E. Harburger, 1885.

Heineken, Amsterdam

Heineken Lager Beer, Special Dark Beer, Amstel

The Heineken group has three breweries in the Netherlands. The oldest Heineken brewery is in Amsterdam and produces the bulk of the beer consumed within the Netherlands. Another brewery at 's Hertogenbosch also supplies the local market, whereas Heineken's export beers are produced at the Rotterdam brewery, which dates back to 1874.

Heineken dark beers and stout are brewed at *De Sleutel* (The Key), the oldest Dutch brewery, which dates back to 1433. Heineken is the major shareholder in this small brewery.

The Heineken kingdom was initiated by Gerard Adriaan Heineken, who in 1864, at the age of twenty-two, purchased De Hooiberg (The Haystack) brewery which had been founded in 1592.

Heineken lager is brewed from barley malt, hops from various countries, and several different water sources. Heineken yeast dates from 1886, and according to the brewery "is the oldest pure yeast culture which has been uninterruptedly used by any brewery." For many years, this yeast strain was sold to foreign breweries but after World War I Heineken ceased exporting its yeast.

This lager is by far the leading import in the United States and considered a standard by many tasters. It is light colored, with a better than average head and medium light bouquet. It is a shade too dry, for my taste, and a bit too salty. Otherwise, it is a respectable lager.

Heineken Special Dark Beer is made from roasted caramelized malts, and a special brewing and fermentation process generates a higher level of malt extract, giving this dark beer a rich, full flavor. It finishes well with a satisfying aftertaste.

Amstel has that characteristic of Alsatian lagers so pleasant when one is drinking heavily, a slight tartness and balanced "nose." The Amstel I had the good fortune of drinking, in considerable quantity aboard a Prudential liner cruise to Canada, was brewed in the Netherlands Antilles. With an average color, medium bouquet and small head, Amstel is recommended.

IRELAND

THE BREWING INDUSTRY OF IRELAND[*]

Brewing in Ireland has existed from the earliest times, the Irish, in common with ancient Britons, drinking both ale and mead. The Hiberi, or Hibernians, are said by the early historians to have used a liquor called

---

[*]One Hundred Years of Brewing.

*The O'Neill, or Brian Boru, Harp, the earliest
known Irish harp and the oldest in existence,
is the basis for the Guinness trademark device,
which was registered in 1876.*

"curmi," made of barley. St. Columbanus, who flourished in the sixth and seventh centuries, found the people and the clergy enjoying their ale, which was "bruised from the juice of wheat and barley," and the Danes, while in possession of the country in the ninth century, brewed their "ael" from heath; hence "heather-beer." It is believed that the saccharine matter, in ancient times, was supplied by the addition of honey, "the flower of the heath being used as a substitute for hops; since it is well known that before the introduction of the latter plant, broom tops, wormwood and other bitter herbs have been employed. According to usual practice, in ancient times, of fermenting worts for the purpose of making beer, the yeast was preserved by means of a furze, or whin bush, kept over in the chimney until the next brewing. This, when dipped in the wort caused the liquor to ferment."

Arthur Guinness Son and Company, Dublin

Guinness: Draught Stout, Extra Stout, Export Stout, Foreign Extra Stout

HISTORY

Arthur Guinness founded the St. James's Gate Brewery on the south bank of Dublin's river Liffey in 1759. Here he brewed Porter (and later Stout) so well that he eventually ousted all imports from the Irish market, captured a share of the English trade and revolutionized the Irish brewing industry.

To achieve wider acceptance the famous Guinness advertising was begun in 1929. Although 85 percent of Guinness production is sold in Ireland and the United Kingdom, it is available in 147 other countries, the best customers being Nigeria and Malaysia.

In 1963, after building up the sales of Guinness in Nigeria from Dublin, Guinness opened a brewery at Ikeja in Nigeria. This has been a very suc-

Front gate of Guinness Brewery at St. James's Gate, Dublin.

cessful operation and the output of the brewery there continues to increase. In 1966 a brewery was built at Kuala Lumpur in Malaysia and this has recently been extended to produce Gold Harp Lager as well as Guinness. The Guinness Brewery at Douala, Cameroun, was opened in May 1970, and the sixth Guinness Brewery was opened in Ghana in 1972. Now another brewery is being built in Nigeria at Benin, initially for the production of lager, and the eighth Guinness brewery has recently been built in Jamaica. The Guinness company supervises the brewing of Guinness in other breweries all over the world.

Different strengths of Guinness are produced to suit overseas markets and the following names are used to describe Guinness products:

Guinness Extra Stout. This is the Guinness sold for bottling in Great Britain and Ireland. Guinness themselves do not carry out the bottling process.

Draught Guinness. This too is virtually confined to Great Britain and Ireland. It is served from metal casks and its characteristic creamy head is produced through a special tap fitting which Guinness have patented.

Foreign Extra Stout. This is the strongest form of Guinness and has a drier flavor than the others. It is brewed in Guinness breweries in Dublin, Malaysia, Nigeria, Cameroun, Ghana and Jamaica. It is also brewed under licence and direct technical control in several other countries.

Export Stout. This, like Foreign Extra Stout, is a strong brew, but is less dry and is exported to Belgium and other European countries.

Extra Stout for Export. This is a form of Guinness similar in flavor to Extra Stout and specially prepared to suit certain export markets, including the United States of America. It is among the darkest of beers, with an almost massive bouquet and body. Thick, like syrup, leaving a dense impression, this beer is *not* for every drinker.

Ingredients. Guinness quality is derived from several principal facts: no adjuncts are used, only barley grown in Ireland and England (this is exported for overseas brewery operations); the flavor and color are natural—derived solely from roasted barley. Hops are from worldwide sources—principally of British, American and European origin. Yeast is a top-fermenting Guinness strain.

Brewing Process. The standard infusion mash system is utilized, with roasted barley or malt added to give the characteristic dark color. While great care is taken to maintain a uniform composition and flavor, different varieties of malt and hops are blended for each brew, and the product which is sold is a blending of several different brewings.

Unrefrigerated storage is used and all production for the Irish and English market is sold naturally conditioned and unpasteurized.

The bottled export variety is a different brew, having a higher alcoholic content, a longer shelf life due to added hops and conditionings and being pasteurized.

The best way to drink the flavorful, rich, dark Guinness outside of the British Isles is on draught. This type is identical with the Irish product locally consumed. The short time it takes for the brew to cross the Atlantic in containerized ships does not require special conditioning or pasteurization.

ITALY

Italy, like Spain and other southern European countries, is predominantly a nation of wine drinkers. Consumption of beer is rapidly increasing in these countries, perhaps due to increased foreign travel.

Italian beer has strong ties with Austrian and German brews. The eleven largest breweries produce mainly light lager beers. Of these Birra Peroni is perhaps the best known. The company began in 1846 and now comprises eight plants located throughout the country.

Birra Peroni, Rome

Peroni Lager

Malt used by the Peroni brewery is purchased mainly from Italian malt producers who grow their barley in central and southern Italy. Small quantities of malt are occasionally imported from other European countries, usually when local shortages occur. Rice of Italian origin, and German and Czechoslovakian hops are also added. Yeast is of the bottom-fermenting pure culture type, which provides a vigorous fermentation, typical of lager beers. Water is treated by water-softening equipment and the addition of various salts, in order to achieve the correct chemical composition. (It should be noted that a large majority of the world's breweries, especially those using municipal waters, treat their water in this way.)

Brewing proceeds by the classic Bavarian two-mash method. Main fermentation takes place both in open or closed vessels, at low temperatures, for seven to nine days. The secondary fermentation and ageing occurs in stainless steel, aluminum, or enameled iron tanks. The cellars in which these tanks are located are kept at 3°C. during the first fifteen days and at −2°C. thereafter. Finished beer is stored for about fifty days and then filtered by use of diatomaceous products, and pasteurized prior to packaging.

Peroni Beer is somewhat cloudy, due to yeast (a good sign), and has an average bouquet but an above-average body and flavor. It is good and sharp, but not bitter, and has the distinction of satisfying thirst while encouraging the desire to drink. Recommended.

JAPAN

As Japan continues to adopt Western habits the consumption of the native *saké* is decreasing while beer consumption (which is still low on a per

Kirin beer helps fatten Kobe beef.

capita basis—only 6.7 gallons in 1968 as compared with 37 gallons in Czechoslovakia) grows at a rapid pace. As the consumption of beer continues, so does the growth of breweries, and Kirin, now the world's third largest brewery even in a nation of relatively small beer drinkers, may soon become the largest in the world.

Kirin, Sapporo and Asahi are the principal breweries in Japan. For the purpose of this book only Kirin, which supplies 60 percent of the domestic market, will be discussed in detail.

Kirin beer was first produced in Yokohama in 1869 by an American named William Copeland who established a small brewery there.

In 1885, a new company called Japan Brewery began producing a premium quality beer, and in 1888 the first *Kirin* (a mythical creature, combining a horse and dragon) label appeared.

What had begun as a novelty drink for Japan became a major item of trade as early as 1918, when Kirin opened a second plant near Osaka to keep up with demand.

By 1974 Kirin had completed its twelfth brewery.

Kirin Brewery, Tokyo

Kirin Lager, Stout, Black Beer

Kirin lager is made from barley grown in Japan, rice, cornstarch and corn grits. Hops are grown on contract farms and imported when needed. Fer-

FRED LYON, TIME-LIFE PICTURE AGENCY

This geisha displays the proper blend of docility and reserve as she presents a light to a diner in a Tokyo restaurant.

mentation lasts eight days. The young beer is then stored for two months before being filtered and pasteurized. Kirin does not add any preservatives to its brews; consequently they are all on a high level.

In taste Kirin is by far the best of Japanese beers. It is light in color, bouquet and body but the dry flavor and smooth finish encourage second and third samples. It's a damned good beer.

Other Japanese Beers

Sapporo Dark Beer pours like Guinness with the addition of a hoppy bouquet. Although the brewers would probably have liked it to be so, it is *not* the darkest colored beer sampled. It has a strong head but the taste is all wrong. It's just a poor Guinness. Descriptions at a recent sampling ranged from "rancid" to "schizophrenic." Ironically, this beer has a remarkably well-designed label, distinguished by a hard, fast star.

Asahi Lager Beer opens nicely with above average bouquet. The light yellow color is typical, while the poor head is disappointing. This beer is so neutral in flavor it is best described as slightly bitter water. In this sense it is recommended for very light drinkers.

KENYA

Kenya Breweries

Tusker Lager

From the very earliest times the people of Kenya drank beer from the tappings of the various palms: coconut, doum and the others. This would mean they would have experienced none of the problems that modern brewers have had to overcome: the scientific processes, particularly those which include the fermentation of a malted cereal, pasteurization, water purity, yeast control and the addition of bitterings. The coastal beer just ran out of the palm; it came in three qualities. The new brew could be taken by children with no ill effects; after a day it was fit for men; left for another 24 hours it had a specific gravity to fell an ox, which put it into the Old Barley Wine category.

Up-country the palm gave way to honey, millet and other grains, but not maize, barley or wheat. There were probably all sorts of brewing ingredients that are now forgotten. There are great disputes on the matter of the arrival date of the maize. A century ago *mahindi* was mentioned, but I once heard a Kipsigis say at a beer-drink that his father when young did not know maize. The Routledge brothers' book on the Kikuyu (1910) states that maize is said to be derived from "the white man of very long ago" and arrived in Kikuyuland via the Akamba. There is a legend that Arabs took maize of various colours to the Kapenguria area before the white men arrived. When they did arrive, wheat and barley were still being imported.

And so we come to the drinking habits of the early Europeans who arrived in Mombasa, recruited porters, and set off for up-country. We cannot discount the missionaries. They were not averse to a half bottle of champagne when recuperating from malaria; indeed David Livingstone, in another part of Africa, makes mention of the wine as beneficial. Beer, however, would, it might be thought, be for the layman. But this was not so. Beer was a heavy load to carry. Brandy, whisky and wine could all be diluted with water and the alcoholic content of a tot was equivalent to the alcoholic content of a bottle of beer. During the years of the Imperial British East Africa Company and the origins of the Uganda Railway, stores stocked imported bottled beer at Mombasa, but unfortunately for the brewing industry, wines and spirits had gained a hold on the local European community. Whisky was king for a strange reason.

The German shipping line that served the East African route was subsidized by the German government. At the same time the shipping company offered large rebates to shippers who fulfilled an annual tonnage quota. If this contract was not met, the rebate was disallowed. To meet the quota, therefore, it was the habit of German shippers to top up their tonnage by sending to Mombasa large consignments of whisky, a commodity sold on the quayside CIF at Shs. 3.50 a case of twelve bottles.

The railwaymen took their choice. Two quarts of beer or twelve bottles of whisky. The price was the same.

The same position applied in German East Africa where the Germans were building their railways. Except, of course, whisky was alien to the German engineers. They knew beer and they drank beer. And because beer was king, a young plantation assistant named Wilhelm Schultz chucked up growing sisal and vegetables and moved to Dar es Salaam where he established a Brauerei. By 1910 Schultz beer had captured the local market and some of his products were being exported to Mombasa and up the line to Nairobi. By this time the German shippers were fulfilling their quotas, and whisky at thirty-odd cents a bottle was no longer obtainable.

But a problem arose. The freight on a case of 48 quart bottles of beer between Mombasa and Nairobi was Shs. 13.50 and there was the freight from Dar es Salaam. In that port, drinkers were served from the barrel and Schultz imported stone beermugs engraved with the name of his brewery. The writer drinks his Tusker to this day from one of these mugs. But let us now dismiss Herr Schultz. Not only was he a brewer of note but he became one of German East Africa's foremost settler politicians. His name and his brewery disappeared from history with the advent of the 1914 war.

So many changes were to come to East Africa with that war. Kenya could not from its own resources of manpower and material grapple with and defeat a people who were trained against *Der Tag* and whose only wish was to hold on African soil an allied force that would deplete the numbers of men who would fight the Fatherland. This the Germans accomplished. Very soon the first of the hundreds of thousands of men began to arrive at Kilindini. Men, horses, mules, donkeys, stores, armaments; all of which joined the ebb and flow of battle.

I have not mentioned that beer was an import. There was no beer in Kenya except the small amount in stock. Tea was the cheapest

CULVER PICTURES

Sipping banana beer.

and the lightest product to transport. The Allied army fought their battles on tea. The Germans had large stocks of wine. When the war ended, the Allied victory was toasted in tea and liquid quinine. Both had helped to bring the campaign to an end.

Very soon, two brothers named Hurst, who were farming at Soy, in Kenya, opened and poured a bottle of imported beer. That simple and social act provided the germ of an idea that was to lead to the establishment of Kenya Breweries which, today, 50 years later, ranks among the great private enterprise undertakings in the country.

—*Edward Rodwell*

Tusker Lager is brewed to local taste and enjoys tremendous sales. Several long-time expatriates tell me it's on par with *Tiger Beer* (Malaysia) but I've only been able to taste the *Tusker Export,* a tart, above-average-bodied lager. Other labels include *White Cap Lager, City Lager* and *Allsopps Pilsener.* Each brand derives its flavor from particular ratios of syrup, hops, yeast and water treatment. All brews are composed of Kenya-grown barley cultivated at altitudes of 2,200 meters and above, with an annual rainfall of 700 to 1,200 mm. Hops are imported from Yugoslavia, Belgium and Germany. Hop extracts are also utilized. White cane sugar is imported from Cuba, and brewing water is drawn from the Nairobi city supply.

The beers are aged for a respectable five weeks, after which time they are "polished" by Kiesulgluir and Carlson sheet filters.

Wartime years in Kenya brought a shortage of glasses which was inventively solved. Tusker bottles were converted into drinking glasses. A piece of string soaked in kerosene was tied around the bottle and ignited. A smart blow took off the top of the bottle above the string; the sharp edge was removed by an emery wheel, and so the people of Kenya drank their Tusker literally from the bottle.

LUXEMBOURG

Diekirch Brewery

Diekirch Pils, Reserve, Grande Reserve, Reservator, Malt

This tiny country brews one of the world's best beers. *Diekirch Pils* is the biggest selling foreign beer in Germany, and that's indicative of fine quality. As in Germany, only barley, hops and water may be used in brewing beer in Luxembourg. No preservatives are ever added.

Founded in 1871, the Diekirch brewery has continually modernized its operations without ruining its products. Brewed according to the Bavarian Purity Decree, Diekirch beers are made from the following ingredients: only Bavarian and Czechoslovakian hops, barley malt (which is malted by Diekirch, a brewing rarity these days), water from the Herrenberg Springs which is distinguished by a low calcium content with an abundance of other minerals.

After "mashing," the early brewing mixture is twice filtered and boiled with hops. It is next fermented for seven to eight days with yeast from Swiss and German strains. It is ripened at 0°C. for the lengthy period of two to three months during which time all malt sugars ferment. Resulting are extremely mellow, clear, aromatic brews of several production types. These are:

Diekirch Pils, a mild, highly hopped, Pilsner type, with 4 percent alcohol.

Reserve, a lager with pronounced malt character, and heavy body; 5 percent alcohol.

Grand Reserve, a finely hopped stout beer, considered a luxury due to the special brewing procedures.

Reservator, a dark 'dopplebock,' Munich type lager.

Malt, a vitamin-rich malt lager with less than 0.5 percent alcohol.

MEXICO

EARLY BREWERIES

The native beverages, *mescal, tequilla* and *pulque* were only slowly supplemented by beer and the native drinks—which are relatively simple to prepare and much stronger than beer—are still very popular. (Pulque is made from the juices of the agave cactus.)

Lager breweries existed in Mexico City as early as 1845. The oldest breweries in the capital were the *Cerveceria de la Pila Seca,* founded by Bernhard Bolgard, a native of Switzerland, and the *Cerveceria de la Candelaria,* founded by Frederico Herzog, a Bavarian. The malt used was made of Mexican barley, sun-dried, and this together with *pilancillo,* made from brown sugar, constituted the raw materials. These breweries prospered until the 1880's when a moderately priced but good lager beer, produced in Toluca, drove them out of business.

There are at present many breweries in Mexico with large production capacities. Some are described below.

Cerveceria Moctezuma, Mexico City

Superior; Dos Equis (XX); Tres Equis (XXX); Noche Buena

The Moctezuma Brewery own its own malting facility, which supplies many breweries in Latin America. Rice is used as an adjunct and hop extracts supplement pure imported hops. During the ageing process only natural carbonation is used, no artificial gas being added to Moctezuma beers.

Some fifteen years ago the semidark XX (Dos Equis) was the brewery's leading label. As national taste moved toward paler beers the Superior label became the leading brand in Mexico. Tres Equis (XXX), a relatively new label, is sold as a premium beer primarily in metropolitan areas.

Superior Light Beer is the top of the Moctezuma line. I would rate it above all other Mexican beers. It is very light in color, with medium bouquet and body. A good head and strong carbonation are plusses. The dryness creates an overall flavor profile that is definitely superior. Recommended.

Dos Equis Beer is, in my opinion, the most overrated import in the United States. I don't know why it is so popular. The deep amber color suggests a dark beer but is due merely to a little caramel coloring. The poor head and watery body speak for themselves. Some call it "malty"; I call it synthetic. It's just nowhere and I could not wait to get its taste out of my mouth.

Tres Equis Beer is another light-bodied, light-flavored lager. It is dry and inoffensive but so are countless other beers.

Noche Buena has a nice reddish tinge and adequate carbonation. The bouquet is strong but smacks of caramel rather than malt or hops. It finishes with a sour taste. Overall it is not all bad, but there are better, more true dark beers. Stick to Guinness or Mackeson.

Other Mexican Beers

Corona Cerveza de exportacion begins well. It is among the most highly carbonated beers, with a very strong bouquet that is difficult to place. (It does not smell of hops or malt; the smell may be of yeast.) The body is very light, the color extremely pale. It is dry but the flavor is poor overall, with a singeing aftertaste.

Carta Blanca, by Cerveceria Cuahtemoc, is almost not a beer at all. The head is nonexistent, the color near white. The bouquet is strong but difficult to place. The taste is surprisingly tart but this is followed by some unpleasant bitterness.

Tecate Cerveza, brewed in Mexico City by the Carta Blanca people, is an alright lager with very light bouquet, color and body. It is also medium dry but unexceptional. I suspect that most Mexican lagers have been computer designed to cooperate with North American tastes. Tecate is one of the few canned beers available in Mexico, and the locals drink it à la Mexicana. Salt and lime juice are sprinkled atop the can, imparting a combination of tastes unlike anything you've ever tried.

Bohemia Ale, also by Cuahtemoc Brewery, is light bodied, colored and flavored. Bouquet is mild; flavor smacks of synthetic ale flavoring.

Indio Cerveza purports to be a dark beer. The color is dark, the body and bouquet of above average intensity. It is sweet and fair for those liking sweet, dark beers.

NEW ZEALAND

Of this country's three breweries, New Zealand Breweries is the smallest and most independent. *Zealandia Half and Half* is a new experience. This interesting blend of mellow stout and lager beer is in a class by itself.

Honey-colored, with above-average bouquet and a weighty body, this blend finishes strong, with a delicious, nut-like aftertaste. Lovers of the blend no longer need mix their own. A winning brew, highly recommended.

NICARAGUA

Cerveza Victoria is a nonoffensive lager, indistinguishable from dozens, if not hundreds, of other similar tasting light beers. Perhaps the sample I tasted had been too long in transit or storage, but all with me agreed it lacked zinginess. In fact, this poor Central American entry was described by one lady taster as "too heavy to even be *called* a light beer." Perhaps Master Brewer Hoar needs to impress upon the Victoria salespeople the importance of proper and rapid transit and storage.

PHILIPPINES

San Miguel Corporation, Manila

San Miguel

The only beer brewed in the country is San Miguel, which became widely popular in the United States following World War Two, when military personnel in the Pacific brought back a confirmed taste for it.

With beginnings in 1890, as a small family-operated brewery, the company has now become a multiproduct public corporation. Aside from beer, San Miguel produces soft drinks, dairy products, glass and plastic containers, poultry and livestock feed and frozen chickens.

San Miguel was the first brewery in the Philippines and in Southeast Asia. The name was taken from a district in Manila where the company's first brewery was located. Today, San Miguel beer is brewed not only in the Philippines, where there are three breweries, but also in Spain (where there are also three San Miguel breweries), in Hong Kong, Guam, and Papua, New Guinea. It has been the recipient of awards in international competitions held in London, Brussels (three times), Paris and Spain.

San Miguel Corporation actually manufactures two different brews in the Philippines—the pilsener (lager) and *cerveza negra,* literally black beer. Both types are distributed in domestic as well as foreign markets.

Ingredients. In the brewing of San Miguel beer, the following ingredients are used: malt made from two-row and six-row barleys from Australia, Canada and France; cornstarch; hops from Germany and the United States; a cultured strain of lager yeast and good brewing water.

Malt is responsible for the body in San Miguel beer. It determines the taste and the golden color and causes the drink to foam on top. Hops from the ripened and dried flower cones of the hop plants provide flavor and aroma.

The base of San Miguel beer is brewing water, the composition of which is determined and controlled according to the specifications of San Miguel brewmasters. The water, whether from deep wells or from the city water systems, is properly conditioned for San Miguel's type of beer before it is used.

Taste. San Miguel Beer is brewed to suit the taste of the people in the areas where the product is distributed.

For instance San Miguel brewed in the Philippines is a light pale pilsen with a slightly bitter taste, because Filipinos are fond of bitterness. San Miguel brewed in Spain is in line with European brews, richer in malt extract, more highly hopped and having a higher alcoholic content. San Miguel brewed in Hong Kong is slightly more bitter than San Miguel in the Philippines, because this is the way the residents of that British Dependency like it. The version exported to the United States is on the sweet side, as is *San Miguel Dark Beer*.

POLAND

If you like a *pronounced* barley malt taste *Krakus* may be your stein of beer. Brewed with the mountain spring waters of Zywiec, by a brewer of the same name, this lager has been aggressively thrust into the lucrative overseas market and is just now enjoying major exposure. People who enjoy robustness of flavor will probably take well to this fine Polish import. Those who have grown up on excessively light beers may find the maltiness too "bitter." As an amateur mountaineer I imagine this beer as the perfect conclusion to a hard climb, preferably at an obscure Carpathian inn on a misty afternoon. It's a damned good beer.

PORTUGAL

Sociedade Central de Cervejas, Vialonga and Coimbra

Sagres

Until 1934 there were four main breweries in Portugal; then, the four joined to form Sociedade Central de Cervejas. This is now the largest brewing company in Portugal (there is only one other large company) and has about 70 percent of the total beer market.

The *Sagres* label was brought out in 1934 and soon became the most popular beer in the nation. It is brewed at two plants, one in Vialonga and the other in Coimbra.

This Portuguese lager is styled on classic lines and made from barley malted at the brewery, corn grits, imported hops for aroma supplemented by bitter hops grown domestically, imported yeast and local waters. All Sagres beer is pasteurized.

As it is for all practical purposes the national beer of Portugal, Sagres is very popular in Africa wherever there has been an appreciable Portuguese presence, namely in the Islands of Cape Verde, Portuguese Guinea, the Islands of St. Tomé, Mozambique, Macao and Timor.

This lager is very pale and mild. It exhibits an average head with minimal bouquet. The aftertaste is mildly bitter, with a slight yeasty quality.

HENRI CARTIER-BRESSON, MAGNUM

A pint in a pub on the Rhine, Switzerland.

SINGAPORE

Malayan Breweries

Tiger Lager Beer

Tiger Lager Beer is reminiscent of those Bremen beers (which I don't like), but lacks the "saltiness" I find offensive. Yet, it tingles the palate with its sharp hoppiness. This beer has long been a favorite among expatriates and locals in Singapore. With their recent export lager, Malayan Breweries, under the direction of P. Rohrig, has produced a serious contender for the huge international market. I find it consistently clear, yeasty and hoppy, with a pleasant bouquet. This is an admirable dry light beer that is recommended for table dressing at appropriate "ethnic" dinners.

SWITZERLAND

Swiss beers are all brewed according to the Bavarian Purity Law—with only malt, hops, yeast and water. No additives are permitted, and one product, *Löwenbräu Zurich Export* beer, is bottled without pasteurization, making it one of the most desirable European beers at present available for export.

Of the fourteen major breweries operating in Switzerland three are described below.

Brauerei A. Hürlimann, Zurich

Sternbrau, Alpenbrau, Birell

HISTORY

In 1836 Heinrich Hürlimann founded the Hürlimann and Company breweries in Feldbach on the Lake of Zurich. He refused to be discouraged by initial failures and with toughness and perseverance repeatedly overcame difficulties, until he could boast an annual production of 4,500 hectoliters—quite a respectable amount in those days.

It fell to his son, Albert Hürlimann, however, to build up an industrial enterprise from the brewery, which had been run as a cottage industry. In 1866 he transferred the plant to what was then the country district of Enge near Zurich. His aim was to win over the growing population of the thriving city of Zurich and make them satisfied and faithful customers. His venture was successful, and his business soon earned the respect of customers at home and abroad.

In 1887 his son, Albert Heinrich Hürlimann took over the direction of the brewery, and it was in his time that the enterprise saw the most active development. Production rose from 30,000 hectoliters in 1887 to 250,000 in 1927. For forty-seven years he led it with great vigor and success. In 1921 the breweries, A. Hürlimann and am Uetliberg Ltd., were amalgamated to become the present-day A. Hürlimann Ltd.

Hürlimann beers are all made of the same basic ingredients. The brewing water, which is high in calcium salts, is softened and adjusted to specifications. Two-rowed barley from major growers throughout Europe is malted to some extent at the brewery, but most of the malt comes from malt houses. Hürlimann Breweries mainly use German Hallertau hops and Saaz hops. These varieties are supplemented by small quantities of hops from Swiss hop-gardens in the region of Stammheim.

The beer is fermented over nine days and then left to settle and mellow in cool cellars, at temperatures of about −1.5°C. During the long ageing period of about three months the beer is naturally krausened (carbonated) under mild pressure.* As a result, almost all of the malt sugars are fermented, and the beer is consequently full, mellow, and rich.

Löwenbräu Zurich, Zurich

Löwenbräu Zurich Export Lager

This Swiss lager is not related to the German Löwenbräu other than by name and type. Both are brewed independently of one another, as a short historical summary will show.

The history of Löwenbräu Zurich goes back to the last century. The brewery at Limmat Street in Zurich was founded at the end of the nineteenth century. *Aktienbrauerei Zurich* as it then was called, took up production in March, 1898. From the beginning *Aktienbrauerei Zurich* shared in the process of amalgamation of the Swiss breweries. The last brewery brought into the corporation, in 1925, gave its name to the *Aktienbrauerei* which henceforth was called "Löwenbräu Zurich AG."

After World War II Löwenbräu Zurich's export expanded considerably. Swiss beer was represented by Löwenbräu Zurich in many countries, especially overseas. In the fifties, when German breweries continually increased their exports, Löwenbräu Zurich was eliminated from several overseas markets, especially in Africa. Today's export markets are mainly Italy and the United States.

Löwenbräu Zurich is made from malt of French and German origin. Hops are from Germany, Yugoslavia, and the United States. Yeast is, of course, from a private strain, while the water comes from Swiss mountain springs. The brewing is conducted in the standard two-mash process and the beer aged from two to four months, depending on the type.

---

*For a fuller explanation of krausening, see page 195.

CULVER PICTURES

The Winter Garden of Tonhalle, Zurich, 1879.

The interesting thing about this label is that it is one of the very few bottled beers available unpasteurized. As a result of a secret filtration process, the brewery guarantees the beer to keep perfectly for a period of six months after bottling.

Löwenbräu Zurich has one of the strongest bouquets of all beers sampled. The body and flavor are also above average but the beer is extremely well balanced and satisfying. Highly recommended.

Sibra, Frenkendorf, Fribourg, Rheinfelden, Waedenswil

Cardinal, Feldschlossen Lager

Cardinal is Swiss beer brewed at five separate breweries. The five brewers joined together to strengthen their stance in the marketplace and have succeeded in establishing this label throughout the country. Cardinal does not suggest any particular geographical location within Switzerland and is also well known as a trademark for "Swiss beer" in Germany.

The five breweries of the Sibra group were all founded between 1788 and 1881, drawing upon a centuries-old tradition. (As early as the year 620, the monastery of St. Gall had a brewhouse.) Still bound by the Bavarian Purity Decree, these Swiss brewers use only barley, water, hops, and yeast.

Another fine Swiss beer, *Feldschlossen Lager* deserves greater recognition. Of medium light amber color, with a gentle, pleasing bouquet and medium body, this dry "mountain" beer is highly recommended.

THAILAND

Amarit Lager is perhaps the most famous beer of Southeast Asia. It is difficult to choose between this brew and Tiger of Malaya, but, in the export versions, I prefer this Thai beer. It is clear, light, and hoppy (perhaps too clear and too light for my taste). Worth looking for, especially fine with hot curries and other spicy food.

Singha Lager has the best-designed label of all beers sampled. Extolled by friends who lived in Bangkok for thirteen years, I'm afraid the export lager has little to offer. Of light body and mild bouquet, the flavor is tart, almost bitter, while the lasting aftertaste smacks of preservatives. (Retasting this beer at a temperature below the "ice-cold" level it was first served at in a restaurant definitely improved the tasting experience.)

UNITED STATES

Beer consumption is at present the highest in our history but the number of beer companies continues to decline. In 1880 most every sizeable town in the country had its own brewery—there were 2,272 in all. By 1963 there were 171; by 1973 only 64 companies remained. It appears as if the fierce competition (in the form of price-cutting on one hand, and the expenditure on the other of several hundred advertising dollars per barrel by at least one national brewer out to capture a local market), a narrow profit margin (the price of beer is about the same as it was in 1955), and the loss of taste discrimination of average Americans accounts for this decline in independent breweries.

Economics in fact seems to be the chief factor in the decline: the larger breweries are able to produce more beer at a lower price with fewer people. About 44 percent of the domestic market is controlled by three companies: Anheuser-Busch, Schlitz and Pabst. Coors, Schaefer and Miller, the next three largest producers account for only 15 percent of the market. However, these figures may be misleading. Coors, for example, could easily move into a higher position if its management chose to a) expand operations by constructing regional breweries, and b) lower the quality of Coors Beer, which as we have seen is about the best of the country's largest selling beers. Coors is in the number four position on a national basis, but it must be remembered that, while it has a limited availability in the East, it is only widely sold in several western states. There it absolutely dominates the market.

If quality were the sole factor in predicting which of the top six companies would survive the next few years of competition, Anheuser-Busch and Adolph Coors Company would be the winners. Both use only natural ingredients, shunning hop extracts, corn grits and other cheaper adjuncts and substitutes. Anheuser-Busch spends about 50 percent more on the production of each barrel than does its nearest competitor, Schlitz. Added costs result from larger ageing facilities and more personnel. Coors incurs even greater expense in using no additives whatever and producing the only major unpasteurized beer, which requires strict refrigeration on the part of wholesalers. Pasteurization kills all living organisms in foods, and it is reasonable to regard pasteurized food as somewhat deadened food. This makes Coors the only live major beer in America, and most likely one of the most nutritious.

Before proceeding to the beers themselves, a list of maximum alcoholic contents for fermented malt beverages, by state, follows. As you will note, the laws vary from state to state. This makes it difficult for brewers throughout the country and the world who send their beer into low alcohol states. Some change their formulations to meet the legal requirements; others change the name of their product to stout, ale, porter or malt liquor. The brew may still be beer, but since the law regarding alcoholic content applies only to beer, the name change gets the product around the law.

This is one reason why some of your favorite beers may not taste the same from place to place. Other reasons are the water used in brewing, storage time, and many other factors outlined in the chapter on brewing.

STATE	MAXIMUM ALCOHOLIC CONTENT
Alabama	4% by weight
Alaska	minimum 1% by volume
Arizona	no limit
Arkansas	5% by weight
California	4% by weight
Colorado	3.2% in dry regions
Connecticut	no limit
Delaware	no limit
District of Columbia	no limit
Florida	3.2% in dry regions
Georgia	6% by volume
Hawaii	no limit
Idaho	4% by weight
Illinois	local regions may limit to 4% by weight
Indiana	no limit
Iowa	4% by weight
Kansas	3.2% by weight; higher in packages

STATE	MAXIMUM ALCOHOLIC CONTENT
Kentucky	no limit, but local regions may limit to 3.2% by weight
Louisiana	6% by volume; dry regions 3.2% by weight
Maine	no limit
Maryland	no limit; Hartford County, 6% by volume
Massachusetts	12% by weight
Michigan	no limit
Minnesota	3.2% by weight
Mississippi	4% by weight
Missouri	3.2% by weight
Montana	4% by weight
Nebraska	no limit
Nevada	no limit
New Hampshire	6% by volume; higher at state outlets
New Jersey	no limit
New Mexico	no limit
New York	no limit
North Carolina	5% by weight
North Dakota	no limit
Ohio	3.2% by weight; to 7% through special license
Oklahoma	3.2% by weight; higher in packages
Oregon	4% by weight; 8% for other malt beverages
Pennsylvania	no limit
Rhode Island	no limit
South Carolina	5% by weight
South Dakota	3.2% by weight; 6% by weight for "high point"
Tennessee	5% by weight; higher by license
Texas	4% by weight; higher by license
Utah	3.2% by weight; higher in state outlets
Vermont	6% by volume; higher in state outlets
Virginia	3.2% in dry regions
Washington	4% by weight; higher in state outlets
West Virginia	3.2% by weight
Wisconsin	5% by weight; higher by license
Wyoming	no limit

A look at some American breweries and their products follows. The list is arranged alphabetically by name of *brewery*. "Capacity" refers to the number of barrels of beer, and one barrel equals thirty-one gallons. In 1973 the United States produced 132 million barrels compared to 76.7 million barrels in Germany, the closest nation in quantitative production.

Anheuser-Busch, St. Louis, Missouri

Budweiser, Busch Bavarian and Michelob

The world's largest brewer (26.6 million barrels, all plants), has not cut costs by reducing quality in several key areas of production. While rice is used as an adjunct, pure hops (not the extract), natural carbonation through krausening, and "beechwood chip ageing"—a relatively lengthy process (at least one month), make Budweiser a genuinely well-brewed beer, equal if not superior to many costlier imports.

Budweiser is made from Western two-row barley which is more expensive than the common Midwest six-row variety (which is the brewing standard in America). As you know, rice is used as an adjunct. Imported hops from Central Europe are combined with high quality domestic blossoms from the western United States. Hop extracts are never used, according to sources at Anheuser-Busch.

Instead of using the "quick" method of artificially injecting carbon dioxide, a second fermentation is conducted under pressure. Krausening, as we have learned, supersaturates the beer with natural carbonation.

The Anheuser-Busch Clydesdales.

Budweiser's second fermentation is staged in special lagering tanks, which contain a dense lattice of natural beechwood strips. These strips offer extra surface area for yeast particles to cling to, helping to clarify the beer and absorb its natural bitterness. This beechwood ageing process is followed by filtration and pasteurization. The rest is history.

Budweiser is one of the lightest colored beers. It reminds me of some German "blonde" beers, notably Wurzburger, but exhibits a flavorful hoppiness that is distinct. Of average head-lasting properties, with a light bouquet; the good, dry flavor and fine aftertaste give this beer a substantial rating in this taster's book.

Slightly different in taste from Budweiser, *Busch Bavarian* is made with corn grits as an adjunct, and a variety of hops from Germany, Yugoslavia and the United States.

Busch is brewed like Budweiser, with secondary fermentation to provide natural carbonation.

First introduced in 1955 in the Midwest Busch is now distributed in almost half the states in the country, with its greatest strength in the South, the Midwest and California. Despite its limited distribution Busch is the largest selling beer in Florida.

Michelob was introduced as a high-cost draught beer in 1896. Originally a high-malt beer, it did not need supplemental grains such as corn or rice to produce its malty flavor. Recently, however, rice has been added to the brewing process, to lighten the flavor to American tastes and perhaps to lower costs. Nevertheless, Michelob is made with the choicest ingredients. Hops are all imported from Germany, Czechoslovakia and Yugoslavia ("hops . . . that the soil and climate of America cannot produce.") It is brewed just like Budweiser except for the use of a special mashing process in the brewhouse.

In 1961 Michelob in bottles was placed on the market for individuals, hotels, clubs, and restaurants without draught beer facilities. While bottled and canned Michelob is a well-brewed beer it is still not as lively as the original draught formula, which is kegged in an unpasteurized form. In fact, Michelob is possibly the best draught beer produced in the United States.

Adolph Coors, Golden, Colorado

Coors Beer

While other major brewers have breweries scattered around the country, the Coors plant in Golden, Colorado, is the largest single beer-production facility in the world (6.2 million barrels per year). An article in *Time* magazine (February 11, 1974) gives good insight into this independent, family-

Bock beer procession in St. Louis at the turn of the century.

owned company, which leads not only the beer industry (in quality on a massive scale) but industry in general in pollution control. If a pilot program develops as anticipated, Coors may soon be using Denver's refuse to provide all the fuel necessary for the brewery.

As for the beer itself, it is a very light, very mild lager, noted for its purity.

A letter from W. K. Coors, the company president, will best describe the conditions under which it is produced.

Coors beer is made principally from our own proprietary variety of brewing barley which we call Moravian. Approximately 2,000 growers in the states of Colorado, Wyoming and Idaho grow this barley under contract to us from our seed. If it meets our specifications, we then buy it and of course malt it ourselves. Our other ingredients are rice and hops. For rice we use a short-grained variety grown in the San Joaquin and Sacramento Valley of California. We find this rice to be superior to all other varieties for brewing purposes, and, of course, we pay a considerable premium for it. We buy our hops for their flavoring rather than their bittering value and as a consequence are committed to the extremely fragrant European variety of hops. For many years, we have been committed to importing these hops from Germany, but recently, varieties of equal quality have been developed in the United States of America, and we are beginning to convert our usage to these.

We brew along traditional continental European lines taking no shortcuts and using *absolutely no additives* in our processing. Our water, incidentally, is a spring water which we call pure Rocky Mountain spring water, and we use it exactly as it comes from the ground—again, with *no corrective salts* added whatsoever.

Because we recognize that any beer will deteriorate in flavor from the time it is placed into the package and that this deterioration will accelerate with temperature, our marketing philosophies are aimed at minimizing both the time and the temperature that our beer is in the distribution pipeline before reaching the consumer. Our beer is *packaged cold* under aseptic conditions so that we *do not have to pasteurize it*. It is shipped to the marketplace, which incidentally averages about 1,000 miles away from our brewery, in either insulated or refrigerated transportation equipment. Our distributors are required to refrigerate the beer that they hold in their warehouses and deliver to the retailers with refrigerated trucks. Approximately 80 per cent of our retailers cooperate with our refrigerated marketing concept and receive delivery of our beer right into their cold boxes. Consequently, when the customer buys the beer, it is about as fresh as is possible to achieve.

In closing, I can assure you that we leave no stone unturned in making our beer the finest beer that is possible to brew and in getting it to our valued customers in that condition. As to raw materials and processing, I believe we can say without qualification that Coors beer is the most expensive beer brewed anywhere.

W. K. Coors

Falls City Brewing Company, Louisville, Kentucky

Falls City Beer, Drummond Bros. Preferred

One of the few independent regional breweries left in the United States, Falls City is the only home-owned brewery in Kentucky. Louisville, located around the only large waterfall between Pittsburgh and New Orleans, was originally called "the City at the Falls," then "Falls City." Finally, in 1780 the city was renamed in honor of King Louis XVI. The brewery prefers the original name for the city.

The brewery was organized in 1905 by local tavern owners anxious to capitalize on a growing beer-drinking market. Some nineteen months later, at its present site, 3050 West Broadway, the first draught beer was ready for delivery to the Louisville taverns. Horse-drawn wagons carried the huge wooden barrels to thriving taverns throughout the city.

A bottle shop was begun in 1907 and the first bottled beer in Louisville was soon marketed in Louisville. Within a short while Falls City bottled beer was shipped across the Ohio River to cities in southern Indiana.

The brewing industry was blacked out from 1919 to 1933 and, like many others in the business, this brewery produced a complete line of soft drinks and a near beer. When Prohibition was repealed, the company made a strong comeback and established itself as a regional brewery. The company has grown so much that *Falls City Beer* is now well known in the southeastern United States. Currently its market includes the seven states of Kentucky, Indiana, Tennessee, West Virginia, southwestern Virginia, Ohio and Illinois. Yearly production of the brewery is 900,000 barrels.

In 1972 the brewery introduced a new label, *Drummond Bros. Preferred*. It is lighter in color and body and milder in flavor than Falls City Beer and quite undifferentiated from numerous other beers on the market; but it seems to enjoy a certain popularity among younger drinkers. This label does have the distinction of being among the first to utilize a new tab-top can. The top pops up, pushes down on the can and stays put. The ring is not thrown out on lawns and roadways, or available for littering in so many other ways. Since Drummond Bros. is as good as many other light American beers, I'd say their concern for the environment earns the brewery the right to declare it a "taster's choice."

Genesee Brewing Company, Rochester, New York

Genesee Lager Beer, Fyfe & Drum Beer, Genesee Cream Ale

The following brewing story exemplifies some details of commercial brewing not yet described. Of special interest is the description of the *krau-*

Delivering growlers, or pitchers, of beer and ale on a Saturday night; an engraving by W. P. Snyder.

sening process, in which carbon dioxide gas is made to form naturally, and the pointers on the effects of sunlight and air on the qualities of beer.

THE PRODUCTION OF GENESEE BEER (1.8 MILLIONS BARRELS PER YEAR)

Malt Mill: This mill cracks the kernels of the barley malt just enough not to damage the husk, but enough to permit the starch in the malt to be available for proper utilization in the brewing. These husks form the filter bed needed in the lauter-tub operation after the brewing mash is converted into wort. Genesee uses only light costly barley in the production, in its own malt house, of quality-controlled malt. It is this light and superior malt which accounts for Genesee's pale golden color, smooth flavor, and the constant and complete uniformity of the end product. And Genesee remains one of the few breweries in America today which does make its own malt.

Adjuncts. Powder-fine and oil-free corn grits comprise the only adjunct used in the brewing of Genesee Lager Beer. This select corn has already been milled before it is delivered to the Genesee Brewery. These completely pure cornstarch grits are used to provide the starch needed to increase its ratio over proteins, thus making the beer even lighter in color, smoother in taste, and more pleasing to the palate. The starch in the malt and the corn undergoes enzymatic conversion to sugar in the course of the brewing process.

Water Purifying System. The Genesee Brewery has the most thorough and elaborate water-purifying system ever devised. Even though its source of water is spring-fed Hemlock Lake Reservoir, Genesee runs the water first through sand and gravel filters, and finally through extensive charcoal filters.

Cereal Cooker. Pure corn grits weighed, along with a small quantity of malt, is placed in the cereal cooker, with enough warmed brewing water to make the desired consistency of cereal mash. This mash is heated in controlled patterns and is ultimately boiled for approximately fifteen to twenty minutes—long enough to rupture the cell structure of the starches to begin their enzymatic conversion into fermentable sugars.

Mash Tub. Most of the malt (the balance of the measured batch) is run into the mash tub along with the product of the cereal cooker, and additional heated brewing water. This mashing lasts from forty-five minutes to one hour, and includes variously timed temperature stages to complete the conversion of all the enzymes into fermentable sugars. The protein from the grain is made more soluble in this way.

Lauter Tub. The purpose of the lauter tub is to leach out or extract all the goodness and the desired properties from the grain and produce what is known as wort. This process continues for another forty-five minutes to an hour, and during this process the liquid wort is separated from the grain husks. The grain is agitated, and fixed nozzles within the tub rain heated brewing water on the mash.

Pre-Prohibition Breweriana Advertising

THE TRAYS, ADS AND CARDS ON THIS AND

THE FOLLOWING PAGES ARE FROM

THE COLLECTION OF MR. JOHN A. MURRAY,

PAST PRESIDENT OF THE NATIONAL

ASSOCIATION BREWERIANA ADVERTISING.

A TROLLEY RIDE IN MILWAUKEE.

FRANZ FALK BREWING CO'S
Milwaukee
EXPORT BEER

OVER

M. BECK BRG Co BUFFALO N.Y.

1899

FRANZ FALK BREWING CO'S
MILWAUKEE
EXPORT BEER

OVER

"Rainier" BEER

"THERE'S NEW VIGOR AND
STRENGTH IN EVERY DROP"

With Compliments of ANHEUSER-BUSCH Brew'g Ass'n.

HIGH LIFE ON MILWAUKEE BAY.

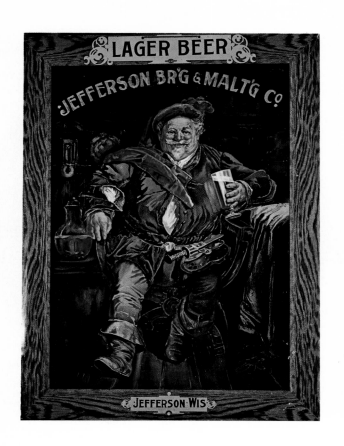

Grain Dryer. Spent grains are dried prior to being sold to farmers as protein-rich cattle feed.

Brew Kettle. The wort is boiled in the brew kettle for approximately three hours which stops the enzymatic conversion of starches into sugars and clarifies the wort, in addition to assuring that all the microscopic flavor-producing enzymes are in complete suspension throughout the wort. (As with milk, most of the ingredients of beer are in delicate balance rather than in solution. That's an important distinction in such matters as shelf life and stock rotation. Bottled or canned pasteurized beer should be consumed within two months and draught unpasteurized within one week after it leaves the brewery to be at its flavorful best.) Throughout the brew-kettle operation varying types of the most expensive and choice hops are added, in measured quantities and at specified times, to impart the needed bouquet, aroma and flavor to the final product.

Wort Coolers. The wort leaves the brew kettle at approximately 200°F., and it is cooled here to approximately 45°F. before entering the fermenting tanks.

Yeast Room. To avoid contamination this room is always off-limits except to those technicians directly involved in the growing or using of the yeast. Genesee carefully grows and guards its own uniform yeast, because the yeast strain is one of the main reasons for the distinctive flavor of the company's beer. In fact, the original yeast strain which Genesee uses was imported from Germany. The brewer's yeast, then, begins its growth as a single cell in the Genesee laboratory where these yeast cells have been taken from the original parent yeast cells. The new yeast is developed in the yeast room at 45°F.

Fermenting Tanks. So that the beer will have and maintain its uniform flavor, aroma and bouquet, it is often blended throughout the brewing process. For example, several fermenting tanks are filled from the brew kettle, so that each fermenting tank contains several brews or batches of wort from the kettle. Genesee's "bottom" lager yeast is added to the blended wort, to convert the sugars into alcohol, and to change the wort into beer. Fermentation is continued for approximately ten days at 45°F. (Ale yeast is top yeast, and is fermented for approximately ten days at 50°F. To avoid any possibility of ale yeast blending into the beer yeast or vice versa, Genesee Cream Ale is fermented and lagered in a separate building, the Cataract Brewery. Although this is an ideal arrangement, few brewers are willing to expend the money for these separated operations though aware that they produce a superior and distinctive product.) At the end of fermentation cycle the beer yeast settles to the bottom of the fermenting tank, and the freshly made beer moves into the lagering tanks.

Sunlight, Air and CO_2 Gas. Direct sunlight cannot be permitted to come in contact with beer at any stage of its development. Bottled beer will spoil if exposed to direct sunlight, though the bottle may be made of the customary dark brown glass to protect it from light. Almost everyone

1874 National Brewers' Congress at Horticultural Hall, Boston, Massachusetts; sketched by E. R. Morse.

who has ever enjoyed a glass of beer is aware of this but few people understand the importance of eliminating air from direct contact with the beer after fermentation. Yeast cells, of course, need oxygen to thrive, develop and grow, and it is the yeast germinating and multiplying which produces alcohol and CO_2 gas during the process of fermentation. However, once the beer enters the lagering tanks, which are located in the refrigerated ageing cellars, no air is ever permitted to come in contact with the product. Beer is of so delicate a nature that substantial exposure to air destroys its flavor. It is advisable to bear in mind that beer is a perishable food product containing some small amount of alcohol. Except when the lagering tanks are being thoroughly cleaned and sterilized after each use, no air ever enters them. After cleaning, they are filled with CO_2 gas. As the fresh new beer is run into the tanks, it displaces enough gas to permit its own entry. From that point forward these tanks and all other receptacles used in production contain beer and measured and controlled amounts of CO_2 gas . . . and nothing else.

Lagering Tanks. The beer is blended again to maintain uniformity as it passes from the fermenting tanks into the lagering tanks, and the brew is cooled at 34°F. in the lagering or ageing process. It is in these huge glass-lined tanks, which are located in the refrigerated ageing cellars, that Genesee beer clarifies and rounds out into its full body and smooth flavor.

Lagering tanks are large vessels. (Genesee has some new tanks that hold some 9,000 barrels of product.) The lagering process continues for a period of twenty to thirty days.

Krausening. During the long lagering process CO_2 gas escapes from the beer, creating a flat beer, or one which is almost devoid of the needed CO_2 gas. It is imperative to restore the pure CO_2 gas to bring back the flavor and sparkle which are necessary characteristics of a fine beer. There is only one natural thorough way to assure that the CO_2 gas permeates every segment uniformly, and that method is known as "krausening." It is an expensive, time-consuming process and not all national breweries krausen their beer. The principle of krausening can be quickly and easily explained. Near the end of the lagering period, fresh, new beer, approximately twelve to twenty-four hours old, is added to the lagered beer in amounts averaging 20 percent of the total gallonage in the tank. This new beer causes that already in the lagering tank to rework, creating new CO_2 gas in small amounts throughout the brew. This additional CO_2 pressure is controlled in the lagering tanks at 5 pounds pressure (and at 34°F.) through the use of tank pressure gauges and valves. The final product maintains CO_2 gas in the amount of 2.6 volume within the beer, which approximates 12 pounds of CO_2 pressure when the beer is served and consumed sometime later at 38°F. to 40°F. The identical CO_2 volume and pressure is used in all Genesee beer packages, whether it be draught, bottled or canned. In the finished product Genesee Lager Beer has an alcoholic content which approximates 3.5 percent by weight or 4.6 percent by volume. Higher alcoholic content could destroy the smoothness and drinkability of the beer, as well as limit the quantities which could be safely consumed.

First Filtration. From the lagering tanks, several fully matured beers are blended, and filtered through the newest and most effective diatomaceous filters at 34°F., to remove any separated materials. Some small additional amounts of natural CO_2 gas are supplied in this process, as a final assurance that the gas within the beer is up to exact and uniform standards.

Final Polishing. The beer is finally filtered through a second and very fine diatomaceous filter, this time at 31°F., to make it clear, to make it sparkle, and to give the product longer shelf life. There are no preservatives, chemicals or minerals used in the brewing of Genesee beer.

Pasteurizer. All bottles and cans are pasteurized at controlled temperatures and for a controlled period of time. The pasteurization process holds the beer at 140°F for fifteen minutes. Pasteurization, of course, is the only completely successful method discovered to date which permits bottled and canned beer to be stored at room temperatures for two months without spoiling. Even the recently developed metal micropore filters, which are used in the filtering of the so-called draught beer in bottles and cans, have not been successful in replacing pasteurization, because that type of filter does not always adequately protect the beer from spoiling.

Draught Racking Machine. In this operation the barrels are filled with natural, unpasteurized draught beer, after which the bung is driven into the keg, sealing up only brewery-fresh beer and CO_2 gas. As draught beer is unpasteurized, it has limited storage life and must be kept at 38°F. to 40°F. until it reaches the consumer.

Theodore Hamm Company, St. Paul, Minnesota

Hamm's, Hamm's Preferred Stock, Waldech

The Hamm's breweries began in 1865 within a small grain mill. At present, in addition to the St. Paul plant, breweries are operated in San Francisco and Los Angeles.

Hamm's Beer is made of malt blended from six-row and two-row barleys. Corn grits are added to lighten the flavor and body. Hops are a blend of domestic and imported varieties. Yeast is of Hamm's own culture and the water is "born in the land of sky blue waters."

The barley is malted in Hamm's own malt house, the beer brewed, aged, filtered and carbonated.

Hamm's Preferred Stock was originally produced in the late 1930's. It has recently been revived and the beer is brewed using the same formula and with the same care that was typical of the brewer of that time.

Malt is made from six-row and two-row barleys, with rice as an adjunct. Domestic hops are from Yakima Valley in Washington, imported hops from Hallertau in Germany. This blend produces a distinct, nonlingering bitterness with a fine hop aroma. The resultant lager is slightly darker than Hamm's Beer, highly sparkling and has a creamy white head.

Waldech is an example of a domestic beer that is easily as good as many imported lager beers, when they are made for export. Waldech is made from expensive two-row barley, Hallertau hops, and Hamm's own yeast, which originated with a culture started in 1865. The barley is malted by the brewer. No cereal adjuncts are added. Waldech is aged for several months and krausened for natural carbonation. A fine-bodied beer. Pleasant aftertaste.

This brand was only recently developed, in an attempt to produce an "Old World" beer in America. The name Waldech is derived from the name of the ancestral home of the brewmaster at that time. Waldech is a hamlet in the picturesque Hesse-Spa province of northern Germany.

The total annual production of all plants is 2.5 million barrels.

Jacob Leinenkugel Brewing Company, Chippewa Falls, Wisconsin

Leinenkugel's Beer, Chippewa Pride

One of the very few old American breweries to have survived the past ten years of cutthroat competition, Leinenkugel is the kind of brewery that respects *local* competition. According to Bill Leinenkugel, the great-, great-grandson of the 1845 founder, "small breweries make for good competition —the kind that results in better beer, not just more of it."

Leinenkugel's is a fine example of the fewer than twenty-five small breweries left in the United States. According to Master Brewer John Cooney, there is no secret to his beer. To him, the ingredients determine the end product. To make *Leinenkugel's* and *Chippewa Pride*, barley malt is augmented by corn grits, then by domestic hops from Yakima Valley, a private strain of yeast and Chippewa spring water. That's it.

Over 75,000 barrels are produced yearly at the brewery, most of it consumed in Indianhead country of Northwest Wisconsin and the Twin Cities area of Minnesota.

Leinenkugel's is a typical American grain-malt beer. It has a very mild bouquet, body and flavor. Of average flavor intensity with little aftertaste, it is certainly equal, if not superior to many "major" lagers presently brewed in the United States.

Olympia Brewing Company, Olympia, Washington

Olympia Beer

This pilsen-type lager from Tumwater, Washington, is made from a blend of two and six-row varieties of barley, with added corn and grits and Sacramento Valley rice. Hops are grown in Oregon, Idaho and California, while the yeast is a strain of *Saccharomyces Carlsbergensis*. The fresh, clean waters are enhanced by brewers who use no artificial coloring or chemicals, only natural products.

It takes approximately ninety days from the beginning of the brewing process until Olympia Beer is packaged for the market. "Oly" is carbonated by krausening, rather than by artificial forcing of CO_2 gas.

The history of the Olympia Brewing Company, which now produces 3.4 million barrels annually, gives a typical picture of the problems experienced by many large American breweries in their development from small, family-owned enterprises.

HISTORY

It was while visiting the construction site of the new capital building at Olympia in 1895 as a member of the Montana State capitol commission that Leopold F. Schmidt first heard of an artesian spring, just outside of Olympia, Washington, near Tumwater Falls. Intrigued by what he had been told, Mr. Schmidt, a brewmaster by profession, visited the spot that had been described to him and tasted the cold, clear water that rushed to the surface. His brewing knowledge led him to believe that this was, indeed, a unique water, one equal to the famous brewing waters of Europe.

Not relying solely on his own judgement, Mr. Schmidt filled two

Hops in the Yakima Valley, Washington.

demijohns with the pure artesian water and sent them east for analysis. The lab report from the Wahl-Henius Institute confirmed his original taste test of the water he had discovered at Tumwater . . . it was one of the few naturally perfect brewing waters to be found in the world.

Immediately, he negotiated to purchase the land on which the artesian springs were located with the owner of the Biles and Carter Tannery. He acquired the land for $4,500 and also obtained the rights to the lower Tumwater Falls, as he knew that he would eventually need a power source for his planned brewery.

Secure with the knowledge that he now owned the rare artesian spring, Leopold Schmidt returned to Montana to dispose of his interest in the Centennial Brewing Company at Butte, Montana. . . . [He] returned to Tumwater . . . [and] though it was the middle of winter, the worst time of the year to start a brewery, Mr. Schmidt began construction at once. It was to be a small brewery as there was no reliable way of knowing how much water could be obtained from the small artesian spring.

The first structure to be built at the sight was a carpenter shop. This was to form the nucleus from which the Capital Brewing Company would rise.

Under the supervision of Louie Schmidt, the tiny brewery took shape. Leopold Schmidt purchased the company's first copper brew kettle and refrigeration equipment from Chicago, where they were once displayed at the world's fair as part of a model brewery exhibit. Brewing commenced at the tiny Tumwater brewery in July of 1896.

The first beer, Olympia Pale Export, was syphoned by hand from wooden barrels, bottled and placed on the market October 1, 1896. . . .

The popularity of the beer was instantaneous and within the first three months of operation, 3,500 barrels of Olympia Pale Export were sold.

Though the company was but a couple of months old, Leopold Schmidt knew that if the beer was to be shipped any great distance at all and maintain its quality, he would have to find a better method of pasteurization to stop the yeast action. The standard cork closure did not allow for this, and therefore, Olympia became the first coastal brewery to adopt the metal cap method of bottle sealing, which made the pasteurization of bottled beer as we know it today possible. . . .

Gold had been discovered at the Klondike River in the Yukon, and prospectors by the tens of thousands trekked north to seek their fortunes. Olympia's gold, a liquid gold, went with them, and this new market, along with a growing popularity of Olympia Beer in its established markets, created the need for further physical expansion of the small Tumwater brewery. Cellars were once again enlarged, new refrigeration machines, engine room, and boilers were added to the plant. . . .

In 1902, the company adopted its own famous slogan, "It's the Water," and a few months later the company was legally changed from Capital to Olympia Brewing Company, so that it more closely identified with the beer from Tumwater that had gained popularity throughout the West. During the same year, more cellars were added to the growing, young company.

The exorbitant cost of freight and the exceedingly long time that it took to ship beer to its destination created problems for the brewery. The natural solution for these burdensome problems was to lessen the distance between the producer and the consumer; this meant building more breweries at central locations. . . .

At each of these four [new] plants, the same hops and barley, the same cereal adjuncts of corn and rice, the same yeast strain, and identical equipment employed by the Olympia Brewing Company were used. Even the brewmasters, who spent many long, uncomfortable hours traveling among the various plant locations, were common to each of the breweries. Yet, they could not produce a beer comparable to that brewed at Tumwater. They could not duplicate Olympia Beer at any of these other locations. The only logical difference was the water; they did not have the rare artesian brewing water that had been discovered by Leopold Schmidt at Tumwater, and consequently, none of the beer produced at the four other locations was ever packaged under the label, Olympia Beer.

In 1906, a new brewhouse was constructed at the site of the original brewery. This, the second brewhouse of the Olympia Brewing Company, still stands today a scant 100 yards or so north of the firm's present location. . . .

In 1914 the states of Washington, Oregon, and Idaho voted dry. The Olympia Brewing Company was given one year to sell its inventory and close up. This grim task of phasing out the company was given to Peter G. Schmidt, who had been elected president following his father's death.

On January 1, 1916, the noble experiment began. The Olympia Brewing Company and the other four breweries—Bellingham Bay, Port Townsend, Acme, and Salem—ceased to operate as breweries. However, in anticipation of the paralyzing effect the 18th Amendment would have on the brewing industry, the Salem brewery had been converted to produce carbonated fruit drinks one year prior to the actual enactment of Prohibition. The plant at Tumwater immediately began producing a drink called Applju. This drink and the Loju produced at the Salem plant were actually the forerunners of today's soda pop and years ahead of their time. . . . But the skyrocketing sugar prices caused by bootleggers and poor economic conditions in the country soon put an end to the fruit drink business.

In October of 1921, the company's 25th anniversary, the last four employees closed and locked the gates across both entrances to the plant, left the night watchman there, and that was it. The Olympia Brewing Company had passed into history. . . .

With the repeal of the 18th Amendment in 1933, renewed life sprang into the community of Tumwater when Peter and Adolph thought it best to open just one plant—the one where the water was—at Tumwater.

However, the cost of reopening the brewery at Tumwater was impossible unless the Schmidt family could get public financial support, and they turned to their friends for help. Times were tough, people still felt the pangs of the stock market crash of 1929. Nonetheless, the response to the stock offer at $1.00 per share was overwhelming.

Immediately, construction began of a modern, $300,000 brewery at a site just south of where the brewery had been operating prior to Prohibition. It was hoped that the new brewery might be in operation within 100 days after the initial ground breaking. Construction crews were doubled from 40 to 80 men, but it still took 150 days to put the new plant into full operation. . . .

The steady growth which the company had known before Prohibition quickly resumed. During the first six years of operation following Repeal, 12 cellars were built and put into operation. The brewhouse capacity was increased with the addition of a second brew kettle, lauter tub, and cooler. The famous "stubbie" bottle was developed and introduced to the public in 1936. This superior bottle with its extra-wide shoulder, short neck, and thinner, but stronger, walls, soon became an industry standard in much of the country.

With our country's entrance into World World II, necessary restrictions were placed on the raw materials needed for the brewing of Olympia Beer. Rather than compromise quality, the firm withdrew Olympia Beer from all sales markets in California, Montana, Nevada, Hawaii, and eastern Idaho. This voluntary decision for the sake of quality brought the rapid growth of the firm to a sudden halt.

Following the end of World War II in 1945 and the removal of the restrictive limitations that had been placed on materials and supplies, the company assumed a course of steady growth. . . .

Henry F. Ortlieb Brewing Company, Philadelphia, Pennsylvania

Ortlieb's Beer, Neuweiler's Cream Ale

HISTORY

Now in its fourth generation of family ownership and management, the Ortlieb Brewing Co. was originally founded in 1869 by Trupert Ortlieb, a Civil War veteran. In the early days Ortlieb's small annual capacity of 3,000 barrels was sold exclusively to an adjoining tavern. The tavern still stands on its original site at American and Poplar Streets but around it has grown a modern brewery which produces 600,000 barrels of beer and ale annually.

Ortlieb's Beer is brewed with select six-row and two-row barley malt along with other choice cereal grains. All hops are personally selected by the Ortlieb family at Western hop ranches. Only the purest of water and only that water which meets the desired mineral requirements (laid down by stringent brewing guidelines and quality-control parameters throughout the years) is used in the brewing of Ortlieb's lager.

Wort is slowly fermented under controlled temperatures and environment by a special strain of bottom fermentation yeast. The young fer-

CULVER PICTURES

The boss beer-jerker in 1880 was a girl from Cincinnati who could carry sixteen glasses of lager at one time.

mented beer is then stored in refrigerated cellars for clarification and maturing—all Ortlieb beer is "sealed processed." Seal processing means that none of the beer is exposed to air during the entire brewing cycle— i.e., all beer is processed in closed vats in order to avoid air contamination.

Neuweiler Ale is brewed with a large proportion of choice six and two-row barley malt—very little cereal adjuncts being used in the production of this ale. Imported Bavarian hops along with specially treated water of the purest quality (similar to the water at Burton-on-Trent) is used to "brew in" the unique flavor characteristics of Neuweiler's.

A special top fermenting yeast (*Saccharomyces Cerevisiae*) of Canadian origin is pitched into the fermenting wort where it is fermented at elevated temperatures. Every drop of Neuweiler's ale is "hand skimmed" (to relieve it of astringent bitterness) before it is transferred to primary storage for maturation. In primary storage the ale is dry-hopped with specially selected imported hops for a period of five to six weeks, after which it is cellared at cool temperatures for additional maturing and clarification. The extended maturation time (two months), along with special fermentation and cellaring techniques, all contribute to a unique, special ale.

Pabst Brewing Company, Milwaukee, Wisconsin

Pabst Blue Ribbon, Andeker

The 130-year-old company that today produces 5.2 million barrels a year and is known as the Pabst Brewing Company was founded in Milwaukee in 1844, four years before Wisconsin became a state. A German immigrant, Jacob Best and his four sons, Jacob, Jr., Charles, Phillip and Lorenz, started the firm and called it, naturally enough, the Best Brewing Company.

In 1862, a Great Lakes steamer captain, Frederick Pabst, married Phillip Best's daughter Maria, an event which would ultimately make him one of the most important figures in United States brewing history.

Historians disagree whether it was ill-fortune on the Lakes or the urging of his father-in-law that caused Captain Pabst to give up his interests in shipping, but in 1864, he became Phillip's partner in the brewery. Within two years, his father-in-law retired, selling the brewery to Pabst and another son-in-law, Emil Schandein.

The captain immediately became the dominant partner and it was his influence and ideas more than any other single factor that charted the brewery's course for the next forty years.

By 1873, he had decided that it was no longer financially feasible to operate the brewery as a family business if it were to realize its full potential, and in that year, the company was incorporated as the Best Brewing Company.

During the next twenty years, under Captain Pabst's leadership, the

A beerhall in Milwaukee, 1873.

company took part in, and often led, a revolution in the brewing industry. This revolution was the changing of the brewing business from a local and regional operation, using methods handed down from generation to generation, to a national organization, using new and scientific methods of brewing and shipping beer. In 1879, in recognition of the captain's leadership, the stockholders voted to change the name of the company to the Pabst Brewing Company.

The culmination of the Pabst efforts came in 1893 when Pabst beer was selected "America's best" in international competition held at the Columbian Exposition in Chicago. Two years later, Pabst became the largest brewer in the United States, selling between 900,000 and 1,000,000 barrels of beer a year.

The captain died January 1, 1904 and management of the brewery passed to his sons, Fred, Jr., and Gustav.

When Prohibition was put into effect, Pabst joined other brewers in finding other products which they could distribute through their existing marketing organization.

As Prohibition was drawing to a close, Pabst completed a merger with the Premier Malt Products Company of Peoria, Illinois. Harris Perlstein, president of Premier, was made president of Pabst and when the breweries resumed production, Perlstein led Pabst back into the dominant position that it had held prior to Prohibition.

In 1934, Pabst acquired a plant in Peoria Heights, Illinois, and pioneered the brewing of the same beer in separate locations. In 1945, the company expanded further by opening a third brewing facility in Newark,

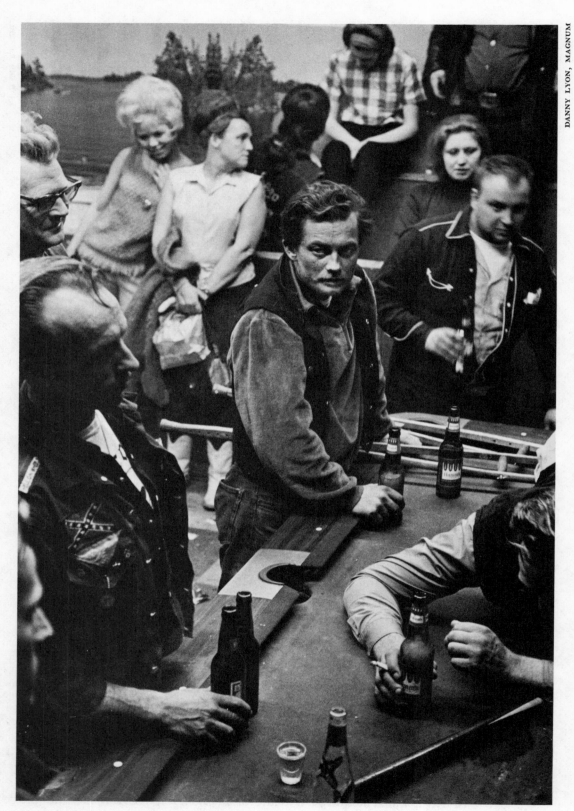

DANNY LYON, MAGNUM

Motorcyclists slaking their thirst,
Cicero, Illinois.

New Jersey, and in 1948, the company added a fourth brewery by purchasing the Los Angeles Brewing Company in Los Angeles, California.

In 1958, the directors and shareholders of Pabst voted to purchase another Milwaukee brewery, the Blatz Brewing Company. James C. Windham, who was president of Blatz at the time, was made president and chief executive officer of Pabst. In 1972, Windham was elected chairman and president of the corporation. Today Windham is chairman and chief executive officer, while Drank C. DeGuire took over the president's position in April of 1973.

At the time Windham assumed leadership of the company, Pabst sales had been declining and the company ranked thirteenth in sales in the brewing industry. A few years after Windham's becoming president, Pabst became the third largest brewer in the nation. The production and sales of Pabst beer jumped from 1.9 million barrels in 1960 to 12.6 million barrels in 1972. A major factor in the company's success is the quality and acceptability of Pabst brands with the beer drinkers.

Like Hamm's Waldech, *Andeker Beer* is another entry by an American brewer into the burgeoning "continental beer" marketplace. Andeker on draught is an exceptionally rich, hoppy, lively pale beer, one that compares favorably with and even exceeds the quality of many imports. While corn adjuncts are used to lighten the flavor, only two-row barley is malted and the hops are all imported varieties.

A multistage double mash process is followed by warm storage and extended cold storage, then by conventional finishing cellar procedures. Andeker is then aged for over thirty days (the poorest beers, known in the trade as "7/7 beer" take less than two weeks to produce, from raw materials to packaged product).

Rheingold Breweries, Orange, New Jersey

Rheingold Lager Beer, Ruppert Knickerbocker Beer, Esslinger Beer, Gablinger's Beer

HISTORY

The founder of Rheingold had been a brewer at Ludwigsburg near Stuttgart, Germany, in 1848. S. Liebmann emigrated to Philadelphia in 1854, then moved to New York and with the aid of a malt and hop merchant, rented a brewery in Brooklyn. Within three weeks S. Liebmann and his young sons were brewing beer at that location.

From that time onward there came an increasing demand for their beer, until the Rheingold brewery ranked fifth or sixth in national output by 1950. Rheingold was unique in that 90 percent of its beer was sold within a radius of about ninety miles of the brewery in New York.

No history of Rheingold would be complete without a review and mention of the Beauty Contest for Miss Rheingold. This tradition of combining beauty and beer began in 1940 when the first Miss Rheingold was chosen. After 1940 the selection of Miss Rheingold was by public vote . . . ballot boxes placed in every outlet where the beer was sold . . . the public voting was for six final candidates among professional models by an election committee. The Miss Rheingold election, regional as it was, had the greatest public response of any advertising or merchandising campaign of its time. As an election it was second only to the United States' presidential election in total number of votes cast.

Another pioneering event by Rheingold took place in 1972. It was the production of a "natural beer" consisting of only brewer's malt; corn; domestic and imported hops; water and yeast. This was a radical departure from conventional brewing as practiced generally in the United States.

Ingredients. Malts from the United States, malted from two- and six-rowed barley varieties; brewers' corn grits from corn grown in the United States; United States hops, mainly cluster varieties grown in Washington, Idaho and Oregon; imported hops from Saaz and Hallertau regions, Bohemian and Bavarian sections respectively; blend of pure-culture pedigree

ARTHUR TRESS, PHOTO RESEARCHERS

Labor Day picnic in Staten Island, N.Y.

yeasts of Carlsberg origin, selected and nurtured in the brewery's laboratory; mountain water from Catskill and Appalachian ranges combined with Delaware system.

Brewing Process. Rheingold is brewed with a two-mash system, a batch method with a semiautomatic extraction process. The brewhouse or extraction operation may be either a mash-filter one, or a lauter-tub type, depending upon which of its two breweries produces the beer. Fermentation is by a blend of pure culture yeasts in the classical wooden vessels of mainly two-inch oak stave construction. Lagering or ageing takes place in glass-lined tanks.

Mild heat process (pasteurization) after packaging ensures stability in bottles and cans. Draft beer in kegs is kept refrigerated until it is consumed, eliminating the need for pasteurization.

Rheingold's particular flavor is derived from many sources. Chief among them is the process of fermentation and the yeast employed. Most brewers use yeast from a single strain but some employ two or three. Rheingold uses several strains of yeast in its blend because each strain produces its own individual flavor.

Few guzzlers realize that one of the best ales in the world is brewed by Rheingold. *McSorley's Ale,* served fresh from the tap at McSorley's Old Ale House in New York City, is tart, sharp, and highly aromatic. Fidelios Brewery used to make this ale but they were absorbed by Rheingold, who now carries the flag. Try it on a Saturday morning, when the alehouse is nice and quiet. Order two at one time, saving a few cents, and retire to the hot area around the potbellied stove. You'll see a few old-timers enjoying their ale, eating some corned beef and cabbage, or just drowsing. The shafts of light break up the smoke, creating a timelessness which lulls you into further drinking. You won't regret it. Ranks with the best.

August Schell Brewing Company, New Ulm, Minnesota

Schell's Beer

Schell's Beer is of the light Pilsener variety. It is a grain malt beer (corn and barley) composed of domestic hops, a private yeast strain going back 110 years, and fairly pure local water. The taste is reminiscent of several German light lagers, with a stronger flavor profile than the very light beers of the United States. Each year 40,000 barrels of Schell's are produced.

HISTORY

The story of this brewery is so touching and so honest just as provided by the president of the company, William A. Marti, that it is included with only minor deletions. After reading this, I suggest we request this brewing establishment be permanently protected as a national monument.

In 1860, August Schell, a young German immigrant, produced Schell's Lager Beer in his modest combination brewery and home. Located on the banks of the Cottonwood River, the new brewery produced two hundred barrels the first year. Good, cool spring-fresh water was obtained from newly dug wells on the property. The enterprising little project was not to progress uneventfully. The Schell family had always welcomed any curious Indians who came to look at their property. They were quick to offer their visitors food and good German hospitality. In 1862 the famous Sioux uprising forced August Schell and his family to seek safety in New Ulm, two miles away. When Chief Little Crow of the Sioux led another Indian attack, the small pioneering community of New Ulm suffered several weeks of pillage, burning and loss of human lives. Chief Little Crow was later tried and hanged at Fort Snelling, Minnesota, when he was found responsible for planning the New Ulm massacre.

After the New Ulm tragedy, August Schell and his family decided to return to their abandoned property even though they anticipated finding it in smouldering ruins. Instead, to their surprised delight, they discovered both the house and brewery intact and relatively undisturbed even though it was evident that the Indians had trailed through everything. The Indians had not forgotten the warm kindness of the friendly German Schell family and refused to harm their property even during an attack.

Through the years since the "Indian Days" Schell's Beer has been consistently maintained as an old world lager. What began as a word of mouth recommendation has progressed to an institution in this area of Minnesota. The beautiful Schell Gardens and Deer Park which adjoin the Schell home are one of New Ulm's show places. Each year tourists visit, to see the many rare and beautiful flowers and taste the beer. Hopefully, the brewery will be able to withstand the onslaught of national competition.

Steam Beer Brewing Company, San Francisco, California

Anchor Steam Beer, Anchor Porter

America's smallest brewery (5,000 barrels annually) has a link with the past that dates back to the days of the Gold Rush.

Anchor Steam Beer is 100 percent krausened. As the krausening occurs, pressure builds up inside the barrels. In the old days as the kegs of beer were set on the far side of a bar to settle for a few days they were bled of some of this pressure or steam hence the name—steam beer. Actually, many old-time beers were steam beers in the sense they were all naturally carbonated by krausening,

The Anchor Steam brewery was purchased a few years back by an energetic, knowledgeable, owner–brewmaster, Fritz Maytag, who has re-created a traditional American beer.

Anchor Steam is made from 100 percent barley malt; no rice or corn

*"The Fountain" beer vaults in San Francisco, 1879;
from a sketch by Walter Yeager.*

adjuncts are added. It is essentially a lager beer that is not artificially carbonated. Being 100 percent krausened, it is sharp and highly palatable. One of the hoppiest beers in the United States, this brand is characterized by a strong body and flavor, average bouquet, good color, and above-average dryness. Finishes well, with an inviting aftertaste. Highly recommended.

Anchor Porter is also an all-barley-malt, krausened beer. It is a solid, very dark beer with a meaty aroma, highly hopped, and a full-bodied, nut-like flavor. The aftertaste is tart. A well-crafted beer. Recommended.

Stevens Point Brewerey, Stevens Point, Wisconsin

Point Special Beer

Point Special, like Leinenkugel's, is local beer holding out against the giant national producers. This brewery is even smaller, and all the production (45,000 barrels per year) is consumed within a seventy-five-mile radius.

Originally known as the Ruder and Wahle Brewery, which originated in 1857, the Stevens Point Brewery is still located on Beer and Water Streets and the beer still made with the local water, which is quite pure. Ingredients include barley malt, corn grits and domestic hops.

The brewing process begins in a unique lauder-mash tun. The solution is filtered into a 185-barrel copper brew kettle and later to a stainless-steel hot-wort tank. After cooling to 50°F., it is pumped to the fermenting room where it is fermented in cypress and oak tanks for one week. After ageing for five weeks Point Special is packaged for its faithful local market.

A light beer, with a distinctive smell of hops. No aftertaste; an easy beer to drink in quantity. Highly recommended.

Tuborg Breweries, Ltd., c/o Carling Brewing Company, Waltham, Massachusetts

Tuborg Beer–U.S.

Tuborg Beer has been brewed since 1873 in Denmark, and is sold in 247 countries. For many years it was imported into the United States from Copenhagen but is now being brewed in three Carling breweries.

After more than sixty full-scale trial brews, in cooperation with the Danish technical staff of Tuborg, a beer was developed using the old European procedures and adapted only to American grain. Malt is made from two-row barley grown from European varieties in North Dakota, Montana and Minnesota. Yellow corn grits is added, and domestic and imported hops combined. The infusion method of brewing is followed with hot wort filtration and double fermentation—including krausening for a slow, secondary fermentation and natural carbonation.

Tuborg Beer–U.S. was the first successful effort in this century at brewing a European beer in the United States. Löwenbräu, of Munich, has now followed suit.

West End Brewing Company, Utica, New York

Utica Club Pilsener, Utica Club Cream Ale, Matt's Premium Lager, Maximus Super

HISTORY

The West End Brewing Company was organized in 1888 by F. X. Matt, who was born in 1859 in Igelschlatt-im-Schichthal, Baden, in the Black Forest region of West Germany. As a boy, he worked for his father, Theodore Matt, in various businesses, including a lumber concern, hotel, farm, and brewery. F. X. learned the art of making beer in his teen-age years at the famed Duke of Baden brewery in Rothaus, Germany. (This brewery, now named the Rothaus Brewery, is still in operation.)

In October, 1878, the senior Matt moved his family to America. F. X. went to work that same year at age nineteen for Carl Bierbauer's Brewery, one of nine breweries then located in Utica.

A year later, F. X. left for Canajoharie to work in the brewery of Louis

Bierbauer, Carl's brother. He remained for seven years with that concern, where he applied himself to learning management, marketing and shipping aspects of the brewing industry from the ground up.

In 1886, F. X. returned to Utica as manager of the Bierbauer Brewery, and in 1888 he reorganized it to form the West End Brewing Company. At that time, the brewery employed twelve people and produced 4,000 barrels of beer annually.

Mr. Matt served as manager and brewmaster during the first few years, and also kept a close eye on sales figures. Before long he decided that sales were not increasing satisfactorily (West End remained the smallest of the nine Utica breweries, and catered only to a local trade). He decided to take over the route of one of his salesmen for one day, convinced as he was that his beer was the finest in the city. By the end of the first day, he had more than doubled the business, and from that day on, he combined the duties of a brewmaster with those of a salesman.

In 1891, F. X. was chosen treasurer of the company, and in 1905 was named president. He held that position until 1950 when his son, Walter, was elected president and he became chairman of the board. F. X. Matt continued to be very active in the business until his death in 1958 at the age of ninety-nine.

The West End Brewing Company survived Prohibition by establishing the Utica Club line of soft drinks, fruit beverages, syrups, extracts, distilled water and malt tonic. The Utica Club brand and popular script logo came into use at this time. Some veterans of the company claim that the new brand name was used on bottles and trucks because of the considerable difficulty of driving a beer delivery truck around town during Prohibition. Production of these "nonbeer" items continued until just before World War II.

After repeal of the Eighteenth Amendment, increased sales and production demanded a vigorous building program. Between 1933 and the beginning of World War II, the brewery added several new buildings, and invested in much new equipment. West End was one of the first to use the then new concept of pneumatic unloading of grain—a labor-saving innovation since adopted by all breweries.

After World War II, the policy of re-investment in the business was continued, for this was Mr. Matt's way. Though a daring and original thinker, capable of great eloquence, he preferred a simple example to make his point. One of his favorite expressions was: "A business is like a man—you have to feed him to keep him alive."

In line with this belief, two new bottling lines were installed when the end of World War II made the machinery available again. And in 1948, work was begun on Mr. Matt's lifelong dream—a million-dollar brewhouse with the most modern equipment and facilities in existence. An article in *Fortune* magazine described it as "the model brewhouse." The

McSorley's, a venerable New York saloon.

equipment included a mash filter rather than the traditional lauter tank, and two huge 600 barrel gleaming copper cooking kettles.

In the 1950s and early 60s, the steady pattern of improvements of and additions to buildings and machinery was continued. Each year brought shiny new machinery or another big building. Highlights of the period were: practical doubling of bottling and warehousing space, new can and bottling lines, a huge new beer storage building capable of holding 750,000 gallons of beer in refrigeration tanks, a new 30,000-square-foot garage, a completely new steam boiler plant, and further renovation of the brewing department.

It was also during this period that the brewery completely converted its case and handling procedures to palletized operation, as well as replacing its fleet of more than 100 vehicles, to fit in with this new and more efficient concept of warehousing. New branch warehouses were built in Schenectady, Binghamton and Glens Falls. Perhaps typical of this period was the new 600-per-minute bottling line installed in 1957. At the time of its installation, it was the fastest bottling line in the country, and its performance still remains unmatched a dozen years later.

Building expenses totalled more than $3.5 million from the end of the war until 1956. During this period, the brewing industry in general was having trouble. An article in *Time* magazine said: "Nothing could be more appropriate to the $2.5 billion U.S. Brewing Industry today than Custer's last fight. Never has there been such whooping, shouting, and scalping. Reason: At the time when nearly everything else in the U.S. economy is bubbling and foaming, beer sales are going down." It was during those very years, between 1950 and 1955, though, that West End saw sales increase from 329,000 to 440,000 barrels per year.

The year 1964 brought the beginning of construction of a new bottling works, and the start of work on what has become a leading tourist attraction in Central New York, the Utica Club Brewery Tour Center.

Two floors of an empty warehouse (formerly the bottling works) were re-created by Walter Pfeiffer, a renowned architect, into a reception area and an 1888-era tavern to handle the ever-increasing number of tourists interested in inspecting brewery facilities. Construction costing more than $600,000 was completed early in 1965. Since then, New York State's only brewery tour has hosted visitors from every state in the nation, and more than eighty foreign countries.

The early distribution network and coverage area of the brewery has greatly changed since 1888. Today, 800,000 barrels of Utica Club beer and ale, Matt's Premium, and Fort Schuyler beer are distributed annually throughout New York State, and in Massachusetts, Connecticut, Vermont, Pennsylvania and New Jersey. Maximus Super is sold in New York State, Pennsylvania, Massachusetts, Connecticut, Rhode Island and Maine. National distribution is being planned for Maximus.

Sales dips have been encountered from time to time during these periods of growth and expansion. Time and again, the power of advertising has proven itself an effective force in combatting sales fluctuations. For example, a sales dip in 1957 and 1958 resulted in the hiring of Doyle, Dane, Bernbach advertising agency, and the complete revamping of the sales and merchandising divisions of the brewery.

The new agency introduced two talking beer mugs, Schultz and Dooley, utilizing the voice of the famous comedian, Jonathan Winters. This campaign must have been one of the most effective in the history of advertising, since sales increased more than fifty percent.

After the effectiveness of Schultz and Dooley began to fade, the brewery contracted for the service of Benton and Bowles, which handled advertising for the firm until a switch was made to Wells, Rich, Green, Inc., in 1966. The brewery's advertising agency has been DKG, Inc., of New York City, since 1968.

A completely new package and label by the San Francisco-based designer, Walter Landor, was instituted in 1968 as a result of the brewery's continuing research program.

From its small beginnings in 1888, the West End Brewing Company now ranks in the top thirty in the nation. (In 1947 there were about 450 brewers in the United States, and at the turn of the century, breweries numbered about 120.)

Utica Club Beer is a light, pilsener type lager beer. It is made of two and six-row barley malt of U.S. and Canadian origin, corn grits, granulated rice and hops from the United States, Germany and Yugoslavia. Water is from the Adirondack Mountains.

Brewed in 600-barrel lots, it uses a rice cooker, main mash mixing tank, mash filter and traditional copper kettles. After the krausening process Utica Club is stored for six to eight weeks.

The ale is brewed by a process similar to that of the beer, except that more hops are utilized, and the cooking process is designed to develop a higher amount of sugar content, to make the ale slightly higher in alcoholic content than beer. The ale is processed separately from the beer, because yeast for ale cannot be mixed with beer yeast. The ale is also stored at warmer temperatures than beer, which ages it more rapidly. The higher temperature also helps develop the ale's characteristic flavor.

Matt's Premium Lager beer differs from Utica Club beer in that only hand-selected, imported malt and imported hops are used in the brewing process. It is a beer that by its very nature must be produced only in small quantities, to insure that its character is maintained.

Maximus Super has nearly twice the alcoholic content of most beers. It differs from ales and malt liquors in that ales are characterized by a noticeable "hoppy" taste, while Maximus has a very smooth taste. This malt liquor is made like a beer, then artificially fermented with enzymes to produce a little more alcohol. Maximus Super starts with 60 percent more grain, and is naturally fermented. Fermentation takes almost twice as long, and the ageing period is longer also. It has a distinctive taste of its own, a taste which is smoother than any normal beer could have, and might be described as slightly malty, mellow, and with an alcoholic sweetness.

YUGOSLAVIA

I recommend you try *Niksicko Tuo,* a fine, light beer, when you're in Yugoslavia. Reminiscent of Pilsner Urquell with slightly more hoppiness, this beer is said to be "a New World type" (whatever that means). In any case, a panel of tasters in San Francisco recently found the export version of this beer clear, very pale, and yeasty. I consistently found it flat, watery, sour and uninspiring. Perhaps it simply was too long in transit and storage.

> Ale, man, ale's the stuff to drink
> For fellows whom it hurts to think!
> —A. E. Housman

GLOSSARY OF BEER TERMINOLOGY

"In which are defined some of the many expressions—serious, comic, colloquial—that have been used by the farmer and the brewer, on both sides of the bar and in the home, during the long and interesting history of this country's traditional drink."*

Adze A tool used by coopers for trussing, i.e. driving a wooden hoop down the staves of a cask while bending them to the correct shape. A similar adze, which has a cutting edge, is used for shaping the chime of the cask.

Albumen One of the natural foods contained in barley grain on which the young plant will feed. It is largely removed in the brewing process, though a small amount remains and help to give a good head to the beer.

Ale (1) Originally a liquor made from an infusion of malt by fermentation, as opposed to beer, which was made by the same process but flavoured with hops. Today ale is used for all beers other than Stout.

Audit Ale, a strong beer produced at the older universities, originally brewed by Trinity College, Cambridge, for the day of audit; hence also *Brasenose Ale. Brown ale,* in bottle is usually a mild ale, though it may also be beer of the Burton type. *Dr. Butler's Ale,* ale flavoured with a variety of spices and tinctures, invented by Dr. William Butler, physician to James I. It was claimed to cure many ailments, and was sold in taverns which bore the sign of the Butler's Head. The sign can still be seen in Mason's Avenue, E.C. *India Pale Ale* (I.P.A) was the name given originally to a fine pale ale specially made for export to troops in India. The name is seldom used now except for certain branded bottled pale ales. *Mild ale (X or XX)* is a dark beer brewed for immediate consumption and normally has a sweeter taste owing to the addition of priming sugar. *Pale Ale,* made

---

*Originally appeared in the Whitbread Publication *Word for Word* (an encyclopedia of beer). Used by permission of Whitbread and Company.

of the highest quality malt, is the driest and most highly hopped beer. It is sold in bottle and (as bitter) on draught. *Penny ale,* 14th-century term for ale at 1d. a gallon. *Scotch ale,* a draught or bottled ale of the Burton type, brewed in Scotland. *Scurvy grass ale,* an infusion of a plant of the cress family reputed to be an antidote to scurvy. *Strong ale,* the strongest ale, usually sold only in winter; hence also *Winter ale* and *October ale. Mulled ale,* a hot drink for a cold night: beer flavoured with sugar and spices and sometimes yolk of egg.

Ale-bowl, an early drinking vessel. *Ale conner,* now obsolescent, an official appointed by City or Borough Authorities, to sample all new brews of ale in his locality. His duties not only cover tasting the brew but also dictating the price at which it may be sold within the limits of the authority's jurisdiction. There are still four ale conners employed by the City of London, although their duties have been considerably curtailed. *Ale Garland,* a garland of evergreens, barley or flowers used on *Ale-stakes* in taverns as a sign of 'festivity, hospitality and good fellowship.' This custom dates back over 600 years and it is thought to be the brewer's sign to replace the Roman Vintners' Bush.

Ale (2) Merry making at which ale was drunk in mediaeval times. *Bid-ale,* benefit feast at which guests were expected to make a contribution. *Bride-ale,* wedding day custom by which the bride received the proceeds from whatever quantities of ale were drunk. *Church-ale,* parish festival (cf. sales of work) to benefit church funds. *Clerks-ale,* period during Easter holidays during which the parish clerk could more readily collect his dues. *College-ale,* festival held at the university. *Cuckoo-ale,* rustic celebration on the day that the cuckoo was first heard. *Give-ale,* free beer, often as the result of legacies. *Harvest-ale,* farmers' celebration. *Lamb-ale,* merry making at lambing time. *Leet-ale,* celebration at the time of the yearly or half-yearly courts of record. *Whitsun-ale,* church feast.

Alecost *Costmary,* aromatic plant formerly used for flavouring ale.

Archdeacon A special beer brewed at Merton College, Oxford.

Axe Shaped like a butcher's chopper and used by coopers for cutting the staves to a rough shape.

B

B-B A popular order. Bitter and Burton, mixed half-and-half.

Bar (1) Counter over which beer or other refreshments are sold.

Bar (2) Place or room where this sale takes place. *Bar billiards,* a game adapted for the bar, based on the 'potting' of billiard balls in a series of holes and the avoidance of hazards in the form of mushroom shaped skittles. *Bar cellarman,* employee who operates between the bar and the cellar.

Barmaid, Barman, assistants in the bar. *Bar parlour,* an inner sanctum patronised by the regulars and surviving only in the older inns and pubs. *Bar rail,* a foot rest on the front of the bar for customers who prefer to stand. *Bar stool,* provided for those who prefer to sit. *Bartender,* barman. *Buffet bar,* occasionally used to describe snack bar or saloon in which food can be served. *Four-ale bar,* term sometimes used for the public bar derived from the old term for mild ale. *Jug-and-bottle bar,* specially reserved for the purchase of drinks for consumption off the premises; only to be found in older pubs. *Ladies' bar,* another Victorian survival seldom seen today. *Private bar,* also fast disappearing, mid-way in the scale between the Public and Saloon bars. *Public bar,* where everything is cheapest and decoration and equipment are simpler than in the *Saloon bar.*

Barley   The prime ingredient of beer; after its conversion to malt, it provides the body and substance of the beverage. *Barley broth;* a form of strong ale (also *Barley wine,* sold in bottle or on draught). *Barleycorn,* a grain of barley. *John Barleycorn,* traditional name for an innkeeper as being the personification of malt liquor.

Barm   A mixture of wort and yeast.

Barm Beer   The wort which results from pressing the yeast and which is returned to the original fermentation.

Barrel   Term in general use among those not connected with the licensed trade to denote any cask; a cask built to hold 36 gallons.

Bulk Barrel   A unit of measure representing 36 gallons.

Standard Barrel   A theoretical unit of measure used by Customs and Excise Officers for assessing duty on the amount of beer brewed. Duty on beer is assessed on the original gravity of beer on the assumption that a barrel of water is 1,000°; the standard barrel of beer is, under present regulations, 1,055°.

Bazil   The technical word used by coopers, meaning bevel.

Beaker   Large drinking cup, fashioned of pewter or glass.

Beer   'Beer' and 'Ale' were Fenton's words to describe all malt liquors, until the 16th century when Flemish settlers reintroduced hops as a flavouring agent. The hopped variety was then called 'Beer' and the unhopped variety 'Ale.' Nowadays both words are used to describe malt liquors, although ale does not refer to stout. There is no bad beer, but some is better than others. *Beer-engine,* machine for drawing draught beer from cellar to bar. *Beer-house,* licensed to supply beer only (no wines or spirits). *Beer-money,* servant's allowance in lieu of beer. *Beer-pull,* handle of the beer-engine. *Beer-*

street, a moral sketch by Hogarth, depicting the prosperity and clean living in Beer Street, contrasting with the horrors of Gin Lane.

Beer-and-skittles. An expression indicating the pleasure and companionable atmosphere of your 'Local.' Normally used in the negative to show that life is not all pleasure.

Free-beer, generally too good to be true. *Ginger-beer,* non-alcoholic drink frequently mixed with beer, when it is known as *Shandy* or *Shandy-gaff.* *Hopping-beer,* early name for the first ale to contain hops (*c.* 1400). *Nettle beer,* brewed from nettles as opposed to barley. *Small-beer,* of lesser gravity hence, figuratively, a trifling matter. In the Middle Ages denoted later strainings from the mash, as opposed to the earlier (strong beer). *Spruce-beer,* an extract from the leaves of coniferous trees, fermented with sugar.

Bellarmine   Jug with a bearded face on the lip, originally a caricature of the 17th-century Cardinal Bellarmine, hated oppressor of Protestant potters in the Low Countries.

Bench   Long wooden seat frequently used in the public house. *Licensing Bench* (see under Licence and Brewster Sessions).

Bevel   The slopes cut on the outer edges of a cask head.

Bick Iron   An iron block used by coopers when rivetting the cask hoops.

Bid-ale   See Ale.

Bin   See Hops.

Binder   Colloquial expression for the last drink, which it seldom proves to be (see 'One for the road'). Also used to describe the person who orders a drink after closing time.

Bine   See Hops.

Binge   (Colloquial). Jollification. The word was borrowed by Field Marshal Lord Montgomery, who used it during the last war to denote soldierly efficiency and spit-and-polish.

Bitter   The driest and one of the most heavily hopped beers served on draught (cf. Pale Ale).

Black and Tan   Stout-and-Mild, mixed half-and-half.

Black Jack   A tanned leather jug of the Middle Ages, companion of the Leather Bottle.

Black Velvet   A mixture of stout and champagne.

Block Hook   Used by coopers for holding the staves while they are "dressing," i.e., shaping them.

Bock   A strong dark German beer. In Belgium and France, the term bock is used to describe a ¼ litre glass of light lager beer.

Boiling Copper   Vessel in which the wort is boiled with hops.

Bombard   Leather jug (16th and 17th century), a companion of the Black Jack and Leather Bottle.

Boniface   Traditional name for an innkeeper (Farquhar, 'The Beaux Stratagem').

Boot   Leather receptacle held between the operator's knees to hold a filled bottle in the days before corking machines. While the bottle was thus held the cork was driven in with a flogger. Also a drinking vessel used in the coaching era for mulled ale.

Booze   (slang) v.i. Partake not wisely but too well. n. The liquid consumed. *Boozer*, or *Boozah*, a pub.

Bottle   An invention almost as important as the wheel. Normally made of glass, it was taken into general use from the middle of the 19th century after the duty on glass was reduced in 1834. *To Bottle*, fill bottles with beer, hence *Bottling Stores*. *Bottle dress*, wartime phrase for drinker's clothing. *Bottle-and-jug bar*, see Bar.

Bottoms Up   A well meaning toast (cf. down the hatch).

Bouge   The 'Belly' of the cask, the middle portion with the greatest circumference.

Bragget   A fancy drink, originally made of fermented honey and ale; a sweetened and spiced ale.

Brasserie   Beer saloon or beer garden (in French, a brewery).

Brew v.t.   To make beer by infusion, boiling and fermentation. n. That which is brewed, a particular brewing of beer (cf. gyle).

Brewer   An artist who, by his choice of barleys and other ingredients and his sensitive control of the entire brewing process, produces your beer the way you like it.

Brewers' Grains   The malt grains which are retained in the mash tun after the maximum economic extraction of liquid malt or wort has been drawn off. These grains are later sold to contractors for use as fresh cattle food or for drying and manufacture of cattle cake (cf. goods, grist).

Brewers' Guild   The Incorporated Brewers' Guild was founded in 1906 in the interests of the trade generally. Its Journal is a recognised trade periodical and its Benevolent Fund has done much to relieve distress among brewers and their dependants.

The Brewers' Society   In 1904 the Country Brewers' Society, London Brewers' Association and Burton Brewers' Association amalgamated into the Brewers' Society. It is now the national organisation of the Brewing Industry.

The Worshipful Company of Brewers   The Brewers' Company was formally constituted by Royal Ordinance in 1406 as the "Mistery of Free Brewers." In 1437, it was granted a charter by Henry VI to control the "brewing of any kind of malt liquor in the City and its suburbs for ever." Membership of its Court is limited to London Brewery directors. The Brewers' Hall was totally destroyed in the Luftwaffe raid on the City on the night of 29th December, 1940.

Brewery   Where the beer is brewed.

Brewhouse   Another word for Brewery, little used today. *Brewhouse hand*, a craftsman in the brewery responsible for the boiling and flavouring of the wort, prior to fermentation.

Institute of Brewing   The world's leading scientific brewing organisation concerned with research and technical problems of great interest to the trade. A recent development was the opening of the Brewing Industry Research Foundation at Lyttel Hall, Nutfield, Surrey, in 1951. The equipment used is the most modern in scientific design.

Brewster Sessions   Special sessions of local Justices of the Peace for the consideration of applications for new licences and renewals of existing licences. (See also Licence.)

Buffet Bar   Occasionally used to describe a snack bar or saloon lounge.

Buffet Car   Means of obtaining beer during a railway journey from A. to B.

Bung Hole   Aperture through which the beer enters the cask at its broadest part and which is finally closed by the shive. *Bung ho!* a popular toast of uncertain derivation.

Burton   A strong ale, dark in colour, made with a proportion of highly dried or roasted malts. It is not necessarily brewed in Burton, and the term is in general use for all varieties of 'strong' or 'old' ales. *Burton Union System*, method of fermentation in large casks, fitted with 'Swan neck' pipes through which the surplus yeast works out.

Bush (1) The ancient symbol for an inn, usually displayed upon a pole (see Ale-stake). The custom presumably derived from the Romans, to whom a clump of ivy and vine leaves was the symbol of Bacchus. Hence the proverb: 'A good wine needs no bush'. Box-bush was also used to describe this symbol.

Bush (2) A small metal ring screwed into the bouge of the cask in which is later inserted a wooden bung. A similar but smaller bush is used for the tap hole in the head of a cask.

Butt A cask holding 108 gallons, and used extensively for the distribution of draught beer to the licensed trade.

Buttered Beer A popular 16th-century drink consisting of spiced and sugared strong beer supplemented with the yolk of egg and some butter.

Buzz A small plane used by coopers.

C

Can Colloquial expression for tankard. Hence *canful*. *Canned Beer*, beer filled into lined tins. More suitable for lager beers for sale overseas.

Carbonation The infusion of CO_2 at low temperature in bottling beer immediately on arrival from the brewery.

Cardinal A 19th-century form of mulled ale.

Cask A hooped oak vessel, cylindrical in shape and having heads in either end, made by coopers for the storage and transport of draught beer. Brewers' casks are made in seven sizes: *Butt* 108, *Puncheon* 72, *Hogshead* 54, *Barrel* 36, *Kilderkin* 18, *Firkin* 9 and *Pin* 4½ gallons.

Casual An occasional visitor to the pub. (c.f. regular.)

Cellar The place in the pub where draught and bottled beers are kept. Upon the proper temperature (55–65° F.) and hygiene of the cellar depends the condition of the draught beer served in the bar. *Cellarman*, assistant who works therein, or in the cellars of the brewery.

Chancellor A special beer once brewed at the universities (cf. audit ale, archdeacon).

Charcoal Fumes of this carbon were used extensively for drying hops before they were compressed into pockets. This form of fuel is now obsolescent as the demand for more modern and efficient types of heating increases.

Chaser   A long drink (beer) drunk with a short (whiskey or rum). The habit is more prevalent in America, Scotland and Ireland than in England.

Check   Special coin used in the hop gardens to indicate the amount of hops picked (see Hop Token and Tally) by a Bin. Checks were collected and formed the basis of the payout at the end of hop picking.

Cheers or **Cheerio**   A toast (cf. bottoms up).

Cheese (1)   The perfect complement to bread, beer and pickles.

Cheese (2)   The heavy wooden ball used in the game of skittles.

Chilling rooms   Where beer is stored and chilled at the Bottling Depot prior to filtration, carbonation and filling.

Chime   The bevel cut at either end of the cask staves.

Chitting   The appearance of the first rootlets while the barley is growing during the initial stage of the malting process.

Chive   A tool used by the cooper to plane a level bed in the ends of the cask staves into which a groove is cut for the head.

Church-ale   See Ale.

Clerk-ale   See Ale.

Closing time   A sad occasion.

Coaching glass   An 18th-century drinking vessel which had no feet and could not stand. Drinks in these were brought out to coach travellers and consumed at a draught.

Coaster   A small circular holder or tray for bottles and decanters, originally fitted with small wheels for easier movement on the table.

Collar   The frothing-head on a glass of draught beer between the top of the beer and the rim of the glass.

College-ale   See Ale.

Cone   See Hops.

Cooling A stage in the brewing process, after boiling and immediately prior to fermentation. Hence *cooling plant, cooler*. (cf. Paraflow.)

Cooper A highly skilled craftsman who makes and repairs casks at the brewery. The Company of Coopers (styled 'The Master and Wardens of the Commonalty of the Freemen of the Mistery of Coopers of the City of London and the Suberbs thereof') was granted a charter in 1501 by writ of the Privy Seal as a fraternity-in-guild for ever. *Cooperage,* where the cooper works.

Copper Vessel in which the wort is boiled with hops.

Copper-Sidesman The brewery hand who operates the copper.

Cork Indispensable companion of the bottle. A stopper so named because of the material from which it is made. *Corkscrew* or *bottle-screw*, instrument for withdrawing the cork. *Crown cork*, a cork-lined metal cap mechanically applied.

Costmary Alecost.

Crate In which beer bottles are transported. Normally made with wooden slats and partitions to hold a dozen or two dozen bottles.

Crinze An earthenware drinking vessel, a cross between a tankard and a small bowl.

Crisps A complementary snack to beer. Cold chipped potatoes sold in a paper bag with a screw of salt.

Crawler One who visits the pubs in a district, drinking a glass of beer in each.

Croze A cooper's tool used for cutting the groove into which is fitted the cask head.

Cuckoo-ale See Ale.

Culms (or Coombes) The rootlets which are sieved from the malt at the end of the malting process; they are used for poultry and cattle food.

Cup A drinking vessel which has been known in various forms throughout the history of beer. *Prunet* (or *Prounet*) *cup*, vessel used for a strong liquor made from wild plums.

Customer Essential to the pub and faithful to that institution throughout its history.

D

Dadloms   A game of table skittles, played with miniature 'cheeses.'

Darts   A game, the origin of which is lost in antiquity, but is said to descend from knife throwing. Although much in vogue at court during the reign of Henry II, the game was not universally popular until the end of the XIXth century, when it was revived as a pastime in public houses. It consists of throwing a dart at a board which is divided into scoring segments. Many variations from the standard board are in use both in local and league tournaments, and the game has now acquired national status. *Dart elbow*, an unpleasant complaint caused by over practice. *Dart widow*, one who waits at home.

Dextrins   Less readily fermentable bodies which are a natural result of the conversion of starch into sugar. The presence of these dextrins in the wort in correct proportions has a direct relationship to its character and the final quality of the beer.

Dextrose   A form of sugar resulting from the conversion of starch in the barley into malt.

Dipstick   An instrument used to measure the quantity of wort in the fermenting squares prior to fermentation.

Dive   A downstairs bar or snack bar.

Dock Glass   A goblet holding exactly a quarter of a pint, used originally by Excise Officers for wine tasting in the docks.

Dog's Nose (colloquial)   Beer 'laced' with gin.

Double (1)   Twice the quantity or strength.

Double (2)   A score in the outer band of the dartboard.

Dowel   A wooden peg used to join together the pieces of timber of a cask head.

Dowling Brace   A tool used by a cooper to bore holes in the pieces of timber into which the dowel is inserted.

Down the Hatch   A toast; usually used for the first drink.

Downright   A cooper's tool used to shave the outside of a cask stave.

Draught (1)   A single act of drinking.

Draught (2)   Adjective to describe cask beer, as opposed to beer in bottle.

Draughts   Game played with twenty-four pieces on a draughts board or chess board.

Dray   Originally used to describe a four-wheeled horse-drawn vehicle employed in heavy transport duties, in contrast with a two-wheeled vehicle, called a 'cart.' The term is now freely used to describe any vehicle used for the transport of beer. *Drayman*   The driver of the dray. Also used generally to describe the horse leader (trouncer) or an assistant. *Drayhorse* Heavy cart horses, often Shires, used to pull Brewers' Drays.

Drip Mats   Small glass or absorbent mats on which glasses are placed to prevent staining tables and counters. There are many shapes and sizes in general use, the most popular being circular or oval.

Driver   A wedge-shaped tool used by coopers to drive down the hoops of a cask.

Dutch   To go Dutch; where each member of a party pays his own way.

E

Eistrich Beer   (Eastern Beer), a product imported from Europe in the 14th century.

Entire (1)   (or *Entire Butt*): The original name for Porter. A special brew, first produced in 1722, equivalent to a mixture of ale, beer and twopenny.

Entire (2)   A house, not necessarily tied, which sells one brewer's beers only or 'entirely.'

Enzymes   Digestive ferments of the malt, which convert the starch to sugar. They are finally destroyed in the boiling of the wort.

Extension   Official permission to remain open beyond the usual licensed hours. Extensions may be granted for special functions, national holidays, Royal occasions, and certain sporting and public events.

F

F-Measure   A liquid measure used in 14th-century London for a farthing's-worth of beer.

Fermentation   A stage in the brewing of beer when yeast is added to the wort. During the course of fermentation the yeast converts the wort into beer.

Fermenting Squares   Copper-lined wooden vessels in the brewery in which the yeast is pitched into the wort to commence the initial part of the conversion of wort to beer.

Fermenting Tanks   Slate or stone vessels in which the conversion of wort beer is completed in the brewery. In these vessels the yeast head is skimmed off in the form of barm beer.

Filler   A long-stemmed glass vessel with a bulb end, pierced by a small hole. It held about a quarter of a pint and was used as an alternative to a ladle for serving punch.

Finings   A preparation of isinglass which is added to the beer in the cask to clarify it.

Firkin   A small cask holding nine gallons.

Flagon   Glass or pewter vessel formerly fitted with a lid and handle for the storage of wine or beer. Today it describes the glass quart bottles in which beer is sold.

Flip   Beer and spirit mixed, sweetened and heated with hot iron.

Flogger   Instrument used before the introduction of corking machines for driving the cork into the bottle, which was held in a boot.

Fob   The word used in a brewery to describe beer froth.

Four-Ale   Old-fashioned term for mild ale. *Four-ale* bar, see Bar.

Frame Saw   A specially constructed saw used by coopers to cut the circular shape of the cask head.

Free House   A house in which the landlord is under no covenant to buy his supplies from any one particular source.

Frog Mug   Originally made at the Sunderland potteries as a form of practical joke. On draining the mug the unsuspecting drinker found a large imitation frog inside.

Froth   The layman's word for 'fob.' It is also commonly used to describe the 'head' on a glass of beer. *Frothblower* (colloquial) beer drinker or member of the Ancient Order of Frothblowers.

G

Gallon   A measure of capacity, 277¼ cu. inches—more happily expressed as eight pints of beer.

Gaspin Leather vessel halfway in size between the bombard and the black jack.

Gill (1) Liquid measure of a quarter-pint.

Gill (2) Ground Ivy.

Gill (3) Beer flavoured with ground ivy instead of hops.

Ginger Ale An aerated non-alcoholic drink flavoured with ginger.

Ginger Beer An effervescent drink flavoured with ginger.

Ginger Wine A liquor made by the fermentation of sugar and water, and flavoured with various spices, including ginger.

Give-ale See ale.

Glass Obtained by mixing silica, limestone or other metallic oxides, and cooking very quickly to prevent crystallisation. Although the art of glass-making dates back to the third millennium, the most famous period for British glass coincided with the coaching era. *Coaching glass*, an 18th century drinking vessel which had no foot and could not stand. Drinks in these were brought out to coach travellers and consumed at a draught. *Firing glass*, so called because Free-masons knocked them simultaneously on the table, in acknowledging a toast, and produced a noise said to resemble the firing of a gun: the foot of the glass was made especially thick to withstand such treatment. *Hogarth glass*, short, wide-based vessel, so called because it so frequently appeared in that artist's pictures. *Last drop glass*, typical of the vessel used for practical jokes. Engraved on the bottom was the figure of a corpse on a gibbet and, even if the glass was turned upside down, the 'last drop' remained. *Long glass*, see Yard of ale.

Goblet A drinking vessel shaped with a wide bowl and smaller rim, without a handle. The name came originally from the Latin *cupa*, a cask, and the shape is similar to a cask which has been cut in half.

Goods The name often used by the brewer to describe the crushed malt grains in the mash tun, c.f. grist, brewers' grains.

Granny Colloquial term for old-and-mild.

Green Malt Malt which has germinated for the full eleven days, but has not yet been dried in the kilns.

Grist Malt grains which have been cleaned and cracked in the Brewery mill machines, whence they are conveyed to the grist cases, preparatory to mashing. After extraction of the malt in the mash tun, the spent grains are sold as cattle food, c.f. brewers' grains.

Ground Ivy   A flower of the genus *Nepeta* of the family *Laviatae*. It produces oils which were used for flavouring beer before the use of hops.

Gruit   A mixture of herbs—bogmyrtle, wild rosemary etc.—formerly used, particularly in Germany, for the flavouring of beer.

Guv'nor, The   The 'regular's' affectionate name for the landlord of a public house.

Gyle   A quantity of beer brewed at one time: one particular brewing. Hence *gyle number,* a number stencilled on a cask to denote the brew or gyle.

Gyngleboy   A leather bottle or black jack ornamented with silver bells.

Haircloth or **Hair sieve**   Blankets of horsehair placed over the slatted floor of the kiln, on which hops are spread and dried.

Half-and-Half (1)   Equal quantities of each of two drinks in a mixture (e.g. Bitter-and-Burton).

Half-and-Half (2)   Old name for a mixture of ale and porter, sometimes used also for mild and bitter.

Halfpiece of wood   Ale measure used in the 15th century.

Have one with me   A sweet sound.

Head   The froth on the top of beer.

Heavy wet   Old term for particularly strong ale.

Hebe   A facetious term for a barmaid or waitress (in Greek mythology, a handmaiden of the Gods).

Heel Tap   Colloquial term for beer left at the bottom of the glass.

Hequ or **Hequp**   Ancient Egyptian name for beer. The earliest records of brewing (c. 2000 B.C.) have been found in Egypt.

Hills   The protective mounds which cover the roots of hop plants. Once a field of hops has been planted, the hills are not disturbed until the plant has lost its virility. This may be up to thirty or more years. When new fields of hops are required, the hops are planted in late March each year in hills, either by cutting from old plants at two-three cuttings per hill, or by perennial roots which are plants grown in the nursery for one year.

Hogshead   Cask made to hold fifty-four gallons.

Hoop   A device displayed outside taverns in the Middle Ages to indicate that beer was on sale (c.f. ale-stake). Later, it became the practice to display certain objects within the hoop in order to differentiate one tavern from another.

Hop   A perennial plant of the nettle family indigenous to Europe generally, which has been cultivated in England since the days of William the Conqueror. Oils and resins in the cones borne by the female plant are used to impart the bitter flavour and preservative values to beer. Hops were first used in English beer (then known as *hopping beer*) at the end of the 14th century, following the example of Eistrich Beer which was then being imported from the Continent. For a few years after its introduction to this country, hopping beer was not altogether popular and on several occasions the use of hops was banned. All beers nowadays contain the resins and oils of hops. (See also Ale, Beer.)

Hop back. Brewery vessel into which the wort and hops are turned out after boiling. The wort is filtered through the hop petals as they lie on a false bottom before it passes to the cooling stage. *Hop bine*, the growing stem of the plant. *Hop cone*, the strobile of the female plant. At the base of the petals of the cones are the seeds and resinous oils of the hops which impart the bitter flavour and preservative properties to beers. *Hop diseases* are Mould, Red Spider, Aphis, Mildew, Downy Mildew and Verticillium Wilt. The latter disease began about 20 years ago *c.* 1935 and caused enormous losses to hop farmers particularly in Kent. New varieties of hops have been cultivated which are wilt-resistant. *Hop farm*, where hops are grown. Approximately a quarter of the farm acreage is normally set aside for hop cultivation. *Hop festival*, an annual celebration of the hop harvest, held at Beltring, Kent, and consisting of two or three days' entertainment for the pickers and camp staffs. *Hop garden*, field in which hops are cultivated. *Hop grower*, one who cultivates hops. *Hop pickers*, men, women and children who come annually to the hop gardens to gather the harvest. *Hop pillow*, pillow filled with hops and reputed to encourage sleep. *Hopping beer*, name given to the first beer flavoured with hops, as opposed to the unhopped ale. *Hop poles*, 11 ft. to 14 ft. poles used to support the wires and strings up which the bines are trained. *Hop strings*. During the early growth of the bines each year strings are strung from the hills to the overhead wires, up which the bines can later be trained. Normally four strings are used for each plant and about 4½ miles of string per acre of hops. *Hop tokens*, local coinage of the hop gardens, until recently used for payments to pickers. See Check.

Hops Marketing Board Under the provision of the Hops Marketing Scheme 1933, the Hops Marketing Board was set up to control all aspects of the growing, marketing, distribution and pricing of hops grown in Britain. It consists of four special members appointed by the Minister of Agriculture and fourteen representatives selected by the producers.

Hopir A 15th-century liquid measure.

Hukster A mediæval term, alternative for *ale-wife,* woman who sold beer.

I

India Pale Ale (I.P.A.).   Name originally given to a fine pale ale made for export to troops in India. The term is occasionally used for bottled Pale Ales by some brewers.

Inn An English institution. A licensed house where beer and other refreshments can be obtained. Often the headquarters of local clubs and sporting occasions (cf. Public House). *Innkeeper,* one who keeps an inn, the landlord. See also Licensee, Tenant. *Innsign,* the symbol of hospitality and welcome.

Isinglass Used as finings.

J

Jack A vessel to hold liquid (cf. Black Jack).

Jacob's Ladder The conveyor which carries beer casks of fined beer from the Brewers cellars to the loading bank. The term is traditional and originated from the reference to Jacob's Ladder in the Bible. *Jacob's Ladderman,* the Brewery hand responsible for the delivery of beers from the cellar to the loading bays.

Jorum Large drinking bowl or its contents.

Jug A deep vessel for holding liquids, fitted with handle. *Jugful,* a pleasing quantity. *Toby Jug* (see also *Bellarmine*), jug of stoneware in the shape of a portly man of the period (18th century). Many variants have since been produced, the most familiar depicting a cheerful rubicund fellow in a three-cornered hat. *Jug-and-bottle bar,* see Bar.

K

Kieve See Mash Tun.

Kilderkin Cask holding 18 gallons.

Kiln That part of the maltings in which the malt is dried after germination. The conical vents of the kilns are the distingushing features of the maltings.

L

Ladle Instrument of china, pewter or silver used for serving punch.

Lager Form of beer brewed principally on the Continent. Less hops are used than in English beer and fermentation is carried out at a much lower temperature. Special yeasts are used which descend to the bottom of the fermenting vessel. Lager should be served cold.

Lamb-ale See Ale.

Lambswool A hot drink of spiced ale with roasted apples beaten up in it.

Landlord Traditional name of the licensee, though he is, in fact, often the tenant installed by the brewer. The licensee of a free house is sometimes technically the landlord.

Last orders, please Doleful sound, frequently accompanied by the ringing of bells and dimming of the light; not as final as *Time, gentlemen, please.*

Lattice In the Middle Ages, few taverns had glass windows. The aperture was covered by a trellis or lattice; this was painted red and served to distinguish the tavern from adjoining houses.

Leather bottle Vessel long used for the transport and storage of beer, most popular during the Restoration. It was made of seasoned hide, double-welted and cross-stitched with waxed thread. Pitch was sometimes used to seal the inside and make the vessel water-proof. There were varied shapes, though none would be recognised as bottles today: the most common were oblong, with flat base and ends, the rounded sides converging on the mouth at the top. Leather bottles were taken into the harvest fields until comparatively recent times. See also Black Jack, Bombard.

Leet-ale See Ale.

Licence Official permit to retail alcoholic drinks. *Licensing Justices,* magistrates empowered to grant such licences (see also *Brewster Sessions*), *Licensing laws,* complex system of legal regulations with which the publican must be familiar. *Licensing hours,* hours during which the licensed premises are open for sale of intoxicants. *Licensee,* the holder of the licence—sometimes the landlord of the premises. *Off-licence,* a licence to sell beer, wine or spirits for consumption off the premises only. *On licence,* a licence permitting sale for consumption on or off the premises. Licences can be *full* (i.e., beer, wines and spirits) *beer on,* for beer only or *beer and* *wine on*. In addition to retail licences, there are others affecting manufacturers and wholesale dealers.

Lifter   Another name for filler.

Light ale   Pale ale (see Ale).

Light and mild   A mixture, pale ale and mild, half-and-half.

Liquor   The term used throughout the brewing industry for water. In earlier days, beers often owed their flavour and popularity to the quality of water from local wells.

Local   The Englishman's affectionate term for the pub round the corner. One of the mainstays of our social system.

Long glass   See Yard of ale.

Long pull   Giving the customer rather more than he ordered. The opposite of *short pull*. For both these offences the publican can be legally prosecuted.

Lord of the Tap   An official appointed to visit all booths at which beer was sold during the annual fair at Cambridge and to test the quality by tasting. The custom did not survive beyond the 18th century.

Lounge   (Sometimes also *lounge bar, Saloon lounge*), an improvement even on the Saloon bar, the best appointed and most expensive bar of the Public House.

Lupulin   The sticky powder in the hop cone, containing the oils and resins which provide the flavour and preservative properties.

Malt   The name given to barley grains which have passed through the malting process. The maltose sugars contained in these grains are extracted with liquor to form the basic wort from which beer is brewed.

Maltings   The buildings in which barley grains are converted into malt. These buildings, with the long multi-windowed walls of the malting floor and the conical vents of the kilns, form a characteristic feature of the countryside in most barley-growing areas.

Malting Processs   The conversion of the insoluble proteins and starch contained in the barley grains into soluble matter and sugars of the malt grains. This is done by steeping the barley in liquor in heaps on the malting floor until it germinates and growth starts. When the growth has extended three-quarters to the length of the corn, the grains are removed from the floor and laid out in the kiln. There they are lightly cooked to prevent further growth and finally sieved to remove the rootlets or culms. Malts for pale ales are now stored until required for brewing. The majority of the barley crop is dried at higher temperatures to provide malts of fuller flavour and richer colour, which are more suitable as malts for darker ales and stouts. These may be kilned over wood chips, heated in a gas oven, or fully roasted to provide a large range of malts for selection by the brewer.

Maltster   The man who controls the malting process.

Malt tower   The highest point of the brewery, from which the malt starts on its journey via the mills to the mash tuns.

Mash   A mixture of crushed malt grains and hot liquor, which is run through the *masher* into the mash tun and from which is extracted liquid malt or wort.

Mash Tun   A large cast iron vessel in which wort is extracted from the grist. The mash is run into the mash tun and lies on a false bottom consisting of perforated plates. It is then "sparged" (sprayed) with hot liquor for several hours after which the wort is run off through the perforated plates and the spent grains retained.

Mazer   A traditional English drinking bowl, of maple wood, silver mounted.

Mead   An early English drink of fermented honey and water. It is still made today, but is probably older than beer, for there are Sanskrit records its existence 3,000 B.C.

Merry-goe-down   Old term describing good ale.

Metheglin   A spiced form of *mead*.

Mether cup   A wooden drinking cup used by the Saxons, probably for *metheglin*.

Mill   Machine in which malt is cracked at the brewery. *Mill hand*, brewery hand in charge of the mill machines.

Modius   A 15th-century liquid measure.

Montieth   An early form of punch bowl, with a scalloped rim, on which glasses could be rested. Said to be named after an 18th-century eccentric who wore a coat with scalloped tails.

Mother-in-law Facetious term for *stout-and-bitter,* mixed half-and-half.

Mud in your eye, Here's Traditional toast, with a meaning far more pleasant than it would sound.

Mug (1) Drinking vessel, made of various materials, with or without handle.

Mug (2) The contents thereof.

Mughouse or mugroom (*c.* 1740) an early form of English music hall. Only ale or stout was sold and a chairman presided over the songs, speeches (often political) and toasts.

Mullet (*Or ale mullet*) Copper funnel with handle, but closed at the narrow end. It was filled with ale and heated in the embers of the fire.

Mum (Or *mumm*) A fancy beer, flavoured with fir bark and herbs, originally brewed in Brunswick. Said to be named after Christian Mumme, who first brewed it in the late 15th century.

N

Nappy Archaic term describing good ale; foaming and strong.

Negus A hot drink, mulled ale or sweetened mead (18th century).

Nine men's monies An old inn game, played in Elizabethan times, with counters or pebbles on a marked board. Possibly an ancestor of *shove ha'penny.*

Ninepins A form of skittles.

Noggin (1) A small wooden mug, still used as a quarter-pint measure.

Noggin (2) Colloquial term for a welcome glass of beer.

Noondrink Mediæval term for ale consumed at noon, when trading was slacker. Previously *high noon* had been popular; this was drunk at about three o'clock, when street trading was finished.

Nuts and bolts Local term, principally used in East Anglia for mild-and-bitter.

Oast The kiln in which hops are dried. The oast consists of a boiler at ground level, a slatted floor above covered by a horsehair blanket on which the "green" hops are laid, and a conical chimney surmounted with a cowl and vane. Hot air and sulphur fumes from the boiler are driven or sucked up through the slatted floor by fans thereby drying out the moisture content of the hops, and the fumes are expelled through the cowls. The drying takes from 8 to 12 hours and the moisture content is reduced to between 7 and 9 degrees. *Oasthouse,* a building containing two or more oasts, and consisting of an arrival gantry, where hops are received, the oasts, and a cooling floor where hops are cooled and pressed into pockets.

October ale   See Ale.

Off license   See Licence.

Old ale   A name sometimes used for a strong ale. Hence *old-and-mild,* mild and Burton mixed half-and-half.

One for the road   Usually the last drink before leaving a house or pub.

Optic   A measuring and dispensing device widely used for spirits. It is usually inserted into the neck of an inverted bottle.

Other half   A return drink.

P

Pale ale   Made of the highest quality malts, the driest and most highly hopped beer. Sold as Light ale or Pale ale in bottle, or on draught as bitter.

Panyers   14th-century term for beer sold at 1d. per gallon, as opposed to better beer at 4d. a gallon.

Pewter   An alloy of tin and lead and other metals, used in the manufacture of tankards and beer drinking vessels. It was well known to the Romans but was not heard of in this country until the Middle Ages, when it provided a cheap substitute for silver. *Pewter pot,* the finest vessel from which to drink draught beer.

Piece   A 15th-century liquid measure.

Piggin   Drinking vessel of pig's skin, similar to the *black jack* and the *bombard.*

Pig's ear   Colloquial phrase (Cockney rhyming slang) for Beer.

Pin   The smallest cask in general use, with a capacity of 4½ gallons. *Pin stage,* in hop growing the first of the three final stages before picking (cf. *hop stage*).

Pin tankard (or *Peg tankard*) Vessel divided into eight sections, each marked by a peg driven into the wood on the inside. They were made on the order of King Edgar in the 10th century, in an effort to restrain heavy drinking; any person drinking past the pin at a draught was to forfeit a penny. Hence the phrase '*to drink to pins*,' a deep draught, and a *peg* as a measure (still used today for whisky).

Pint A liquid measure of ⅛th gallon. Hence also *pint glass, pint mug, pint pot, pint tankard, Imperial pint*, a liquid measure of 20 ounces. *Reputed pint*, a bottle of beer having a capacity of approximately 12 ounces.

Pitcher A leather vessel so called because it was treated with pitch on the inside to make it waterproof.

Pocket A large sack made to contain roughly one and a half cwts. of dried hops. The hops are pressed into the pockets after cooling, and are thus stored until their arrival in the brewery.

Polishing A process by which the beer is made brilliant and crystal-clear before bottling. The beer is filtered through asbestos sheets to remove sediment and minute yeast cells, and then refiltered. This process "polishes" or makes the beer brilliant.

Pony A liquid measure of one fifth of a pint. It originated during the 19th century when landlords served saloon bar customers with five measures to the pint, and four measures to public bar customers, charging each the same price.

Pope A spiced drink similar to *Negus* and *Cardinal*.

Porter (see also Entire) A brew popular in the late 18th and 19th centuries, equivalent to a mixture of *ale, beer* and *twopenny*. It is reputed to have been so called because of its popularity amongst London market porters. *Porterhouse*, a house at which porter was retailed; hence also *porterhouse steak*, choice cut of beef to be obtained there.

Posset-pot A two-handled vessel used for making posset; a drink made of hot milk curdled with ale or other liquor, and often flavoured with spices. Used to be drunk as a remedy for colds.

Pot A rounded drinking vessel; hence *pot of pewter. Pothouse*, alehouse. *Potman*, publican's assistant. *Pot-pal*, drinking companion. *Pot valour*, courage of a man who has emptied several. Hence also *pot valiant*.

Potell 15th-century liquid measure.

Pottle (1) Half gallon liquid measure. Now obsolete.

Pottle (2) Pot to contain this quantity.

Priming The addition of a small quantity of cane sugar solution to mild ales and stouts after they have been fully fermented. The effect is to produce a slight extra fermentation and create a sweeter palate. *Priming house*, department in the brewery where this sugar is dissolved.

Private Bar see Bar.

Prunet (or Prounet) Cup Archaic vessel used for drinking a liquor made from wild plums.

Pub An affectionate diminutive for the most democratic of all British institutions, the *Public House*. An establishment licensed to sell beer and alcoholic liquors for consumption on or off the premises. A social centre which is frequently the meeting place of local sports clubs and associations. A native product which is unexportable. *Pubgoer, pubman*, one who knows the truth of the above definition.

Public, The *The Public Bar* (see under **Bar**).

Publican That man of all the virtues who runs the pub—a man with a smile for his customers and impartial to all their arguments; above all an expert on the conditioning and serving of beer. (See also Landlord, Licensee.)

Punch A hot drink of wine or spirits mixed with ale or water and seasoned with sugar, lemons, spice, etc. (cf. *wassail*).

Puncheon A cask made to hold 72 gallons.

Purl A type of mild ale brewed with plant roots, fruit peel and spices, and matured for about one year. Purl was much in vogue up to the end of the 17th century.

Puzzle jug Form of practical joke popular in this country until about a hundred years ago. Puzzle jugs were made in a variety of shapes and were usually presented to the newcomer to an inn; many had concealed holes which spilled beer over various parts of the drinker's body.

Quaff To drink in large draughts or to drink from quaich or cup.

Quaich Literally a cup or bowl (Latin *caucus*, Greek *kauka*). In its most usual form, a quaich consists of a shallow bowl made of silver, pewter or china, with two handles.

Quart   Twice as good as a pint. A liquid measure, quarter gallon, the approximate contents of a *flagon*. *Quart mug, quart pot*, drinking vessels to hold this quantity; these are now not normally used in the pub. *Put quart into pint pot*, attempt the impossible. *Still takes his quart*, likes his beer.

Quartern   A liquid measure of ¼ pint.

Quartering (1)   A term used in coopering to describe the part of the cask between the chime and the bouge. The quarter hoop is placed midway between the chime and the bouge.

Quartering (2)   A term used to describe one method of sawing timber suitable for use as cask staves. This method tends to waste some of the timber as only a small proportion can be used for staves.

Quintain   A vertical post with two horizontal arms one of which was a mark and the other a sandbag. The quintain was used for beginners to tilt at, or for the skilled horseman to display their prowess. Today the sport is often played in modified form, a wheelbarrow replacing the charger of bygone days. The last remaining quintain in this country is close by *The Red Lion*, Offham, Kent.

Quoits   A game in which an iron hoop is thrown to encircle a peg on the ground, supposed to be developed from throwing the discus. Although it was available for the entertainment of visitors at most public houses up to the end of the 19th century, it is not often seen there today.

R

Rack (1)   To fill a cask or container with beer in a brewery, hence *racking cock, racking machine*. The term is also used for wines.

Rack (2)   To draw off wine to clear it from dregs or lees, hence *racked wine*. *Racked beer*, beer which has been fined in bulk in the brewery and then racked into casks for distribution and immediate consumption. Most beer is fined in cask before delivery to the trade.

Raise   A term used in coopering to describe setting up cask staves into a chime hoop in readiness for trussing. An ash hoop is placed over the bouge as a measure to ensure that the cask will ultimately hold the correct amount of beer.

Regular   One of the mainstays of the licensed house. A customer who is a regular visitor to a pub.

Rough   The beer in the drip-cans, overflows from draught beer or the residue from bottles. This is also called ullage.

Rings Once very popular game in the inn. Rings were thrown at hooks in a board hung on the wall. A sort of vertical quoits.

Rosemary A flowering shrub whose leaves were used to flavour some varieties of beer in the 16th and 17th centuries.

Round An order for drinks for more than one person.

Rouser A long-handled instrument, often in the form of a wooden stick, used to 'rouse' or stir the yeast and wort in the fermenting vessels thereby aerating the yeast and promoting maximum fermentation. Hence *rousing*.

Rue Perennial evergreen shrub whose bitter leaves are believed to have been used by ancient Egyptians to flavour their beer.

Rummer A traditional English glass, long associated with the inn. It has a large bowl and a squat stem.

Rundlet or **Runlet** A small cask, often of earthenware, used mainly for storage of wines and spirits.

S

Sage Ale An infusion of sage leaves used in the 17th century for medicinal purposes (cf. scurvy grass ale).

Saloon or **Saloon Bar** Normally enjoying better amenities than the public bar and therefore more expensive to the customer. *Saloon lounge*, is generally to be found only in the larger public houses or hotels.

School Collective noun for group of beer drinkers for whom a round is bought.

Scotch Ale See Ale.

Screw Stopper A device for sealing bottles, first introduced in 1885. In the smaller size bottles, i.e. ½ pint and reputed pints, it has been largely superseded by the crown cork, but is in general use for both pint size and quart bottles. *Bottle Stopper Washer*, one employed on cleaning and checking screw stoppers in a bottling depot.

Scurvy Grass Ale See Ale.

Shades Cellars, or a bar below ground level (see also Dive).

Shandy or **Shandy Gaff** A drink of beer mixed with ginger beer; sometimes served as a mixture of beer and lemonade, though this is perhaps more correctly termed *lemon shandy*.

Shanghai   A popular variant of the standard game of darts, usually played by four or more people. Each player is given a number which he must first score; he then proceeds to score the numbers of all the other participants.

Shive   A circular wooden plug, partly bored in the centre which is hammered into the bush of a cask when it has been filled. A solid shive or bung, smaller in diameter and with a counter-sunk centre, is used to seal the tap hole.

Short   A colloquial name for a gin or whisky drink, usually taken before a meal (cf. snifter).

Shove Groat   The parent of *shove ha'penny,* played in the days when the groat was a coin of the realm (value 4d. issued 1351-1763).

Shove Ha'penny   A popular inn game. Metal discs the size of a half-penny are balanced on the edge of a small board marked laterally in sections. The discs are 'shoved' by a smart tap with the palm of the hand. The object is to steer three discs into each section or 'bed.'

Shovelboard   A large scale version of shove ha'penny, played with heavy metal weights. The game is seldom seen in inns today, though it is still played on ships' decks.

Six Out   Measure used today principally for spirits, which gives six out of a gill. See Optic.

Skittle Board   An adaptation of skittles, popular in the West Country. Sometimes called *Devil among the tailors,* since there are nine skittles and 'nine devils make a tailor.' A small wooden ball is attached by cord to a pole set on the left-hand side of a large tray. In this tray are nine skittles placed in a box. The ball is swung to the left, round the pole and the object is to knock down as many skittles as possible (cf. Dadloms).

Skittles   A traditional inn game, revived in recent years, due largely to the enthusiasm of Sir Alan Herbert. It is played in an alley (a narrow space enclosed with wooden guards) and heavy wooden cheeses are directed at nine pins (skittles).

Small Beer   See Beer.

Smeller   A man employed in the brewery to examine casks after they have been washed and prior to their being filled with beer. He smells the interior of the cask to ensure that it is 'sweet', has not been contaminated by oil, rain or mould, and then removes any pieces of broken shive with an iron fork. His correct title is *examiner and smeller.*

Snack Bar   A public house bar equipped for the service of food. Though there are sometimes hot dishes available, these are more often exclusive to the restaurant. In most houses the snack bar confines its activities to sandwiches, salads and cold food.

Snifter   Colloquial term for a drink.

Snug or **Snuggery**   Semi-private apartment in the pub, reserved usually by custom for the regulars. Similar to the bar parlour.

Sparge   To spray hot liquor on to the grist in the mash tuns. This is to ensure that the 'goods' remain suspended in the wort during the extraction process.

Spell, To Take A   To trot round to the local for a glass of beer. Phrase coined by Mr. Peggotty in Charles Dickens' *David Copperfield*.

Spile   A small peg of either soft or hardwood or cane which fits into a hole in the shive. It is loosened to facilitate the drawing of the beer from the cask, or tightened to thumb pressure to keep the beer in condition when not in use.

Spruce   See under Beer.

Stave   See Barrel.

Steeping   The first part of the conversion of the malting process, soaking the grain in large cisterns at the maltings. *Steep ripe*, describes the steeped barley when it has absorbed approximately 60 per cent of water.

Stillion   The wooden cradle in which the casks are stood in the cellars of a public house.

Stingo   A strong ale, similar to barley wine, popular during the winter months and usually sold in bottle.

Stock Ale   A term sometimes used for beers of the Burton type.

Stool   Useful piece of furniture for the customer who likes to remain at the bar, but is anxious to take the weight off his feet.

Stout   Beer brewed from roasted, full-flavored malts, often with an addition of caramel sugar, and a slightly higher proportion of hops. Stouts have a richer, slightly burnt flavour and are dark in colour.

Strong Ale   See Ale.

Sugar One of the ingredients of beer, extracted from sugar cane grown mainly in the West Indies, and imported into Britain. It is refined in this country and arrives in the brewery as an invert sugar, i.e. treacle in casks or metal containers. It was not generally used until 1881, when Mr. Gladstone repealed the malt tax and allowed the brewer more liberty in his choice of materials. *Invert sugar*, cane sugar which has been changed slightly in composition by the action of catalysts, usually weak acids. It is added to the wort before it is boiled with hops. It is not used at this stage to sweeten the beer, but to increase fermentability. *Priming sugar*, see Priming.

Sundowner Term imported from South Africa used for the first glass of beer in the early evening.

Swig n. Slang phrase for a draught of beer, generally a large one. v.t. and i. To take such a draught.

Swipes Waste beer.

T

Tables Another name for backgammon, once a popular inn game: name derived from the fact that the table for this game folded in half and either section was known as a table.

Tally, Hop Tally or **Tally Stick** A flat piece of wood 9-12 inches in length used in the hop gardens until comparatively recent times as a means of assessing a grower's debt to his pickers. The stick was split down the middle for some two-thirds of its length and cut across so that a portion could be removed; the latter was issued to the picker, while the talleyman kept the remainder. A record of the picker's work was kept by fitting the two sections together and scoring a notch across both with a file, each notch representing five bushels. Tallies were later replaced by special coins known as hop tokens or checks.

Tankard Originally a pint or quart size drinking vessel made from wood, leather or pewter with either one or two handles, and occasionally fitted with a lid. It is more usual nowadays for tankards to be made of pewter, silver or glass in ½ pint or pint sizes.

Tap (1) Cock through which beer is drawn from cask. *To tap a cask*, to drive in the wooden or brass tap into the cask in preparation for serving draught beer,, i.e., drawn from the wood. *Tap-borer*, auger for boring the tapered hole in the cask.

Tap (2) A particular brew or guile e.g., *an excellent tap*. This use is now uncommon.

Tap (3) Abbreviation of *tap-room*, room where beer is served direct from the cask. *Brewery Tap*, a bar or public house attached to a brewery from which beer could be bought on draught. The name is no longer in common use although a few public houses retain the title. *Taphouse*, alehouse where beer is served on draught. *Tapster*, an old-fashioned name for barman or cellarman.

Tappit Hen A lidded pewter drinking vessel fitted with a handle, and having a slim neck and broad body. It is so-called owing to its shape, which resembles a hen.

Tavern Traditional English name for a public house for the supply of food and drink. *Tavern keeper*, the landlord or licensee. *Tavern song*, one of the many colourful ditties which have sprung from such an historic meeting place. *Tavern tale*, anecdote told over a glass of beer and generally not too reliable.

Taverners, The A company formed in 1937 for the production of plays and the reading of poetry in pubs. They have performed plays by Shakespeare, Shaw, Galsworthy and many modern authors chiefly in the London suburbs and the Home Counties.

Tenant The landlord or licensee of a licensed house held under a tenancy.

Third 15th-century liquid measure.

Thirst Suffering enjoyed by beer drinkers.

Three threads Term originally used for a mixture of ale, beer and two-penny. It was superseded in 1722 by the production of a single brew called entire and, later, porter.

Tied House A house in which the licensee is under covenant to buy his supplies from a particular brewer. The tied house is normally owned by a brewery company.

Time, gentlemen, please A sad occasion, necessary but never welcome.

Tipple v. To drink slowly and repeatedly. n. The liquid thus consumed. Hence the question *What's your tipple? Tippler*, one who suits the action to the verb. *Tipling house*, [sic] mediaeval term for ale-house.

Toast (1) n. A drink to the health of a person, thing or sentiment, derived from the old custom of placing a piece of toast in the wine cup.

Toast (2) Phrase used, sometimes not too seriously, in announcing such a drink. v.t. To drink someone's health. *Toastmaster*, person who announces toasts at a public dinner.

Toby Jug   See under Jug.

Tokens   See under Hops.

Trade, The   The Licensed Trade, collective term for the wholesalers and retailers of beer, wines and spirits.

Trimmer   A senior cooper who examines each faulty cask thoroughly on its arrival in the cooperage, collects the materials required for its repair and allocates the cask to a cooper. He is responsible for keeping records of all repair work carried out in the cooperage.

Trouncer   The drayman's mate; so-called because, before the improvement of roads under Telford and MacAdam, he had to 'trounce,' i.e., push and manhandle the dray over the innumerable potholes and hazards.

Truss   Expession used in coopering, meaning to bend the staves of a cask into the characteristic elliptical shape. In hand coopering this is achieved by heating the cask over an oak chip fire and hammering down different sizes of ashen hoops. In the saw mills mechanically made casks are trussed by a hydraulic trusser after being steamed. *Trusser,* operator of an hydraulic trusser.

Trussing the Cooper   Traditional ceremony at which, after five years' apprenticeship, the new journeyman-cooper is initiated by his fellows. He is flung into a cask of his own making and water poured over his head. After being rolled in the cask up and down the floor of the cooperage he is tossed in the air by his tormenters. (See Cooper.)

Tumbler   A flat-bottomed drinking glass, derived from the original Saxon vessel which was so made that it could not stand upright and must therefore be drained at a draught or held in the hand.

Tun   Large beer cask, formerly used as a measure of capacity (252 wine gallons); the word is now generally used to describe many vessels in a brewery, e.g. Mash Tun. *Tun Room,* a department of brewery where fermenting takes place.

Twist one's arm   To 'persuade' one to have a drink, when no persuasion is needed. A facetious action and remark.

Twopenny   A pale, small beer introduced to London from the country and sold, in the 18th century, at 4d. per quart.

Twos   Colloquial term in general use in Norfolk, for mild and bitter, mixed half-and-half.

U

Underletting A means of heating the contents of the mash tun by admitting hot liquor through the bottom of the tun.

Underback A control vessel in the brewery through which the wort flows and from which samples are taken by the brewer and chemist.

V

Vat Large vessel in which fermentation may take place; often used to store beer; frequently described as a tun.

Verticillium Wilt A wasting virus disease which affects and wilts hops. Although it has been known for many years among strawberries and tomatoes, it is only since 1938 that it has attacked hops. It is highly contagious and can spread very rapidly through a hop garden, wiping out several acres in a few days. Control is effected by growing wilt-resistant varieties of hops.

Vessel Hollow receptacle for liquid.

Wallop Colloquial term for mild ale.

Wassail (1) Hot ale flavoured with sugar, nutmeg and roasted apples.

Wassail (2) Festive occasion at which wassail was consumed. Hence *wassail cup, wassail horn,* vessels for the purpose.

Wet one's whistle (Colloquial) To slake one's thirst.

What's yours An invitation which sums up the companionable atmosphere of the public house.

Whiskin 17th-century drinking vessel.

Whitsun Ale See Ale.

Wilt See Verticillium Wilt.

Wompo Local name for ale, used particularly in the East End of London.

Wood The cask. "Beer from the wood" is that served direct from the cask, instead of being pumped from the cellar by beer-engine.

Wormwood Ale See Ale.

Wort   The solution of malt extract in water, derived from the grist in the mash tuns. The solution is known as wort from the time extraction has taken place in the mash tun until fermentation in the fermenting vessels has been completed, when it is known as beer.

XX   A guarantee of quality originated by the monks during the Middle Ages, when each monastery was equipped with its own brewhouse. Later, when brewing companies were formed in the 17th and 18th centuries, the sign was retained to denote the strength of beers, thus XX was Mild Ale, XXX a slightly stronger beer, and XXXX strong ale. Today, beers are often marked with multiple X's or K's, XXXX or KKKK being a strong ale.

Yard of ale   Known also as a *long glass,* an old form of practical joke, companion of the puzzle jug of earlier centuries. Although the length varied, the yard of ale was approximately 3 feet long, shaped like a horn with a glass bulb at one end and open at the other. It held between 2¾ and 3½ pints and needed to be drained in one steady drink; if tilted too steeply, the beer ran out over the drinker's face.

Yeast   The fermenting agent which transforms the wort into beer. The *yeast head* grows and multiplies until it is some 3 or 4 feet high. By its action the sugars of the wort are converted into alcohol and carbonic acid gas. The gas is generally trapped and used for the carbonation of bottled beers, and after fermentation is complete—approximately three days—the yeast is removed and kept for further use. The brewer's supplies of yeast are thus continually increasing and the surplus is sold to firms who manufacture yeast foods. *Brewers' Yeast* is recommended by the medical profession as a blood purifier.

TASTER'S GUIDE TO BEERS OF THE WORLD

🍺 POOR BUT DRINKABLE   🍺🍺🍺🍺 GOOD INGREDIENTS

🍺🍺 PASSABLE   🍺🍺🍺🍺🍺 BETTER THAN AVERAGE

🍺🍺🍺 AVERAGE, COMPUTERIZED   🍺🍺🍺🍺🍺🍺 ALMOST PERFECT

🍺🍺🍺🍺🍺🍺🍺 THE WORLD'S BEST

BEER (country)	COMMENTS	RATING
Alpine (Canada)	Average light beer	🍺🍺🍺
Alt Seidelbrau (Germany)	Fine German lager.	🍺🍺🍺🍺🍺
Amarit (Thailand)	Perhaps the most famous beer of S.E. Asia. Clear, light and hoppy. Worth looking for. (Try it with hot, spicy food.)	🍺🍺🍺🍺🍺
Amstel (Holland)	A highly rated lager. Slight tartness and balanced nose. Average color, medium bouquet, small head.	🍺🍺🍺🍺🍺🍺
Anchor Steam (U.S.A.)	A well-crafted lager from one of America's smallest breweries. Sharp and highly palatable. Highly hopped; characterized by strong body, flavor and bouquet. Mellow amber color, dry. Finishes well with inviting aftertaste.	🍺🍺🍺🍺🍺🍺
Anchor Steam Porter (U.S.A.)	A solid, very dark beer; malty aroma, hoppy, full-bodied, nut-like flavor. Tart aftertaste. Recommended.	🍺🍺🍺🍺🍺
Andeker (U.S.A.)	An exceptionally rich, hoppy, lively pale lager. Compares well against "continental" lagers. Aged over 30 days.	🍺🍺🍺🍺🍺
Asahi (Japan)	Opens well with above-average bouquet. Typical light yellow color with poor head. So neutral in flavor, is best described as slightly bitter water.	🍺
Astra Ale (Germany)	Pale amber, lasting head, distinct malt flavor. Balanced by a tartness which leads to a satisfying finish.	🍺🍺🍺🍺🍺
Ballantine Ale (U.S.A.)	"America's largest selling ale." No longer brewed in New York, but in regional breweries. A delicious, tart ale but difficult to determine whether it's an authentic brew. Is ale flavoring used? Recommended with reservation (pending ingredients data).	🍺🍺🍺🍺🍺
Ballantine Beer (U.S.A.)	Much better than average light lager. A definite flavor profile.	🍺🍺🍺🍺🍺
Bass Pale Ale (England)	One of the world's finest ales. Full, rich flavor with above-average bouquet and head. Tart and inviting. Highly recommended.	🍺🍺🍺🍺🍺🍺🍺
Beck's (Germany)	Medium-light amber with above-average flavor and bouquet. Firm head, average body, dry. Quite salty with sharp aftertaste. (Nevertheless, the ingredients are faultless.)	🍺🍺🍺🍺🍺

BEER (country)	COMMENTS	RATING
Berliner Kindl (Germany)	If you like Dr. Brown's Celery Tonic *you might try this peculiar beer.*	🍺🍺🍺🍺 (4)
Berliner Weisse (Germany)	*Naturally cloudy, as this is top-fermented beer and fermentation takes place in the bottle. The yeast left inside contains vitamins of the B-complex. A specialized beer, a wheat beer; tart and consumed like dessert wines, often with raspberry or cherry syrup.*	🍺🍺🍺🍺🍺🍺 (6)
Black Horse (U.S.A.)	*Sorry, but the sample we tasted was flat and tasteless. Mild and light, almost nonexistent flavor. Negligible bouquet. On the sweet side when it should be tart.*	🍺 (1)
Blatz (U.S.A.)	*Big in Wisconsin.*	🍺🍺🍺 (3)
Blitz-Weinhard (U.S.A.)	*Very big in Portland. Unique flavor profile.*	🍺🍺🍺🍺🍺 (5)
Bock Dark Malt Liquor (Germany)	*A mild dark beer. Lacks any special characteristics.*	🍺🍺🍺🍺🍺 (5)
Bohemia Ale (Mexico)	*Light body, color and flavor. Mild bouquet. Smacks of synthetic ale flavoring.*	🍺 (1)
Brahma Chopp (Brazil)	*An average computerized lager.*	🍺🍺🍺 (3)
Brewmaster (England)	*Delicate pale amber color, light hoppy bouquet. Well-balanced body and flavor. Highly recommended for those who like astringent flavors.*	🍺🍺🍺🍺🍺🍺 (6)
Budweiser (U.S.A.)	*One of the lightest-colored beers. Exhibits a flavorful hoppiness. Average head, light bouquet. Good, dry flavor; fine aftertaste. Good ingredients.*	🍺🍺🍺🍺🍺 (5)
Busch Bavarian (U.S.A.)	*Above-average body, rich flavor.*	🍺🍺🍺🍺🍺 (5)
Cardinal (Switzerland)	*A fine Swiss lager.*	🍺🍺🍺🍺🍺 (5)
Carling Black Label (U.S.A.)	*Run of the mill.*	🍺🍺🍺 (3)
Carling Pilsener (Canada)	*Not a "pilsener." An average light lager.*	🍺🍺🍺 (3)
Carlsberg Light (Denmark)	*A light, dry, fully flavored beer that finishes well.*	🍺🍺🍺🍺🍺🍺🍺 (7)
Carlsberg Special Dark (Denmark)	*Dark without being heavy or sweet. Well-flavored, with a good malty bouquet. Pleasant aftertaste.*	🍺🍺🍺🍺🍺🍺 (6)
Carta Blanca (Mexico)	*Almost not a beer. Nonexistent head. Color nearly white. Surprisingly strong bouquet and tart taste. Unpleasant bitter aftertaste.*	🍺🍺 (2)
Ceres Red Eric (Denmark)	*Heavy and bitter.*	🍺🍺🍺🍺 (4)
Cerveza Victoria (Nicaragua)	*Nonoffensive lager indistinguishable from thousands of similar brews.*	🍺🍺🍺 (3)
Champale (U.S.A.)	*A sparkling but average beer.*	🍺🍺🍺 (3)
Chippewa Pride (U.S.A.)	*Very mild bouquet, body and flavor. Little aftertaste. Equal, if not superior, to many major U.S. lagers, with a loyal following.*	🍺🍺🍺🍺🍺 (5)
Club Colombia (Colombia)	*Average computerized lager.*	🍺🍺🍺 (3)
Cold Spring (U.S.A.)	*A Minnesota favorite. Above-average flavor, body. Good aftertaste.*	🍺🍺🍺🍺🍺 (5)
Colt 45 (U.S.A.)	*Strong, but average in flavor characteristics.*	🍺🍺🍺 (3)
Columbia (Canada)	*Not too bad at first, but taste disappears on swallowing. Average lager.*	🍺🍺🍺 (3)
Coors (U.S.A.)	*Very light, mild lager noted for its purity. Unpasteurized.*	🍺🍺🍺🍺🍺 (5)
Corona Cerveza de Exportacion (Mexico)	*Average computerized lager.*	🍺🍺🍺 (3)

BEER (country)	COMMENTS	RATING
Courage Strong Draught Bitter (England)	Deep amber color, mild head, very hoppy. Solid body, true strong flavor.	🍺🍺🍺🍺
Damm Estrella Darado (Spain)	Nothing special.	🍺🍺🍺
Diekirch Pils (Luxembourg)	Extremely mellow, clear, aromatic brew. Mild and highly hopped. Delicious and recommended.	🍺🍺🍺🍺🍺🍺
Dinkelacker Bock Extra (Germany)	A good strong bock. Above-average body, high yeasty flavor. Fine light amber color, small but lasting head. Pleasant and balanced.	🍺🍺🍺🍺🍺🍺
Dinkelacker Malt Liquor (Germany)	Golden amber, strong head. Well-carbonated. Full body and bouquet. Marvelous taste—sweet at first but good tart aftertaste.	🍺🍺🍺🍺🍺🍺
Dixie Beer (U.S.A.)	Big in Louisiana, but fairly average.	🍺🍺🍺
Dortmunder Hansa (Germany)	Good body, balanced flavor.	🍺🍺🍺🍺🍺🍺
Dortmunder Kronen Malt Liquor (Germany)	Blonde lager, average bouquet, above-average body and flavor with average dryness. Pleasant hoppy finish.	🍺🍺🍺🍺🍺🍺
Dortmunder Union (Germany)	Awarded important prizes worldwide for fine qualities and taste.	🍺🍺🍺🍺🍺🍺🍺
Dos Equis (Mexico)	Perhaps the most overrated import in the U.S. Poor head and watery body. Caramelized color. A synthetic taste.	🍺🍺🍺
Double Diamond (England)	Britain's top-selling ale. Not as good as other, lesser-selling British ales.	🍺🍺🍺🍺
Dragon Stout (Jamaica)	An average stout.	🍺🍺🍺
Dressler's Export (Germany)	Too salty and bitter.	🍺🍺🍺🍺
Dunk's Beer (U.S.A.)	From a very small brewery in Florida. A surprisingly unique flavor.	🍺🍺🍺🍺🍺
Esslinger Beer (U.S.A.)	Average light lager.	🍺🍺🍺
Falls City (U.S.A.)	Very big in Kentucky. Fairly straightforward.	🍺🍺🍺
Falstaff (U.S.A.)	Richer-than-average computerized beer.	🍺🍺🍺🍺
Feldschlossen (Switzerland)	Medium-light amber color; gentle, pleasant bouquet, medium body. Dry and highly recommended.	🍺🍺🍺🍺🍺🍺
Fiji Bitter (Fiji)	Very strong, very bitter. (Fijians love it.)	🍺🍺🍺
Fix (Greece)	Amber yellow in color, a good sharp taste. Flavor is full with a good nose. Look for it.	🍺🍺🍺🍺🍺
Foster's Lager (Australia)	Opens well with a golden amber color and fabulous head; bouquet of an average American lager; flavor is weak with a nonexistent aftertaste. Very little character. Popular nevertheless.	🍺🍺🍺🍺🍺
Gablinger's (U.S.A.)	Average American lager.	🍺🍺🍺
Genesee (U.S.A.)	Pale golden color, smooth flavor. Brewery manufactures its own malt.	🍺🍺🍺🍺
Geyer's Lager (U.S.A.)	A holdout in Frankenmuth, Michigan, with a very loyal following.	🍺🍺🍺
Gold Fassl (Austria)	Superb light flavor; of medium body, with mildly euphoric aftertaste.	🍺🍺🍺🍺🍺🍺
Gosser Stifts Brau-Dark (Austria)	Ochre-colored, above-average bouquet and hoppiness. Head firm. Overall, a bit on the sweet side.	🍺🍺🍺🍺🍺
Grolsch (Netherlands)	The Dutch never make bock beer. This tangy lager is finally available for export. The medium-amber color, sharp aroma, and rich, malty flavor separate it from the mass.	🍺🍺🍺🍺🍺🍺

BEER *(country)*	COMMENTS	RATING
Guinness Extra Stout for Export *(Ireland)*	Among the darkest of beers, with a massive bouquet and body. Thick, like syrup, leaving a dense impression. Bitter. *(Not the same as the domestic Guinness which is one of the world's finest stouts.)*	🍺🍺🍺🍺🍺
Hamm's *(U.S.A.)*	Fairly average.	🍺🍺🍺
Hamm's Preferred Stock *(U.S.A.)*	Slightly darker than average, highly sparkling with a creamy white head. Distinct nonlingering bitterness with fine hop aroma.	🍺🍺🍺🍺🍺
Harp Lager *(England)*	Medium amber-colored beer, strong bouquet and body; dry and well-balanced. Good, but not a true British beer such as Donnington's, which is naturally carbonated and unpasteurized.	🍺🍺🍺🍺🍺
Heidelberg *(Canada)*	Indescribable odor and flavor. Aftertaste fine if you need a strong purgative. (Spoiled?)	🍺
Heineken Lager *(Holland)*	Light color, above-average head, medium-light bouquet. A shade too dry and salty.	🍺🍺🍺🍺🍺
Heineken Special Dark Beer *(Holland)*	A good thick dark lager. Well-balanced.	🍺🍺🍺🍺🍺🍺
Henninger *(Germany)*	A perfect light amber lager with delicate bouquet. Comes on tart, with a good dry taste and pleasing aftertaste. One of the best.	🍺🍺🍺🍺🍺🍺🍺
Hudepohl *(U.S.A.)*	Folks in Cincinnati swear by it. Try it.	🍺🍺🍺
Hull's Cream Ale *(U.S.A.)*	A real sleeper. Try it in Connecticut.	🍺🍺🍺🍺🍺
Indio Cerveza *(Mexico)*	Dark color, body and bouquet. Above-average intensity. Sweet and fair; for those who like sweet, dark beer.	🍺🍺🍺🍺🍺
Jamaica Red Stripe *(Jamaica)*	Computer beer.	🍺🍺🍺
Jever German Pilsener *(Germany)*	Pale yellow lager. Very mild bouquet. Bitter flavor, harsh aftertaste.	🍺
Jupiler *(Belgium)*	A good, trustworthy, sprightly lager.	🍺🍺🍺🍺🍺
Kirin *(Japan)*	The best of all Japanese beers. Dry, rich flavor; smooth finish.	🍺🍺🍺🍺🍺
Knickerbocker Natural *(U.S.A.)*	A tart, sparkling light lager. Brewed without additives; medium bouquet, body and flavor. Slightly hoppy finish, sharp inviting aftertaste.	🍺🍺🍺🍺🍺
Kokanee Pilsener *(Canada)*	Ratty aroma, sour flavor, small head, average body; yet, surprisingly, a very good aftertaste. Overall, not as bad as its features.	🍺🍺🍺
Kootenay Bière Pale Ale *(Canada)*	A tangy light beer. Good bouquet, mild yellow color, average body. Tart, good flavor. Spoiled by a sour aftertaste.	🍺🍺
Krakus *(Poland)*	Pronounced barley-malt flavor; robust. Recommended.	🍺🍺🍺🍺🍺🍺
Kronenbourg *(France)*	An Alsatian beer; the best of Germany and France. Fine, alive, good body, sprightly nose. Highly recommended.	🍺🍺🍺🍺🍺🍺
Kronenbrau *(Canada)*	Slightly more amber than average Canadian lagers; medium body, poor head, mild bouquet. Lively sweet taste. Very drinkable.	🍺🍺🍺🍺
Kulmbacher Light Beer *(Germany)*	Another fine German light beer.	🍺🍺🍺🍺🍺🍺
Kulmbacher Monkshof Dark Beer *(Germany)*	Reddish amber with a strong bouquet, average body and lasting head. Not sweet, highly malty with a flavor profile and pleasant aftertaste.	🍺🍺🍺🍺🍺🍺
Labatt's 50	Average amber color, good head, fruity, pronounced bouquet. A delicious taste unique to light lagers.	🍺🍺🍺🍺🍺
Lederer-Brau *(Germany)*	Delightfully tart. A fine alternative to the hubris of the "big" German imports. Recommended.	🍺🍺🍺🍺🍺🍺

BEER (country)	COMMENTS	RATING
Leinenkugel's (U.S.A.)	Typical American grain-malt beer, with its own flavor characteristics. A loyal following.	🍺🍺🍺🍺
London Stout (Canada)	An interesting Canadian stout.	🍺🍺🍺🍺🍺
Lone Star (U.S.A.)	Big in Texas, but fairly average lager.	🍺🍺🍺
Long Life (England)	Largest-selling canned beer in Britain.	🍺🍺🍺
Löwenbräu (Germany)	A standard, one of the world's best lagers.	🍺🍺🍺🍺🍺🍺
Löwenbräu (U.S.A.)	Weaker body, lighter all around, yet better than average.	🍺🍺🍺🍺🍺
Löwenbräu Zurich Export (Switzerland)	Very strong bouquet. Body and flavor above-average; overall, extremely well-balanced. A sleeper—highly recommended.	🍺🍺🍺🍺🍺🍺
Lucky (U.S.A.)	Straight computer beer.	🍺🍺🍺
MacEwan's Edinburgh Ale (Scotland)	Highly carbonated, strong, rich. Full malty bouquet. Followed by a too-rapidly-dissipated head.	🍺🍺🍺🍺🍺
MacEwan's Scotch Ale (Scotland)	Makes beer drinking an artful pleasure. Honey-amber color and creamy head, aided by a mildly sharp bouquet, prepares your palate for a solidly tasty drink. The aftertaste is delicious. Highly recommended.	🍺🍺🍺🍺🍺🍺
MacEwan's Tartan Ale (Scotland)	Creamy dark brown; loses head almost on pouring. Above-average malty bouquet; smooth, pleasant aftertaste.	🍺🍺🍺🍺🍺
Mackeson Stout (England)	The standard for dark beers. Most stable head of all. For those who like dark beers but not bitterness.	🍺🍺🍺🍺🍺🍺
Manuia Pia-Tiurai (Tahiti)	Tahiti's water is pure and this lager is agreeably like some Alsatians.	🍺🍺🍺🍺
Marathon (Greece)	Bitter where it should be tart; tart where it should be mellow. Forget it.	🍺🍺
Matt's Premium (U.S.A.)	Brewed in small batches to maintain flavor characteristics.	🍺🍺🍺🍺
Maximus Super (U.S.A.)	Stronger than average through fermentation after standard brewing process. Slightly malty, mellow, with alcoholic sweetness.	🍺🍺🍺🍺
McSorley's Ale (Draught) (U.S.A.)	On draught, the best ale in the U.S.; among the sharpest, most aromatic in the world. Tart and hoppy. (Bottled version is mediocre.)	🍺🍺🍺🍺🍺🍺
Michelob (U.S.A.)	A very smooth lager. (Don't underestimate it.)	🍺🍺🍺🍺🍺
Miller High Life (U.S.A.)	Highly overrated by too many drinkers. An average computer lager.	🍺🍺🍺
Moldaubrau (Germany)	Original Burvar-Budweiser brewed in South Bohemia. Excellent.	🍺🍺🍺🍺🍺🍺
Molson Ale (Canada)	Largest-selling ale in North America. Light in color, sprightly in carbonation; firm, white head. A mild beer with good flavor characteristics.	🍺🍺🍺🍺🍺
Molson Lager (Canada)	A typical light lager. Above-average body but acidy flavor, meaty aroma. Aftertaste tart and pronounced.	🍺🍺🍺
Moosehead Ale (Canada)	Brewed in Nova Scotia, where it enjoys a loyal following. Highly hopped, tart and sharp.	🍺🍺🍺🍺
Narragansett Ale (U.S.A.)	Very big in Rhode Island. Not bad.	🍺🍺🍺
Neuweiler's Cream Ale (U.S.A.)	Hand-skimmed, dry-hopped, with above-average maturation time. Better than average.	🍺🍺🍺🍺🍺
Newcastle Brown Ale (Scotland)	Fine, full-bodied, tangy ale. Dark amber, nut-like aroma, solid head. Captivating aftertaste. Tastes like a mixture of light and dark lagers tossed together, one of the author's favorite blends.	🍺🍺🍺🍺🍺🍺

BEER *(country)*	COMMENTS	RATING
Niksicko Tuo *(Yugoslavia)*	*Reminiscent of Pilsner Urquell with slightly more hoppiness. The export version sampled was flat and watery, sour and uninspiring. Transit and storage problems?*	🍺
Noche Buena *(Mexico)*	*Nice reddish tinge and adequate carbonation. Smacks of caramel rather than of malt or hops. Finishes with a sourness.*	🍺🍺🍺
O'Keefe's Extra Old Stock Malt Liquor *(Canada)*	*Strong and tart. Winey bouquet, average body and flavor. Mild head. Above-average dryness. Sharp aftertaste.*	🍺🍺🍺
Oktoberfest Malt Liquor *(Germany)*	*Strong, tart and inviting. Aftertaste a bit too harsh.*	🍺🍺🍺🍺🍺
Old Blue Pilsener *(Canada)*	*Rich and flavorful. Above-average bouquet, body and flavor. Dry, pungent, delicious. Another winner from Uncle Ben.*	🍺🍺🍺🍺🍺
Old Chicago *(U.S.A.)*	*A leftover from the old Chicago days but still fairly average stuff.*	🍺🍺🍺
Olympia *(U.S.A.)*	*A good, basic light lager. Nothing special.*	🍺🍺🍺🍺
Optimator Doppelspaten *(Germany)*	*Reddish color, medium sweet, above-average bouquet. Nothing special.*	🍺🍺🍺🍺
Oranjeboom *(Netherlands)*	*Good and sharp. (The Dutch never seem to fail at beermaking.)*	🍺🍺🍺🍺🍺
Ortlieb's *(U.S.A.)*	*Average lager, above-average ingredients.*	🍺🍺🍺🍺
Pabst Blue Ribbon *(U.S.A.)*	*A full-bodied lager. Somehow richer than average.*	🍺🍺🍺🍺🍺
Pearl Premium *(U.S.A.)*	*Big in Missouri, but fairly straightforward lager.*	🍺🍺🍺
Pelforth Pale *(France)*	*Rather poor flavor in spite of a creamy head and amber appearance. Passable.*	🍺🍺
Peroni *(Italy)*	*Somewhat cloudy (a good sign—yeast). Average bouquet, above-average body and flavor. Good and sharp but not bitter.*	🍺🍺🍺🍺🍺
Pilsner Urquell *(Czechoslovakia)*	*The standard for all pilseners. (Much better on draught.)*	🍺🍺🍺🍺🍺🍺🍺
Point Special *(U.S.A.)*	*Aged for 5 weeks, this light beer has a distinctive hops aroma with no aftertaste. Highly acclaimed by locals.*	🍺🍺🍺🍺🍺🍺
Primo *(U.S.A.)*	*They've tried everything, but it's still a laughing stock in Hawaii. (It's premixed and shipped over by Schlitz.)*	🍺🍺
Pripps *(Sweden)*	*A big, big seller in Sweden. Nothing unique, however.*	🍺🍺🍺
Puntigam *(Austria)*	*Substantial but not great.*	🍺🍺🍺🍺
Rainier Ale *(U.S.A.)*	*Good and sharp, but not a McSorley's or even a Ballantine; very popular nonetheless.*	🍺🍺🍺🍺
Reininghaus Lager *(Austria)*	*Another basically sound Austrian lager.*	🍺🍺🍺🍺
Rheingold *(U.S.A.)*	*One of the first mass-market "natural" beers in the U.S. Basically sound but uninspiring.*	🍺🍺🍺🍺
Ringnes *(Norway)*	*Making it big in the U.S., but a fairly straightforward light beer.*	🍺🍺🍺🍺
Rolling Rock *(U.S.A.)*	*A real sleeper from Pennsylvania. It is alive, tart, sharp and very unusual.*	🍺🍺🍺🍺🍺🍺
Russian Imperial Stout *(England)*	*Very strong. Smooth, rich, velvety. Sweet, yet carries the bitter tang of hops.*	🍺🍺🍺🍺🍺🍺
Sagres *(Portugal)*	*Very pale and mild. Average head, minimum bouquet, mildly bitter aftertaste, with a yeasty aroma.*	🍺🍺🍺
St. Edmund Ale *(England)*	*A full, malty flavor.*	🍺🍺🍺🍺

BEER (country)	COMMENTS	RATING
San Miguel (*Philippines*)	Brewed to regional tastes. The Spanish version, being richer in malt extracts, hoppier and higher in alcoholic content, is the best. A delicious beer.	🍺🍺🍺🍺🍺
Sapporo (*Japan*)	Taste is all wrong, just a poor imitation of Guinness.	🍺
Schaefer (*U.S.A.*)	Average computerized lager.	🍺🍺🍺
Schell's (*U.S.A.*)	Taste reminiscent of many German light lagers. Flavor stronger than average light beers. Good.	🍺🍺🍺🍺🍺
Schlitz (*U.S.A.*)	Just awful. Sour, weak. A poor computerized lager.	🍺
Schmidt's (*U.S.A.*)	Better than average in taste, body and flavor.	🍺🍺🍺🍺🍺
Schoenling (*U.S.A.*)	From a very small but strong local brewery in Ohio. Worth looking for.	🍺🍺🍺
Schwechater (*Austria*)	A basic, solid lager. Good flavor characteristics.	🍺🍺🍺🍺🍺
Shiner Premium (*U.S.A.*)	One of America's smallest breweries. Look for it in Shiner, Texas.	🍺🍺🍺
Singha (*Thailand*)	The export version has little to offer. Of light body and mild bouquet, the flavor is tart, almost bitter, while the aftertaste smacks of preservatives.	🍺
Skol (*England*)	Very big in England and Europe, but quite average.	🍺🍺🍺
Spaten-Munich Light (*Germany*)	One of the lightest-colored beers tasted. Strong body, very sweet flavor.	🍺🍺🍺🍺🍺
Stella Artois (*Belgium*)	One of the best. Distinct hoppy flavor, good body, sparkling.	🍺🍺🍺🍺🍺🍺
Sterling (*U.S.A.*)	An Indiana favorite; unique flavor profile. (Try it when in Evansville.)	🍺🍺🍺
Stoney's Gold Crown (*U.S.A.*)	One of Pennsylvania's strong local breweries. Available only in the Smithton region.	🍺🍺🍺
Stroh's Beer (*U.S.A.*)	A strong local holdout in Detroit. Fairly average.	🍺🍺🍺
St. Pauli Girl (*Germany*)	Well made, but a bit too tart for my palate.	🍺🍺🍺🍺
Superior Light (*Mexico*)	The best of all Mexican beers sampled. Very light in color, medium bouquet, good head and strong carbonation.	🍺🍺🍺🍺🍺
Swan (*Australia*)	Very pale, pleasant fruity aroma, weak head, malty flavor. No body whatever. Uninspiring.	🍺🍺
Takara Masamune Sake (*U.S.A.*)	All you've heard about sake, but unratable since it's so different.	
Tecate Cerveza (*Mexico*)	Medium dry, very light bouquet, color and body. Drunk in Mexico with salt and lime juice.	🍺🍺🍺
Ten Penny Ale (*Canada*)	A distinct flavor profile. Worth looking for.	🍺🍺🍺🍺🍺
Tennent's Lager (*Scotland*)	Unlike many light lagers this one has good density, sprightly taste and mellowness. Unique to Scotland.	🍺🍺🍺🍺🍺🍺
Thor (*Denmark*)	Alive, sharp and interesting.	🍺🍺🍺🍺🍺
Tiger (*Singapore*)	Consistently clear, yeasty and hoppy with a pleasant bouquet. Admirable, dry, light beer, recommended with spicy food.	🍺🍺🍺🍺🍺
Tres Equis (*Mexico*)	Another light-bodied, light-flavored beer. Dry and inoffensive like countless others.	🍺🍺🍺
Tsingtao (*China*)	Disappointing. Heavy, overly dry finish.	🍺
Tuborg-U.S. (*U.S.A.*)	Better-than-average lagers, but not anywhere as well crafted as the Danish version.	🍺🍺🍺🍺🍺
Tusker (*Kenya*)	Don't be misled by the country of origin. The brewers have been there a long time.	🍺🍺🍺🍺🍺
Uncle Ben's Malt Liquor (*Canada*)	Thick body, strong head, more substance than average. An aged quality—mellow and good. Soothing texture, inviting aftertaste. A winner!	🍺🍺🍺🍺🍺🍺

BEER *(country)*	COMMENTS	RATING
Utica Club Cream Ale *(U.S.A.)*	Not too bad, but definitely not the best. Worth trying.	🍺🍺🍺
Vat 7 Draft *(U.S.A.)*	From a small brewhouse in Iowa. It's got something genuine about it.	🍺🍺🍺
Waldech *(U.S.A.)*	A good, strong-bodied beer. Pleasant aftertaste. Easily as good as many continental lagers.	🍺🍺🍺🍺
Watney's Red Barrel *(England)*	Sharp, tart and biting. Excellent.	🍺🍺🍺🍺🍺
Whitbread Gold Label Malt Liquor *(England)*	Honey-amber liquid with filaments of nutritious yeast. Strong and tart, pronounced malt flavor.	🍺🍺🍺🍺🍺
Whitbread Pale Ale *(England)*	Burnished copper in color; fine-bodied ale delivering rich molasses-like flavor. Firm, thick head.	🍺🍺🍺🍺🍺
Wurzburger Dark *(Germany)*	Dark Export: Mellow, robust, old Bavarian flavor. Special Bock: Featured during cooler months (October to May); rich and sprightly.	🍺🍺🍺🍺🍺
Wurzburger Light *(Germany)*	Edequell: Light color and Body. Crisp, hoppy flavor. Marzen: Above-average body. Rich.	🍺🍺🍺🍺🍺
Young's Stout *(England)*	Young produces 8 labels popular in England and surrounding countries. Not available overseas. Strong, rich and dark.	🍺🍺🍺🍺🍺
Yuchuan *(China)*	Tastes like Alsatian beer at first, but peculiar chemical aftertaste indicates a heavy hand with the chlorine.	🍺
Zealandia Half & Half *(New Zealand)*	A fine blend of mellow stout and lager beer; in a class by itself. Honey-colored, above-average bouquet, weighty body, strong finish; delicious mead-like aftertaste.	🍺🍺🍺🍺🍺
Zywiec Beer *(Poland)*	Dead and flat. (Perhaps the sample was spoiled?)	🍺

BIBLIOGRAPHY

Anderson, Will. *The Beer Book*. Princeton, N.J.: Pyne Press, 1973.

Baron, Stanley (1962). *Brewed in America*. Boston: Little, Brown and Co., 1962.

Beer in Britain. London: The Times Publishing Co., 1960.

Berry, C. J. J. *Home Brewed Beers and Stouts*, 6th ed. Hampshire, England: The Amateur Winemaker, 1971.

Bickerdyke, John. *The Curiosities of Ale and Beer*. London: Spring Books, 1889; Reprinted 1965.

Brewing in Canada. Ottawa: Brewers Association of Canada, 1965.

Brewing Through the Ages, vol. 1 of 3. Philadelphia: C. Schmidt and Sons, 1945.

Cairncross, S. E., and Jöström, L. B. S. "Flavor Profiles—A New Approach to Flavor Problems." Food Technology vol. IV(8):308–311, 1950.

Campbell, Andrew. *The Book of Beer*. London: Dennis Dubson, 1956.

Emboden, William. *Narcotic Plants*. New York: Macmillan Publishing Co., 1972.

The Flavor Profile. Cambridge, Mass.: Arthur D. Little, Inc., 1972.

Gayre, G. R. *Wassail! In Mazers of Mead*. London: Phillimore and Co., 1948.

Gray, Barry, and Savage, John. *Ale: In Prose and Verse*. New York: John Taylor's Sons, 1866.

Hill, Kenneth. *Beer for Beginners*. London: Mills and Boon, 1971.

Jacobsen, Michael and Anderson, Joel. *The Chemical Additives in Booze*. Washington, D.C.: Center for Science in the Public Interest (1972).

Jones, Dean. *Home Brewing Simplified*. Hampshire, England: The Amateur Winemaker, 1971.

King, Frank A. *Beer Has a History*. Hutchinson's Scientific and Technical Publications, London.

Marchant, W. T. *In Praise of Ale*. Detroit, Mich.: Singing Tree Press, 1888; reissue.

Mew, James and Ashton, John. *Drinks of the World*. London: Leadenhall Press, 1892.

Monson-Fitzjohn, G. J. *Quaint Signs of Olde Inns*. London: Herbert Jenkins, Ltd.

————. *Drinking Vessels of Bygone Days*. London: Herbert Jenkins, Ltd., 1927.

Neilson, Anne J. "*Significance of the Flavor Profile to the Master Brewer*." *Technical Quarterly of the Master Brewers Assoc. of America*, vol. 3(1): 69-75 (1966).

One Hundred Years of Brewing. Chicago: H. S. Rich and Co., 1903. Reprinted 1973 by Sonja & Will Anderson, Newton, Conn.

Parkes, B. *The Domestic Brewer and Family Wine-Maker*. London: Wetton & Jarvis, 1821.

Porter, John. *The Beer Book*. New York: Doubleday and Co., 1974.

Romer, Frank. *Reviewing American Brewing*. Baltimore, Md.: Crown Cork and Seal Co., Inc., 1942.

Shales, Ken. *Brewing Better Beers*. Hampshire, England: The Amateur Winemaker, 1971.

The Story of Whitbread's. London: Whitbread and Co., 1964.

Strong, Stanley. *The Romance of Brewing*. Privately circulated, 1951.

Weeks, Morris. *Beer and Brewing in America*. Washington, D.C.: United States Brewers Assoc., 1949.

Word for Word: An Encyclopedia of Beer. Introd. by Ivor Brown. London: Whitbread and Co., 1953.